GEOGRAPHIES OF CARE

For my parents

Geographies of Care

Space, place and the voluntary sector

CHRISTINE MILLIGAN
Institute for Health Research
Lancaster University
Lancaster, UK

Ashgate

Aldershot • Burlington USA • Singapore • Sydney

Published by
Ashgate Publishing Ltd
Gower House
Croft Road
Aldershot
Hants GU11 3HR
England

Ashgate Publishing Company
131 Main Street
Burlington, VT 05401-5600 USA

Ashgate website: http://www.ashgate.com

British Library Cataloguing in Publication Data
Milligan, Christine
    Geographies of care : space, place and the voluntary sector
    1. Public welfare - Great Britain
    I. Title
    361.9'41

Library of Congress Control Number: 2001088772

ISBN 0 7546 1624 X

Printed and bound in Great Britain by Biddles Ltd
www.biddles.co.uk

Contents

List of Figures, Tables and Maps

Preface

This book presents the results of a research project undertaken in the late 1990s about health and social care restructuring in Scotland and the likely impacts of reform on the informal sector.

The environment of community-based care is a complex one, in which numerous different actors and agencies operate at across various different spatial and organisational levels of the policy process. The actions and responses of these actors are in part mediated by their inter-relationships with other actors also involved in the caring process. This book has sought to tease out some of these inter-relationships through examining the experiences of statutory and informal care providers concerned with the provision of care to the frail elderly in Scotland. Taking the voluntary sector as the lens through which these inter-relationships are explored, the book examines how voluntary supports become mediated by differing local contexts of care. To do so, it explores the social and spatial implications of these linkages in two ways: firstly, it examines how deinstitutionalised care is effecting changes in the inter-relationships between formal an informal sectors in two differing local authority environments in Scotland and what this means in terms of locally-based care outcomes; and secondly, using a networked approach to analysis, it explores the social and policy environment within which community-based care is mediated. In this way, the research adds a new dimension to our understanding of the ways in which the restructuring of social care can vary between places, and across various spatial scales, and what this can mean for those concerned with the provision of care supports to community care groups.

Lancaster
January 2001

Acknowledgements

I would like to thank Robert Rogerson at the University of Strathclyde for his invaluable help and support throughout the progress of this research. I would also like to acknowledge all those participants whose willingness to help allowed me to undertake the study. In particular, I would like to thank those informal carers who gave up their time and knowledge despite the enormous burden of care they undertake - often with very limited help and support. Finally, I would like to thank my husband who frequently found himself a 'pressed volunteer', listening patiently (and sometimes less patiently!) to all my ideas, moans and groans throughout the research process.

List of Abbreviations

APT	Area of Priority Treatment
EU	European Union
GGHB	Greater Glasgow Health Board
JAG	Joint Action Group
JSG	Joint Strategic Group
LA	Local Authority
MISG	Mental Illness Specific Grant
MSC	Manpower Services Commission
NHS	National Health Service
PPA	Priority Partnership Area

Key to Quotes

I	Interviewer
R	Respondent
DG (+ number)	Voluntary Organisation - Dumfries and Galloway
DGC (+ number)	Carer - Dumfries and Galloway
G (+ number)	Voluntary Organisation - Glasgow
GC (+ number)	Carer - Glasgow
PDG (+ number)	Private Sector - Dumfries and Galloway
PG (+ number)	Private Sector - Glasgow
H	Housing Department
HB	Health Board
LA	Local Authority
SWD	Social Work Department
VO	Voluntary Organisation
Code + (1) or (2)	Denotes sequence of interviews
Bold	speaker's emphasis
[pause]	speaker's pause
...	break in quote
****	indicates identifying name has been removed

1 Introduction

Since the 1970s, and more evidently throughout the 1980s and 1990s much emphasis in the UK has focused on the way in which successive governments have attempted a retrenchment of publicly provided social welfare. A major change effected by this restructuring has been a shift in the location and mode of the delivery of care to service dependent populations - that is, the frail elderly and those experiencing mental, physical or sensory impairment. One element of this shift has been a move away from the prevalence of publicly provided services located within large, centralised institutional environments towards domiciliary and small community-based sites of delivery.

Hand in hand with the changing locus of care has been a change of emphasis in the *mode* of service delivery. Care is no longer viewed as the prerogative of public services. Rather, there is growing consensus amongst policy-makers that the informal sector (defined as comprising voluntary/non-profit organisations, the private sector and informal carers: Cm. 849, 1989) could and should play a key role in the provision of social and welfare services. Legislation from the late 1980s has thus sought to promote a mixed provision of care to include voluntary, private and informal care supports. Such options are seen as offering flexible and cost effective ways of delivering social and care services within local communities. As a consequence, provision is said to be breaking away from the 'binary choices' of public or private sectors, toward the development of a social market that incorporates the voluntary/non-profit sector (Amin et al, 1999).

Within this changing environment of social welfare, there are a number of issues that merit research that is sensitive to the ways in which social processes related to welfare reform operate in specific places. Of particular relevance, here, has been the call for research that explores the extent to which recent developments in social welfare have either improved or constrained the lives of specific groups of people in specific regions (see for example, Pinch, 1997). This book aims, in part, to explore these issues by considering one facet of the changing environment of social welfare; that is the restructuring of care provision to service dependent populations in the UK.

1

Geographers' interest in welfare reform and deinstitutionalised care is not new. It is evident in work that spans more than two decades, from Wolpert and Wolpert's (1976) early study of the relocation of mental hospital patients, through to more recent studies by Dear and Taylor (1982), Dear and Wolch (1987), Smith and Giggs (1988) and Kearns and Smith (1994). These works have focused largely on the exclusionary and locational experiences of deinstitutionalised individuals and the spatial implications of the new geography of care practice. Few, however, have sought to examine the role of non-statutory agencies in this process. Those geographical studies on voluntarism that *do* exist have tended to focus either on the role of the voluntary sector in regional economic growth and decline (e.g. Wolpert, 1977; Wolpert and Reiner, 1981), or the uneven nature of the spatial distribution of voluntary organisations (e.g. Wolch and Geiger, 1983, 1986; Wolch, 1989, 1990). Such studies make little connection between the impact of geographical variations in informal care supports on the lives of service users, and the ways in which voluntary supports can influence, and be influenced by, differing local contexts. Indeed, it is only in the last few years that a small body of geographical work has emerged whose concern has been to examine the place of the voluntary sector in the lives and experiences of community-based service users (see for example Milligan, 1996; Brown, 1997; Parr, 1997; Kearns, 1998).

With this in mind, the book aims to make two key contributions to our understanding of care reform. Firstly, it goes some way toward redressing gaps in the geographical analysis of the informal sector by examining how deinstitutionalised care is effecting changes in the interrelationships between public and informal sectors. These changes are viewed through the lens of the voluntary sector. The book sets out to explore the collective experiences of voluntary organisations in the process of care restructuring, to reveal how this restructuring is manifest within two different spatial environments in Scotland. The first of these sites is the urban-based locality of Glasgow City in central Scotland; the second is the semi-rural locality of Dumfries and Galloway in south west Scotland. Whilst urban/rural issues form one of the spatial dimensions discussed, the book also draws attention to additional geographical factors that are of equal importance in understanding how care restructuring is manifest at local level. The changing environment of care provision in Scotland has been further complicated by the implementation of the Local Authorities (Scotland) Act of 1996. The Act, which fused together district and regional councils into one single tier of local government, resulted in a re-drawing of local authority boundaries in Scotland. As a consequence, some local authorities have experienced major change. These factors are shown to have had additional implications in terms of the spatial outcomes and experiences of care restructuring within localised contexts.

Theorists of care highlight the importance of the interconnectivities and interdependence that characterise care as a relationship (see for example, Gilligan, 1982; Tronto, 1993; Daly and Lewis, 2000). In Daly and Lewis's terms, such relationships are defined as "the activities and relations involved in meeting the physical and emotional requirements of dependent adults and children, and the normative, economic and social frameworks within which these are assigned and carried out" (2000, 285). So care is seen as involving labour, obligation and responsibility with costs that are both financial and emotional. Such care extends across both public and private space. Yet such interconnectivities are not uniform over time or space, and local conditions can interact with broader trends to produce specific geographies of care. The influence of space and place in shaping care outcomes is an issue that is all too often ignored by care theorists. This book seeks to go some way toward redressing this omission by examining how such variations act to influence evolving patterns of formal and informal sector care in the Scottish context, and hence the experience of care provision.

Four themes, in particular, are explored. First, the book examines the influence of the voluntary sector in the development of social care provision. Second, it considers factors contributing to geographical variations in access and availability of voluntary sector supports and third, it examines the interrelationships occurring between formal and informal sectors at locality level. Finally, the book focuses attention on the ways in which key agents operating within specific spatial arenas impose their own agenda/interpretation on voluntary action. The outcome of such action reveals a complex spatial manifestation of care restructuring which is seen to be generated at various spatial levels.

Through its focus on informal care provision, the book illustrates how variations in access to informal care can arise as a consequence of political, economic and historical factors that vary both between local authority areas and within them. It, thus, highlights how social welfare restructuring is shaping the ways in which care is made available within different geographical settings. These issues are implicit throughout the analysis of the substantive chapters of the book, and are drawn together more explicitly in chapter eight.

In considering the progression from institutional to community-based models of healthcare, the book moves away from the more traditional focus on biomedical models of health and illness to examine how social, cultural and political factors impact on experiences of health

3

and healthcare. While recognising the importance of the individual, the book also points to the importance of understanding *how* decisions are made with regard to care. This points to the need to understand the policy environment within which social care is mediated. While legislation emanates from central government, numerous influences are brought to bear as it is translated and transformed by actors operating at various levels of the policy process - many of which occur within localised contexts. Local authorities, health authorities and the informal sector, for example, play a key role in the implementation of policy at local level. Hence, though action by central government is important - serving as a guideline for interpreting both the spirit and intent of the law - it is only by examining how policy is mediated by actors operating within and across various spatial and organisational environments, that the connections between care policy, and the many local scenes within which it is translated and practiced, can be made.

Any narrative of health and social care restructuring must necessarily take cognizance of those relationships occurring between actors operating at various spatial scales. So, while the book acknowledges the wider social, economic and political context within which change occurs, it is also concerned to examine those relationships occurring at the meso- and micro-levels[1] of the caring process. To enable these issues to be explored within two different geographical settings, the empirical research has been linked through the development of a conceptual framework within which these relationships can be examined. This forms the second major strand of the book. This proposes the basis of a model - the 'dependency network' - that seeks to build on wider frameworks of network theory. While these approaches have been employed as a means of interrogating developments within regional and economic geography in recent years, their utility for examining issues of health and social welfare have yet to be explored. Thus, in addition to illuminating geographical issues pertaining to the changing role of the informal sector, the book also seeks to contribute to our understanding of how care restructuring impacts on actors and agents at local level through the development of the 'dependency network'.

Within any such inter-related framework, it is difficult to understand the whole. The network approach adopted here reflects a need to examine the various influences of actors operating within and across landscapes of care in order to understand how outcomes are manifest within localised contexts. Inevitably, this means that this approach to the examination of care restructuring is, to some extent, deductively driven by the context, in that the wider framework of health and social care restructuring can be said to predetermine those actors operating within

4

the network. Restructuring, however, cannot be viewed simply as a backdrop to the study - in emphasising the role of different actors, it also serves to shape the form of network participation. In this way, relationships *within* the network can be seen to arise as a consequence of the dynamic process of change. Thus, by examining the outcomes of restructuring from within the network, the book aims to contribute to a wider understanding of the social and spatial influences on the caring process.

The predetermination of actors operating within this conceptual framework has played a pivotal role in the methodological construction of the study. As noted above, the focus of the book is on *one* particular set of actors - the voluntary sector. While this sector has long played a role in British welfare (Taylor, 1992), the magnitude and importance of key relations between the voluntary sector and the state have altered significantly in recent decades. Legislation defining the restructuring of health and social care to community care groups, for example, assigns an elevated role to the informal sector in the network of care services (Cm. 849, 1989; Cm. 4100, 1998). Not only is the voluntary sector viewed as having a more prominent role to play in the *provision* of health and social care delivered within local communities, but it is also assigned an elevated role in the policy and planning process. The voluntary sector has, thus, formed the point of entry to the network, and relationships are viewed largely through this lens. This is not to suggest that the voluntary sector is more, or less, important than other sectors within the network or that other sectors could not equally be investigated in a similar fashion. Rather, it is offered as *one* window through which to examine the impact of health and social care restructuring within localised contexts.

The 'anatomy' of the voluntary sector is explored by building a description of that part of the voluntary sector involved in health and social care provision to the frail elderly and their carers, and its relationship to both the statutory sector and private care providers. The framework for understanding this process focuses on the ways in which actors located within the network transform - and are transformed by - other actors also situated within it. However, as access to, and the characteristics displayed by the various actors examined within the study varied significantly, it was necessary to innovate and specifically tailor the research design to maximise data collection opportunities from within each group. The design adopted an in-depth approach that increased the depth of data collected within the overall project. This approach is presented as being sensitive to the dynamic nature of change in agents involved in the provision of care to frail elderly populations. It is also one that places actors, and the linkages *between* actors, at the heart of the analysis, by undertaking interviews with key informants from within various agencies sited within the network. The book, therefore, seeks to uncover the inter-relationships and social processes occurring within the network based on understanding the experiences of actors operating within it.

It is acknowledged at the outset that the researcher's position is one that is located outside the network. The research design, however, attempted to work with this, by adopting a methodological approach that facilitated an increased depth of study. By using in-depth interviews and diaries as methods of data collection, the study reflects the voices of those actors within the network. Secondly, the book aims to present this data in such a way as to maximise the voices of those actors participating in the study.

Legislatively, deinstitutionalised - or community-based - care focuses on four key care groups: the frail elderly, those experiencing mental ill-health, the physically and the mentally disabled (Cm. 849, 1989). Each of these 'groups' can vary enormously in their internal composition as well as the care needs of individuals located within them. Whilst there are differences, there are also many overlaps between the needs of individuals falling within particular care groups. To this extent, the composition of these groups is necessarily blurred, and attempts to draw boundaries around them are inherently flawed. In an aging population, for example, a key issue must be the point in life at which an individual becomes defined as 'elderly'. Similarly dichotomies arise over the 'boundaries' between care groups when considering issues of aging and (i) chronic mental ill-health; (ii) physical disability; and (iii) sensory disability. Given that the 'frail elderly' are frequently presented as the care group consuming the highest proportion of community care funding, these are not idle questions. Nevertheless, these are the legislatively defined groups that researchers must seek to work with if they are to attempt to understand the impact of care restructuring. Thus, while acknowledging the flaws inherent within such definitions, the study attempted to work *with* the legislative context. The book has, thus, focused on care provision to just *one* of these community care groups - the frail elderly - in order to examine how policy enacted by central government is translated and transformed by actors operating at the meso- and micro-levels of the caring network.

While the definition of this group is open to debate, within the context of this book it is less immediate. The focus here is on care *providers* as actors within the network rather than service recipients. As such, the frail elderly are not, in themselves, central to the study. This is not intended to infer that service recipients are not actors within the dependency network. Rather, because of their experience as end-recipients of care provision, they are envisaged as the focus of a separate (though clearly inter-linked) piece of research.

The book has been constructed as two inter-related parts. The first locates the study within a contextual framework. As such, it weaves a path through a changing context of care which has at its root a policy framework that has shifted and developed over both time and space. This shifting context highlights the fluidity of research in this field. Care policies and their implementation are subject to constant revision and change arising from circumstances occurring at particular points in time. Given that the context is constantly changing, research in this area can never be 'up to date' - this is a situation that is both recognised and acknowledged. The book represents an investigation of relationships within the care network over a three-year period from 1996-1998. The effects of restructuring cannot be viewed adequately through a 'snapshot' approach, the interactions and effects of change in social care systems occur slowly. Such complex processes require time for exploration, with the interactions between people, policy and place demanding a longitudinal in-depth engagement with the social world of the informal provider within the chosen localities. Thus, rather than presenting the study as a 'snapshot' of care restructuring which is seen in isolation from past and future events, the analysis is viewed more as a 'still' from a moving film. In doing so, it allows us to recognise that not only is the situation subject to constant change, but also that while the focus may switch between arenas from time to time, these arenas are inter-linked by the medium of the 'film', and as such, are representative of the dynamic of the network.

The three chapters that follow lay the foundation and framework for the analysis of the substantive material contained in the remainder of the book. Each of these chapters contributes to the overall process of the study by illuminating a number of key themes through which it is possible to examine how the restructuring of health and social care is impacting on the voluntary sector - themes which are explored in the remaining chapters.

In chapter two, the book explores the development of different approaches to the examination of problems of health and illness. These serve as a means locating the study within its geographical context, and in particular, it considers the perspectives offered by medical geographers. Any discussion on the subject of care restructuring, however, also needs to incorporate an understanding of the key factors contributing to the development of newly emerging spaces of caring and an appreciation of the forces that have shaped their history. These issues are explored in chapter three. The final chapter in this section serves to locate the study within a conceptual framework, by exploring the utility of a networked approach as a means of understanding how care policy and practice is mediated within locally-defined contexts.

The second part of the book lays out the analysis of the substantive data. Each chapter explores how care restructuring is experienced by one set of actors within the dependency network and their inter-relationships within it - in particular with the voluntary sector. Chapter six is concerned with care restructuring as experienced by the voluntary sector itself. Chapters seven and eight consider the role of informal carers and the private sector experience of care restructuring respectively, and their influence on the shape of voluntary care provision. These three chapters are, thus, concerned with the experience of care restructuring within the informal sector. Chapter nine, however, focuses on a second aspect of this restructuring. Here, the emphasis is on the redefinition of state responsibilities for the social welfare of the population - effected by public sector retrenchment - and the move toward alternative informal and private sector care provision. The nature of the relationship between the formal and informal sector within the context of the dependency network is an integral part of this project, in that the book attempts to illuminate how and why actors and agencies respond in particular ways. Within health and social care, this may be particularly evident in the differential ability of agencies to exert influence within the policy, planning, purchasing and implementation processes. Chapter nine thus, examines the ways in which the statutory sector translates and transforms policy and its care outcomes within locally embedded networks of care. In doing so, it also discusses some of the ways in which restructuring has become manifest in shifting power relationships both within the statutory sector, and between the statutory and voluntary sectors, and what this may mean for voluntary organisations located within the dependency network. The following chapter serves to draw together the social, spatial and temporal issues alluded to in preceding chapters. Finally, the book concludes by discussing the utility of the dependency network as a framework for understanding care restructuring at the meso- and micro-level and its potential for examining geographical problems in health and social welfare.

Note

[1] Meso- and micro-levels are used, here, to describe interactions occurring at the level of local governance and those taking place at the level of the individual respectively.

2 Geographical Perspectives on Health

Introduction

As care has moved from institutional to community-based sites of delivery, concern has focused not only on the relocation of the locus of care, but also on the new sets of actors and agencies involved with its planning and provision. Attention is drawn to the ways in which decisions are made and how the social processes of care reform operate in particular places. The relationship between healthcare and the means through which social, cultural, political and economic influences alter the experience of health and illness across space and within places has been of particular interest to medical geographers in recent years.

The study upon which this book is based builds on work that has emerged from several strands of contemporary geographical thinking. Such work maintains that for a clearer understanding of how and why specific patterns of health and healthcare emerge in particular places at particular times, there is a need to extend the focus of medical geography to incorporate a wider view of health and healthcare. These broadly embody the recognition of a need to move away from biomedical approaches to the geographical analysis of health issues, to incorporate social models of health and healthcare. Such approaches also highlight the potential benefit of integrating multi-disciplinary perspectives to geographical analyses, and the need to understand how wider contextual factors impact on experiences of health and healthcare. To understand why these issues are of importance here, this chapter gives a brief history of the development of medical geographical thinking, identifying some of the main elements that have informed the study. In doing so, I discuss some of the main 'traditional' theoretical and epistemological positions through which aspects of health and illness have been examined within medical geography, and how development in thought across the discipline as a whole has become manifest in terms of 'contemporary' perspectives in geographies of health and healthcare.

The range of studies and subject matter encompassed within medical geography make it both a complex and diverse sub-discipline. From the outset, it should be noted that labels such as 'traditional' and 'contemporary' positions are not viewed as reflecting a 'past and present' in research; all strands continue to be found in current works and all continue to offer valuable insights into geographical problems of health and ill-health. Further, the strands identified here are seen as neither all encompassing nor mutually exclusive, for within some current work, it is possible to discern a fusion of those 'traditional' and 'contemporary' perspectives. Indeed, Philo (1995, 36) explicitly warns us, that due to the 'messy' nature of medical geography (in terms of the overall eclecticism of approaches taken) any attempt to categorise the approaches adopted within it are doomed to be flawed and partial. Whether this 'messiness' is representative of chaos or a healthy diversity within medical geography is currently the subject of debate within the sub-discipline itself (see The Proceedings of the IXth International Medical Geography Symposium, Montreal, 2000). Despite this 'messiness' much of the geographical literature relating to changes in health and social care is influenced by one or more of these positions. As a consequence, the chapter aims to provide an overview of some of the main strands currently evident within the sub-discipline. It does so firstly, in order to 'place' the conceptual framework adopted within this book; and secondly, to draw attention to the increasingly multi-faceted approaches through which medical geographical research is examined.

'Traditional' Perspectives

Geographical approaches to health have a long and respected history traceable to Ancient Greece. Hippocrates' treatise on *Air, Water and Places* stressed the importance of water quality, climate and a scenic environment for health and well-being (Gesler, 1993). Nineteenth century British and European colonialists with an interest in the potential dangers to health in their newly annexed territories, also highlighted the importance of geography to the understanding of health and disease (May, 1952). An often cited example of the early mapping of disease is the work of John Snow in the 19th century. His inability to explain the cause of cholera in a specific part of London, led Snow to map the incidence of cholera-induced death, with the result that prevalence rates were shown to be highest closest to a particular source of water. Such clustering enabled Snow to demonstrate a link between cholera and infected water, pointing to the utility of mapping disease both at locality level and at the wider spatial scale.

As a sub-discipline, the emergence of medical geography has been attributed to the German Zeiss. In 1932, he maintained that "by *geographical medicine* or *geomedicine* is understood the branch of medicine which attempts to clarify and explain the results of medical research by geographical or cartographical treatment" (quoted in May, 1952, 1). Howe (1976, 19-20) further defined it as, "the comparative study of the incidence of disease and the distribution of physiological traits in people belonging to different communities throughout the world and the correlation of these data with features of the environment". In this way, Howe mapped out a more distinctive role for the medical geographer, emphasising the spatial aspects of environmental relationships and health related behaviour. This particular view of medical geography is one that bears a close relationship to epidemiology.

These 'traditional' approaches to medical geography have tended to view disease as a naturally occurring and culture-free entity (Litva and Eyles, 1995). The focus has been on Western biomedical discourses on health and disease. These have emerged from the Cartesian paradigm, which views disease as a temporary impairment in the functioning of a component making up an individual, or of the relationships between these components. More succinctly, this has been summed up by Curtis and Taket (1996) as the consequence of a breakdown in the machine - the doctor's task being one of 'repairing' the machine. Such an interpretation of health and ill-health views disease as a deviation from 'normal' biological functioning, that emerges as a consequence of causal factors such as vectors, pathogens or micro-organisms. This biomedical approach is also one that views disease as generic; that is, it is believed to display the same symptoms and processes over time and space. Such a conventional view of biomedicine has tended to resist any encroachment of social models of health and ill-health, with the emphasis being on science, technology and rationalism - cure rather than prevention. Health thus becomes an absence of disease.

Epistemologically, such approaches have been most closely aligned with the positivist school of thought - tending to rely on theories of natural science and quantitative approaches to method.

11

Within geographical thought, two main strands of 'traditional' medical geography are identifiable. The first strand, most closely associated with those definitions given by Zeiss and Howe, has been concerned with geographies of disease and ill-health, 'mapping' the correlates of disease and disease distribution and assessing actual and possible environmental associations. The second strand focuses largely on geographies of healthcare, exemplified in research concerned with the spatial analyses of patterns of service provision and healthcare.

The following discussion of work within these strands makes no claims to being all-encompassing, rather the selected studies have been used to illustrate particular points or developments within medical geography, and as a basis for providing a critique of these developments.

Ecological approaches to medical geography

Ecological approaches to medical geography have been largely concerned with the influence of geography on agents or vectors of disease; the main purposes being to locate and establish geographical correlations arising from identified phenomenon. This has been illustrated through as variety of techniques from mapping to sophisticated statistical analysis. May (1952), for example, viewed medical geography as the study of disease and factors contributing to disease over the earth's surface. His work on the plague regions of India highlighted the links between the intensity of the occurrence of the plague and climatic conditions, attributing it to the animal and insect vectors of disease (in this case, rats and rat fleas) whose prevalence was found to increase and decrease under specific climatic conditions (WHO Bulletin, 1951, 4, 75-109).

At a more local scale, Girt (1972), too, considered the links between ecology and disease. In particular, he maintained that diseases such as bronchitis arose as a consequence of the interactions between the individual and his or her environment and demonstrated a strong positive correlation between the incidence of bronchitis and overcrowding and dampness in housing. The risk of developing such a disease was, thus, shown to increase with prolonged exposure to a causal factor in the environment. While the link between health and environment is clearly an important one, these studies ignored the influence of alternative variables - for example, the influence of social and behavioural factors such as smoking - variables that can greatly alter the relationship between bronchitis and the ecological environment (Eyles and Woods, 1983). The relative importance of social versus behavioural and environmental factors in contributing to poor health are still evident in health inequality debates that continue to rage on today (e.g. MacIntyre, 1993; Wilkinson, 1996; Curtis and Rees Jones, 1998; Ecob and Macintyre, 2000; Haynes and Gale, 2000).

The limitations of these relatively simple correlations lead other medical geographers to undertake more sophisticated associative studies, with Pyle and Rees (1971) using factor analysis to consider the relationships between eighteen variables plus population density across seventy-six districts in Chicago. In doing so, they revealed an ecological patterning of socio-economic status, that highlighted a close correspondence between poverty and overcrowding in the inner city and the incidence of diseases ranging from tuberculosis and gonorrhoea, to infant mortality and childhood diseases such as mumps, chickenpox, and whooping cough.

Cartography has played a major role within ecological approaches to medical geography. With geographers such as Stamp (1964) and Howe (1963, 1976) emphasising the importance of the map as an analytical tool for identifying suggestive patterns which may (or may not) point to some causative factor. The utility of such maps, was argued to be evident not just in their ability to identify the prevalence of disease in certain locations, but also in their ability to identify geographical environments which are conducive to physical and mental well-being (Stamp, 1964). Cartography has been used at the global scale to map not only the incidence of disease ranging from leprosy to heart disease but also the geographical aspects of nutrition and malnutrition, and their implications for health. Stamp (1964), however, also drew attention to the need for research into other geographical aspects of health and ill-health, suggesting that suitable subjects for study might be the linkages between health and factors such as housing, occupation and micro-climate - issues which still form the basis of much contemporary research in health geography (see for example Smith, 1989; MacIntyre, 1994; Dorling, 1996; Smith et al, 1997).

Thus, to confine a review of the mapping of health and disease to studies undertaken in the 1950s and 1960s would be to undermine their continued relevance in medical geography today. Studies in the late 1980s by Cliff and Haggett (1988) provided a comprehensive review of contemporary methods in medical cartography including computerised techniques such as linear programming and stochastic modelling. Other studies incorporating the techniques of medical

13

cartography have been undertaken by geographers such as Gardener et al (1983), Jones and Moon (1987) and Dorling (1995, 1996, 2000). In Dorling's (1995) work, for example, cartographic models are used extensively to illustrate the degree to which social factors such as access to housing, employment, demography and economic indicators, can be used to explain changing patterns of health in Britain. When and why we are most likely to die is attributed to where an individual lives, variations in the way the health service operates between localities, and how governments both organise health provision and regulate society. While such studies have been largely concerned with the mapping of health related occurrences, they do, nevertheless, begin to highlight the importance of examining the influence of social and political factors as a means of understanding spatial difference in health outcomes.

Other geographers (e.g. Haggett, 1972; Pyle, 1973) attempted to combine the ideas of spatial diffusion (deriving from the work of Hägerstrand, 1968) and graph theory. This was adopted in an attempt to understand the causative processes in the spread of disease, and as a means of accurately forecasting its geographical spread. Pyle (1973), in particular, used diffusion modelling not only to illustrate the age-specific attack rates of measles, but also to highlight the role of socio-economic indicators in the prevalence of the disease. The origins of the disease were found to be in the poorest location of the area studied with a clear pattern of diffusion thereafter. Additionally, however, the relatively expensive cost of the vaccine was shown to present a barrier to the diffusion of inoculation to the entire population at risk. Hence, in work of this nature, we can see medical geography beginning to go *beyond* diffusion and spatial patterning, to look at causation - not just in a medical sense, but also in socio-cultural terms - to explain differentials in the incidence of disease amongst populations.

Ecological studies of health and disease have tended to use aggregate measures of health and risk factors for populations resident in different geographical areas. In Giggs's (1973) work, for example, aggregate measures were used to study the distribution of Schizophrenics in Nottingham. His work revealing a distinct agglomeration of such individuals within areas that displayed high levels of social deprivation. Giggs thus advanced the notion that it was possible to identify specific 'risk' areas within the city, where increased incidence of mental illness was likely to arise as a consequence of adverse environmental conditions - the so-called 'breeder' hypothesis (Giggs, 1973). Later studies by Dear and Taylor

(1982) and Dear and Wolch (1987), however, have pointed to alternative explanations for the incidence of mental ill-health in the inner city. Here, agglomeration in the urban core was viewed as the consequence of urban drift, as individuals become excluded from more affluent areas by NIMBY attitudes and the exclusionary tactics of such communities. As a consequence, individuals with mental ill-health were shown to migrate toward the urban core in search of affordable housing and support systems not found elsewhere. Here again, medical geographers have drawn attention to a need to consider the contribution of social, political and economic factors in shaping the spatial incidence of health and illness.

So despite an increased sophistication in ecological analyses, and their ability to demonstrate *associations* between health/ill-health and ecological/environmental factors, these studies have rarely been able to isolate the causative mechanisms. So, while studies using aggregate data can highlight *incidence* of health/ill-health, they cannot provide conclusive explanations, and as a consequence, their utility as a means of examining the experience of care restructuring is subject to limitations. This is not to undermine the utility of this work; the search for the spatial patterning of disease is a necessary component in any search for causation and amelioration of ill health and disease. Consequently, while there is a need to place geographical distribution and environmental factors within a wider framework, such analyses can still provide a useful tool for generating hypotheses with regard to possible causal factors. As such, they are a useful means of illustrating how the combination of people and place have implications for health.

Nevertheless, in focusing on aggregate measures, ecological approaches to health and disease have a tendency to overlook possible links between ill-health and environmental risk-factors at the level of the individual. This has led to criticisms that they are subject to an 'ecological fallacy' (Curtis and Taket, 1996) or the misinterpretation of assumptions about causal factors contributing to health and illness. Recent studies by Jones and Duncan (1995) and MacIntyre et. al. (1993) question whether the focus on aggregate data is an appropriate level at which to examine spatial differences in chronic illness. Jones and Duncan (1995) argued, that whilst ecological explanations are potentially important, much aggregate data does not hold at the level of the individual. Rather than an ecological fallacy, they maintain that the issue is one of an 'aggregative fallacy' (p.28). Consequently, there is a need to focus on the ecology within which individuals live and work. So while acknowledging the importance of individual

15

characteristics (such as age, gender, class) work in this vein maintains that to understand health outcomes, it is also necessary to consider whether people of similar characteristics experience different health outcomes in different places. Nevertheless, they also recognised the potential problem of an 'atomistic fallacy', in which an exclusive focus on the individual level can miss the context within which individual action occurs. Hence, they call for a 'multi-level' approach, which places an emphasis on the modelling of individual and ecological interactions.

The spatial analysis of healthcare

A second key strand within this 'traditional' approach is concerned with the spatial analysis of service provision and healthcare; that is, examining the systems that have been developed under differing political and economic administrations in order to combat environmental adversities to human health and well-being. Here, geographers have adopted methods such as location-allocation modelling, correlation and regression analyses, to focus on the spatial and temporal relationships between the distribution and requirement for services and characteristics of the environment (e.g. Pyle, 1974; Haynes and Bentham, 1979a; Joseph and Phillips, 1983; Phillips, 1981, 1990).

Based on concepts developed by Christaller (1966) and Lösch (1954), Pyle's (1974) study of the geography of healthcare in North America in the post-war period demonstrated the non-systematic manner in which the response to healthcare needs has developed as a result of a laissez-faire economy. Such a response was shown to be manifest in an uneven distribution of resources across locales. Pyle also demonstrated the existence of a theoretical hierarchy of facilities in North America, within which degrees of patient attraction, and distance travelled, were shown to be dependent on the facility size and range of specialities offered. Hence, the largest hospitals with the most specialisms attracted patients from the whole of a metropolitan area plus its rural hinterland, with successively smaller hospitals in turn having correspondingly smaller service areas.

Pyle and Lauer (1974), however, also revealed how external factors can impact on location-allocation models, highlighting the role of *income* as a major contributory factor in the creation of irregularities in the expected pattern of location-allocation models. Consequently, this work was able to illustrate that regularities of fit, as demonstrated within the location-allocation model, are often non-existent. Nevertheless, such studies are useful in that they offer an important point of departure for undertaking more in-depth analyses.

Location-allocation modelling is also at odds with the work of Shannon and Dever (1974) who drew attention to the distance-decay effect (so-called Jarvis' Law). This indicated that lower admission rates to mental hospitals was not attributable to any spatial variation in psychiatric morbidity, rather it arose as a consequence of a greater *knowledge* of the potential benefits of facility usage amongst those living proximate to it. This line of argument has guided empirical studies such as those of Haynes and Bentham (1979b), whose work attempted to quantify distance as a variable in attendance/utilisation of a facility. However, as Phillips (1981) maintained, in emphasising the numerical frequency of utilisation, studies in this vein fail to capture important differences in the *need* to use services, and the rationale behind such decision-making variables. Thus, while such studies can have a useful role to play in the planning process, the conclusions drawn from such work offer only a partial explanation.

One consequence of these criticisms of 'traditional' approaches to medical geographical problems has been that some studies began to move away from simple and deterministic assumptions regarding human behaviour. Phillips (1981), for example, used census enumeration districts to demonstrate how distance, social status, personal mobility and previous residence were all influential in the selection of which GP surgery an individual attended. Hence, while usage patterns were seen to bear some relationship to distance, this was not the whole story. Rather, he was able to demonstrate that many patients preferred to remain with their GP even following a change of residence, so highlighting an historical inertia to surgery use. Previous residence was, thus, seen to play a significant factor in explaining the spatial patterning of GP utilisation behaviour.

In challenging the presumptions of a spatial hierarchy (as proposed by Christaller, 1966), work of this nature highlighted the importance of behavioural perspectives to the analysis of health issues. The interaction between the patient and the medical facility was shown to be dependent not only on the medical setting and the patient's attributes, but also on expectations taken to the setting by the patient. More recently, Kanzanjian and Pagliccia (1996) used a similar approach to explore the locational influences on physicians in Canada, illustrating how such influences can contribute to the twin problems of physician surplus and geographical inequity in provision.

Behavioural perspectives have been useful in challenging the assumptions built into such theses as central place theory, and begin to focus attention on the role of human motivations in exploring health related behaviour. Nevertheless, by focusing on the individual, these approaches make it problematic to obtain a sense of the social context from which the individual derives. Hence, it is possible for behaviour practised and exhibited by a majority of individuals to become theorised as the 'norm', leaving all other behaviour to be treated as a deviation from this 'norm'.

Towards 'Contemporary' Approaches in Medical Geography

By focusing on the relationships between biomedical phenomena and the environment, 'traditional' approaches have been seen as closely related to epidemiology - a factor that has often led the sub-discipline to be viewed as essentially a biomedical tool. Its utilisation of biomedical discourse has led to a number of identifiable assumptions within these 'traditional' approaches:

- disease is defined as a deviation from 'normal' biological functioning;
- disease is assumed generic;
- a scientific neutrality to medicine is assumed;
- they identify the presence of vectors of disease requiring medical/scientific interventions to both identify and eradicate the problem, and to provide preventative/therapeutic measures; and
- their advocation of 'technofix' solutions are essentially non-economic - that is, they assume financial resources are available to allow such technical solutions. However, in doing so, they fail to identify competing wants and limited resources (Eyles and Woods, 1983).

The positivist epistemologies associated with such approaches have lent themselves to methodologies that reduce health problems to measurable, quantifiable 'facts'. However, while positivist research may answer questions of where, when, what and how, it has, however, been unable to explain *why* phenomena occur. Within human geography as a whole, this has resulted in the emergence of a vigorous response to the general trend of positivist analysis over the last two to three decades. 'Traditional' approaches to medical geography have been subject to criticisms in that they provide only cause and effect models which cannot explain *why* specific individuals in specific places become sick/ill, and which tend to be divorced from the social, economic and political environment within which they are located. Further, their essentially western-centric approach to health/ill-health, it is claimed, overlooks both lay perceptions of health, and socio-cultural differences in definitions of sickness and care. Hence, as Gesler (1993) notes, western medical systems are seen to have become subsumed by a scientific approach to health and healthcare. Such medical systems tend toward high-cost technological interventions rather than prevention, a discourse focused on cost containment over non-monetary factors, and an emphasis on individual need. Further, in its largely unquestioning adoption of a biomedical approach to health and illness, there has been a tendency to consider the human experience of service provision as exclusively the domain of actual or potential patients. This has been argued, by some, to have diminished the human experience in its failure to consider the ways in which individuals can consume spaces of healthcare in non-medical ways (Dyck and Kearns, 1995).

Within medical geography, such criticisms have become manifest in new approaches to healthcare and health-related behaviour. Thus, the simple twofold division discussed in the preceding sections of this chapter, is no longer an accurate reflection either of the research, or the epistemological position of those working within the sub-discipline. Geographers have begun to question both the unproblematic adoption of biomedical and reductionist terms of reference - in which it is assumed that illness and disease can be reduced to 'dots on a map' - and the failure to acknowledge the ways in which health and identity can be experienced and constituted through difference (e.g. race, gender, sexuality, disability).

In general terms, the implication of this 'contemporary' response for medical geography has been that it should be informed by social and cultural theory. This can be broadly subsumed under humanistic and structuralist perspectives. In the process of exploring such social constructions of health/ill-health, and with an increased emphasis on the individual, these developments demonstrate a significant growth in the body of research within medical geography that embraces and recognises the value of adopting qualitative approaches to the analysis of a particular research problem.

19

While it is possible to identify a number of strands that can be said to fall within 'contemporary' perspectives on medical geography, Curtis and Taket (1996), usefully identify [at least] three new strands which adopt very different approaches. Each arises from a variety of critiques of both positivism and the biomedical model.

'Humanising' medical geography

The first of these 'contemporary' strands concerns itself with the humanistic turn, and has been linked to the Chicago School of Sociologists (e.g. Park). Such studies move away from the simplistic normative behavioural assumptions which formed the basis of earlier work, to focus on the nature of the motivations behind individual health-related behaviour, and a concern with understanding individual decision-making. Thus, they take as their focus a concern with socio-cultural constructions of health and illness.

Such interpretative epistemologies consider health and health services with reference to the individual actors themselves, their intentions, and the context within which their interactions occur. Their use of a largely ethnographic approach seeks to allow individuals to express themselves in their own way (Eyles and Donovan, 1986), and attempts to find out what health and illness mean to ordinary people. Such material allows for an understanding of the ways in which 'others' make sense of their lives. Thus, there is not one truth, but many truths related to the ways in which people perceive and act in the world. The concern is consequently one of exploring peoples' lived experiences - as they relates to health - in terms and concepts derived from their own narratives about the worlds they inhabit. Such perspectives move away from the more 'traditional' bio-medical models of health, towards a social constructionist approach to research. Within medical geography, the works of Cornwell (1984), Eyles and Donovan (1986), Takahashi (1997) and Parr (1997, 1998) have all adopted qualitative approaches as a means of considering not just the *causes* of ill-health, but also to examine both concepts and perceptions of health and illness.

Cornwell (1984), for example, illustrated how any understanding of an individual's conceptualisation of health needs to begin with a consideration of the relationships between individuals, the constraints within which they act and the ways in which meanings are negotiated within those constraints. Using a qualitative case-study approach, she explored influences on the lay perceptions which govern people's relationships with health and illness in East London.

20

In doing so, she was able to demonstrate how an individual's response to illness was grounded in their way of life - determined by a combination of the social, gendered and physical environment within which they reside.

The study revealed how illness within a working-class community was perceived as falling into 'acceptable' and 'unacceptable' categories, placing an onus on the individual to establish the legitimacy of their illness by grounding it within those categories perceived of as 'normal'[1] and 'real'[2] (i.e. falling either within or just outside the bounds of medical treatment). This work, however, also revealed how lay perceptions could be altered by the development of medical treatment, so 'legitimising' an illness by changing it from a natural occurrence (thus a non-illness) to a medically treatable, 'normal' illness. Work in this vein not only revealed a preoccupation with the moral aspects of health and illness, but it also established the 'otherness' of some forms of ill-health (Cornwell, 1984).

By illustrating differing societal negotiations surrounding illness, geographers working within this strand of medical geography have highlighted the importance of recognising the rules and moral definitions surrounding illness and disease, and how these can vary *between* societies. Recent work on AIDS/HIV by Takahashi (1997), for example, has also focused on constructing health geographies that provide an alternative to the epidemiological approaches to illness. Moving away from spatial analyses that consider AIDS/HIV through the bodies of those infected with the illness, Takahashi explored local knowledge and community responses to the disease. In doing so, she was able to demonstrate how stigmatisation surrounding the illness amongst Latino and Vietnamese populations in California emanated in large part from the social construction of AIDS/HIV as an 'imagined community of gay men' (1997, 196). Stigma and resultant denial were seen to place a major obstacle to the provision of healthcare facilities to serve the needs of individuals with HIV/AIDS. Denial leading to a community belief that AIDS/HIV facilities were not needed by the host community, and hence represented a noxious intrusion that should be located elsewhere.

Geographers such as Pinfold (1996) and Parr (1997, 1998) have also used ethnographic approaches in health related research to examine the place and presentation of the researched and researcher's bodies as they interact within the research process. Parr (1998), for example, illustrated how the ideas, bodily actions and concepts of time for individuals with mental ill-health can often differ from the socially constructed norm. In researching difference, there is, hence, a need to confront notions of the corporeal self as 'same' or 'different'.

Work falling within this strand of medical geographical thought indicates the potent influence that the social construction of health and illness can have on community responses to human service facilities. It also highlights how such socially constructed definitions can affect both the behaviour of the individual and the practice of health professionals. The move from institutional to deinstitutionalised modes of health care delivery, for example, can be seen to arise from changing societal responses to care for particular groups of individuals. It further illustrates how such conceptions can arise from the particular socio-cultural and historical circumstances within which the attitudinal and institutional structures of society are embedded.

Spatial inequality and the political ecology of health

The second of these more contemporary strands derives from an essentially welfarist approach within human geography (Smith, 1977) that focuses on issues of spatial inequality in health and welfare and their importance for the well being of the individual. In does, however, move beyond Smith's concern with who gets what, where and how, to incorporate the role of political and socio-economic processes in the production of health and resource distribution.

Eyles' (1987), for example, maintained there was a need to incorporate a focus on the policy process and the mechanisms by which resources are allocated to particular territories and groups. "Policy", he suggested, "is simply the visible outcome of the operation of allocative mechanisms that are themselves shaped by power relations and conceptions of need and justice" (1987, 216). From this perspective, disease and healthcare systems are viewed, in large part, as the product of the wider socio-cultural context. To illustrate this point, Eyles focused firstly, on the relationship between health, work, poverty, housing, class and culture in Britain; and secondly, on the ways in which powerful vested interests (e.g. health professionals and industrialists) attempt to shape policy in order to maintain a technical approach to healthcare. Such work illustrated the need to consider the social and spatial context within which national health services operate, and the geographically and socially uneven effects of policy. Health outcomes, within this approach, are seen to arise as a result of variations in the historical legacy of locales combined with the uneven implementation of policy, organisational problems and financial stringency.

Other researchers have also highlighted the importance of political factors in considering aspects of health geography. More recently, work by Mohan (1995a), has examined the macro-political environment in Britain post-1979, maintaining that changes in the health sector should not be viewed as a consequence of technological determinism, post-Fordist organisational reforms, or convergence. Rather, they should be seen in terms of particular political responses to choices at particular times. In emphasising this point, he focused on the ways in which the macro-influences of government, changes in the economic structure and the uneven historical legacy of capital stock have contributed to an inconsistent development of the 'national' health service over time. He further highlighted spatial differences in the capacities and resources of localities. These are seen to be manifest in the public-private mix of care, the rejection of any resource allocation formulae that incorporate social factors, variations in family structures that may facilitate/inhibit community care, and the variable support local authorities are able to generate through charitable or entrepreneurial activity. Mohan further highlighted the ways in which government policy in Britain throughout the 1980s and early 1990s has sought to relocate the perceived determinants of health and illness from collective to individual responsibility. Such factors draw attention to the importance of considering both macro- and micro-environmental influences on health related behaviours.

Approaches within this strand of thought have also been concerned with the interactions between structure and agency, the material constraints that contribute to people's experiences of health and health services, and the role of health services in society. Dear and Wolch's (1987) study of deinstitutionalisation, for example, drew upon the theories of the duality of structure and agency in social life, and the role of political economic factors in social change as a means of interpreting the historical experience of social welfare provision for individuals with mental ill-health.

Rosenberg (1988), too, maintained that there was a need for medical geographers to develop new frameworks of analysis that incorporate both socio-cultural and political economic influences in the environment to their analyses of healthcare delivery systems. He further argued that any such framework needed to set analysis within its geographical, historical and epidemiological context. Using a case study of abortion service utilisation in Ontario, Canada, Rosenberg

(1988) revealed how the socio-cultural influences of parents, partners, peers groups and community can all affect an individual's decision to seek an abortion and where it is sought. He further illustrated the importance of the role of the primary care-giver in providing *access* to the formal health care system, the geographical organisation of service provision, and how political-economic factors affect both the individual and the delivery system.

In pointing to the need to incorporate the wider economic, socio-cultural and political perspectives within the study of health and healthcare delivery, researchers working within this strand of geographical thought have focused attention on the need to draw upon multi-disciplinary perspectives in examining health-related behaviour. In terms of the study presented within this book, such work is important in that it highlights the need to integrate political and social theory into the examination of geographical problems as a means of exploring the interconnections between societal structures and health.

Health, culture and the 'therapeutic landscape'

A third strand of thought which has relevance within this discussion of 'contemporary' perspectives in medical geography is the emergence of work that has been associated with the 'cultural turn' in geography.

In particular, Philo's (1987, 1989) work on 'the mad business' illuminated how health and illness is both produced and reproduced by a host society that both labels and treats accordingly. Madness and its treatment from this viewpoint becomes a social construction that varies over both time and space. In adopting this view, Philo moves away from a 'traditional' focus on biomedical models of health and illness towards the integration of social models in the analysis of problems within medical geography. Work in this vein also raises awareness to *difference* in the ways in which new concepts of caring for the 'mad' become manifest across space and within places. Philo (1987), for example, illustrated how no one model of the asylum could be said to have prevailed; rather the picture is one of a number of variants, based on 'moral treatment', but whose concrete manifestation stems largely from the views of officials and 'experts' operating in different locales. Such work is of particular importance to this study, in that it draws attention to the ways in which responses to care become differentially embedded within places. Consequently, while there are wider elements that relate to one another in analysing

24

the treatment of the insane, we are also alerted to the fact that these do not add up to some 'tidy, articulated and (grand) theorizable whole' (p.283).

Gesler (1991, 1992, 1993, 1996) using examples at Lourdes and Epidaurus, developed the concept of the 'therapeutic landscape'. In particular, he explores the role of landscape in the healing process, demonstrating how healing in Ancient Greece was perceived as a combination of both secular and spiritual purification. Patients were helped to make sense of their illnesses and their cures, through an attachment to well known rituals and routines in an atmosphere of peace and tranquillity. While such work has largely consisted of an analysis of historical landscapes, it nevertheless draws attention to alternative modes of healing, illustrating how it might be possible develop environments conducive to healing in contemporary society. It also points to the need to move away from an over-arching emphasis on western bio-medical approaches to health, to incorporate more holistic approaches and alternative landscapes of healing (see for example Madge, 1998; Williams, 1998; Armstrong, 2000). These concepts have subsequently been taken up by other geographers interested in aspects of health and environment, who have explored such diverse topics as: the role of the National Forest in middle England in contributing to quality of life (Bell, 1996); the ways in which those with mental ill-health interact with the public city (Parr, 1996); and the ways in which the Cuban government has constructed a landscape of healing in the capital as a means of serving a particular political agenda (Scarpaci, 1996). Kearns and Barnett (1997) have also used this concept to link culture, place and health by examining the contribution of healthcare facilities and their underlying ideologies of competitive provision, to contemporary urban landscapes in New Zealand. More recently, Frazier and Scarpaci (1998) use this concept to reveal the inextricable link between ill-health, place and human rights in post-Pinochet Chile.

While emphasising the importance of notions of place to health and well-being, the work of Gesler (1993) and others also highlights the underlying structural forces within the medical system (e.g. the inherent power structure underlying the clinician/patient relationship, medical territoriality etc.) Consequently, such work makes an explicit attempt to incorporate a blend of emphasis both on the power of human agency or individual action, and the impact of structural constraints.

The above discussion draws attention to the ways in which medical geography has developed. Key points from the above discussion have been summarised in table 2.1. Work within the sub-discipline highlights a number of factors that are of particular import to the ways in which people experience health and illness across space and within places, and which are of relevance to this book. In particular, attention is drawn to:

- the association between health and illness and the environment;
- the relationship between the experience health and illness, the spatial distribution of healthcare services and access to services;
- the need to address the ways in which temporal, socio-cultural, political and economic factors can act to shape variable experiences of health and healthcare across space and place;
- the need to examine how the policy process and resource allocation mechanisms impact on health outcomes;
- the importance of motivation and intentionality in responses to healthcare and health related behaviours;
- the ways in which health and illness, and hence responses to health and illness are socially constructed across time and space; and
- the ways in which changes in the ideology of healthcare become manifest in the landscape of care.

These are all considerations, which in varying degrees, are of relevance to the examination of care restructuring. In particular, the above issues emphasise how the experience of health and healthcare is shaped both by factors operating across the wider spatial context, and those operating at a more localised place-based level; thus drawing attention to the multi-levelled contexts within which health and healthcare is mediated.

While the above factors arise from developments that are evident across various strands of medical geography, this book can perhaps be most closely associated with 'contemporary' responses to health and illness. However, though this study may be viewed as being situated both conceptually and methodologically within a

Table 2.1 Developments in Approaches to Medical Geography

Approach	Typifier	Characteristics	Innovator	Innovation	Recent Work	Study
Ecological Approaches	Snow (1855)	Attempt to uncover associations between disease and the environment through mapping.	Pyle and Rees (1971)	Linked ecological patterning of disease with socio-economic status.	Dorling (1995)	Linked spatial variations in health in UK to social factors.
Spatial Analysis of Healthcare	Pyle (1974)	Focus on distribution and need for services with spatial and temporal characteristics of the environment.	Phillips (1981)	Maintained frequency of use and rationale for use not the same. Highlighted need to consider role of behavioural perspectives in analysis of health issues.	Kanzanjian and Pagliccia (1996)	Demonstrated role of community and spouse in GP locational decisions.
Humanistic Approaches	Waxler (1981)	Focus on motivations and intentionality of individual, combined with socio-cultural environment.	Cornwell (1984)	Demonstrated how individual lay perceptions of health and illness are grounded in lifestyle combined with the social, cultural and gendered environment.	Takahashi (1997)	Demonstrated how responses to AIDS are shaped by the socio-cultural environment.
Political Ecology Approaches	Eyles (1987)	Focus on how policy, process and resource allocation mechanisms act to influence care outcomes.	Dear and Wolch (1987)	Drew on theories of structure and agency and political economic factors in social change as means of interpreting experience of social welfare provision for those with mental ill-health.	Mohan (1995b)	Demonstrated link between uneven development of health services and political responses to change over time.
Cultural Responses to Health	Philo (1987)	Focus on difference, and how social constructions of health and illness vary across time and space.	Gesler (1991)	Demonstrated the role of the 'Therapeutic Landscape' in healthcare and the treatment of ill-health.	Kearns and Barnett (1997)	Linked manifestation of urban landscape of health with culture, place and ideology of competitive provision.

'contemporary' approach to health and health geography, it draws on elements that are evident within a number of these strands. As a result, it does not claim to fit neatly within the parameters of any one particular strand identified above. Nevertheless, in developing a conceptual framework within which to examine a restructured landscape of care, the study acknowledges and incorporates a number of elements that have emerged within 'contemporary' approaches to medical geography.

First, as the context of care has moved from institutional to community-based models of healthcare, the study acknowledges the need to move away from those bio-medical approaches to health and illness evident in earlier medical geographical thought. The conception of health and ill-health can no longer be viewed as a culture-free entity, consequently the study recognises the need to move towards the incorporation of social models of health and healthcare as exemplified here in the work of geographers such as Waxler (1981), Cornwell (1984) and Takahashi (1997).

Second, as a consequence of the above, health and ill-health are viewed as intimately linked to the social construction of society and the power relations inherent within it. This highlights the need to explore not just the relationship between the physical environment and health, but also the ways in which an individual's health and his/her experience of healthcare may be linked to the cultural and socio-economic environment within which he/she is located. These issues are of particular import to the examination of a restructured landscape of care.

Third, geographers such as Cornwell (1984) and Rosenberg (1988) have also drawn attention to the utility of integrating multi-disciplinary perspectives to the analysis of geographical problems. In particular, such work highlights the potential for incorporating social theory as a means of providing insights into the ways in which health and health related behaviour may be mediated through the social networks of individuals within a particular community.

Finally, while acknowledging the role of the individual, the study also recognises the importance of understanding *how* decisions are made with regard to care. This highlights the need to understand the ways in which policy implemented at the national level may be mediated by the meso- and micro-environment in the implementation process. Philo (1987), Rosenberg (1988); Mohan (1995a); and Curtis (1997) have all illustrated in their various ways, how geographical inequities in service provision can arise as a consequence of factors operating at the macro-, meso- and micro-levels. Work in this vein not only highlights the need to place the analysis of care within its wider social, economic and political context, but also illuminates how historical, socio-economic and political factors can be differentially embedded within locales.

To examine a restructured geography of caring thus requires a framework that acknowledges the multi-levelled contexts within which change is mediated. To do so, the study explores the role of actors and agencies operating within the field of community-based care, and the ways in which players within this field can both influence and be influenced by the physical and the social environment within which change occurs.

Notes

[1] Illnesses that were viewed as commonplace and medically treatable e.g. mumps, measles, influenza etc.

[2] Those illnesses which were unusual or severe, and either *just* within the province of medical treatment or just beyond it, i.e. cancers, cardio-vascular diseases, epilepsy, diabetes.

3 Policy and Place: An Historical Geography of Caring

Introduction

Any geographical discussion on the subject of care restructuring requires an understanding of the key factors contributing to the development of newly emerging spaces of caring, and an appreciation of the forces that have shaped them. The previous chapters have drawn attention to two specific elements that are of relevance to these issues. Firstly, the introduction alludes not only to a changing legislative framework of care, but also to the spatial context within which care is located. Secondly, work within 'contemporary' strands of health geography, as discussed in the previous chapter, has highlighted not only how policy can act as a setting for care restructuring, but also how the experience and social construction of care can vary across time and space. So while changes in landscapes of care are, in part, shaped by policy emanating from central government and implemented by formal and informal actors across space, these responses do not develop in a vacuum but are, in part, shaped by their historical context.

In the light of the above, this chapter seeks to fulfil two key functions. Firstly, it provides a discussion on some of the main historical factors that have played a role in shaping the contemporary caring environment. After briefly addressing the significance of the frail elderly in terms of care restructuring, the chapter gives an overview of the historical development of care in the British context, and the ebb and flow of the voluntary sector within this process. While early responses to frail elderly care were located largely within institutional environs, changes in the philosophy of care from the mid-20th century (and more particularly from the late-1980s) combined with its translation into a social programme, have become manifest in a changing landscape of care. Emphasis is now placed on care support located within the community, rather than within institutional spaces, with a concomitant [re]elevation in the role of voluntary, private and informal care supports. This forms the second strand of the chapter, in which the contemporary legislative context within which care policy is translated and produced is discussed. In this way, representations of care are shown to be manifest in new texts, spaces and treatment, new occupational roles and social policies that alter across both time and space (Prior, 1993). These changes also highlight a move away from care responses, which, in the past, have been almost exclusively located within a biomedical framework, toward an increased emphasis on the importance of social models of care. The relevance of this changing framework for the study of geographical problems of health and health-related issues is also discussed.

The Significance of the Frail Elderly

While it is acknowledged that the elderly are a diverse group of people that cannot (and should not) be defined under some homogenous banner, community care legislation nevertheless designates 'the elderly' as one of the key care groups falling within its remit. No definition is given of what is meant by this group. Rather, reference is made to the fact that the majority (around two thirds) of those individuals with mental, physical or sensory disabilities are over the age of sixty five, and thus rely to some extent on social or health services that are provided locally, in order to live as independently as possible within the community (Cm. 849, 1989, para. 2.11). The OECD (1994) embraces a more concrete terminology, viewing this segment of the population as the *frail elderly*, which it defines as 'those aged 65 and over who have a chronic illness or other condition, physical or mental, which causes some long-term loss of function' (p64), a definition also adopted by Tinker et al. (1994) in their report on the frail elderly in UK. The General Household Survey further defines such dependence as pertaining to those who 'could not get about unaided or [who] needed help with one or more aspects of daily living' (Goddard and Savage, 1991, Supplement A, p.4). Particular reference is made to impaired mobility, and a reduced ability to undertake domestic and personal tasks. Such frail, sick or disabled elderly are likely to spend large periods of time at home, and as a consequence, the quality of that environment is likely to be crucial to their mental health and general well-being (Means, 1991).

The significance of the frail elderly for any policy of care lies, in part, in their sheer numbers and the growth of the *very* elderly (Curtis, 1989; Henwood, 1990). As figure 3.1 illustrates, whilst the proportion of over 65s in 1901 had totalled just under 5 percent of the population, by 1991 this had risen to 16 percent - a total of 9 million people.

Figure 3.1 Rise in Over-65s in Britain 1901-2021

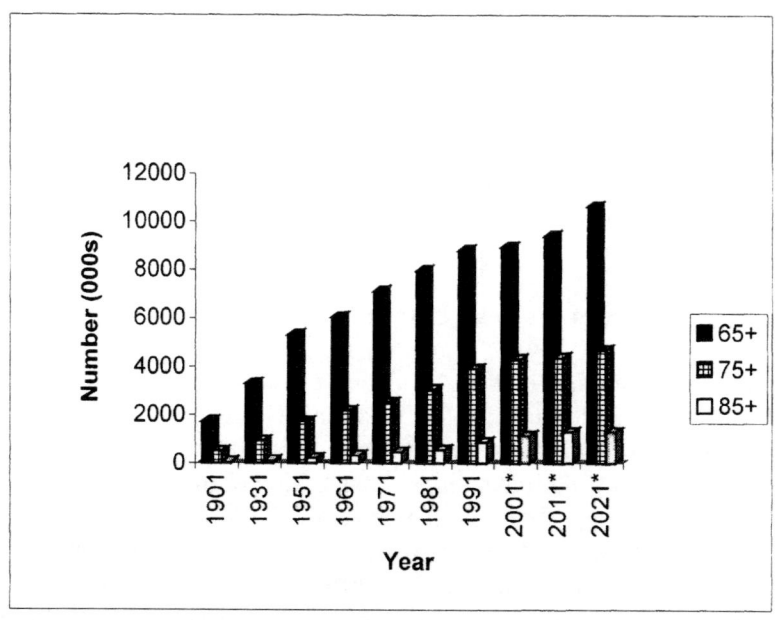

* Projected figures (Coombes, 1996, 12)

This figure is projected to increase further, to just over 18 percent (11 million people) by 2021 (Coombes, 1996, 12), so trebling both the total number *and* proportion of the elderly population in UK since the turn of the century. In addition, there has been a marked growth in the very elderly (those aged seventy-five and over) rising from just 1.4 percent of the population at the beginning of the 20th century to 7 percent by 1991. This figure is further projected to increase to 7.9 percent by 2021. Consequently, there has been a five-fold increase in this age group since the beginning of the century, with a further projected increase into the new millennium. Such a demographic change is significant, in that this age group, in particular, are known to be high consumers of health and social care services. For while old age is not synonymous with ill-health and dependency, increasing age *is* connected with frailty; 70 percent of disabled adults are in the sixty plus age grouping (Tinker et al, 1994, 27).

In Scotland, the total number of over 65s has been projected to increase by 44.5 percent, between 1991-2031, with an even greater increase (64.9 percent) in the 75+ age grouping (GRO Scotland, 1994). Yet despite the long predicted growth in the numbers of elderly throughout this century - with its concomitant health and social policy implications - attitudes towards the prospective care needs of the frail elderly have largely been met by a 'demographic myopia' (Parker, 1990, p.13). As the following section illustrates, government responses to care for the frail elderly has been slow and piecemeal.

An Historical Geography of Care for the Frail Elderly

Prior to the 19th century, social care in UK as a whole was characterised largely by informal community care. A private system existed for those who could afford the services of medical practitioners, nurses and other care support. For the majority, however, the only available source of help beyond the informal system was that provided by charitable organisations or the parish. Social care at this time was seen to be closely inter-twined with religion - philanthropy being intimately linked to support directed at those deemed as suitable subjects of 'Christian care' (Checkland, 1980). Religious institutions of the time were involved in the delivery of many forms of philanthropic support including material support for the mentally and physically infirm, orphans, and the elderly. Such philanthropic giving was characterised by a paternalistic class system, in which aristocrats and landed gentry were the controllers of local charities, and thus influential in the management of the Poor Law at parish level (Wolfenden, 1978).

Elderly care pre-welfare state

By the mid-19th century, the economic opportunities created by industrialisation, combined with the emergence of the new industrial and commercial class, led philosophers such as Smith and Bentham to extol the virtues of a laissez faire economy - such an approach was argued to be a prerequisite for economic prosperity. Proponents of laissez-faire emphasised the detrimental effects of interventionism in the form of regulation and charity, resulting in the 1834 Poor Law Amendment Act. It is in this Act, that Means and Smith (1994) maintain it is possible to identify the roots of statutory care provisioning. The Act introduced a centrally controlled 'deterrent' system of support, aimed at minimising non-institutional relief and leaving the workhouse as the only alternative. Much charitable giving at this time was focused on ensuring that philanthropic policies were in line with the administration of a system of poor relief, which sought to separate out the 'deserving' from the 'undeserving' poor. In line with this policy, attempts were also made to rationalise charitable work. The founding of the Charitable Organisations Society in 1869, for example, aimed to co-ordinate activities within areas with a view to encouraging a 'scientific' evaluation of individual cases as a means of preventing the excessive allocation of help to any one individual.[1] As a consequence, throughout much of the 19th century there was little recognition of any social group defined as 'frail elderly' that may require special provision due to their age. Elderly people with no visible means of support either worked until they died, or, if unable to do so, often ended up in the workhouse. No distinction was made between the elderly and other indigent groups at this time.

By the early 20th century, further technical and industrial development was beginning to force a rethink on attitudes to the elderly. Such change was seen to exclude the elderly from the labour market through no fault of their own, so increasing their dependence on poor-law relief. At the same time, studies (e.g. Rowntree, 1901) were beginning to demonstrate that the conditions imposed by industrialisation had a direct effect on poverty and disease. Collective action was being increasingly viewed as the only solution to this problem. Responses to these changes during the early part of the century, however, were predominantly based around the concept of retirement. Concern was focused largely on pension legislation, rather than the introduction of social care supports - a factor driven more by high unemployment rates (and thus the perceived need to remove the elderly from the workplace) than any real concern with the elderly themselves (Means and Smith, 1994).

The voluntary sector thus remained a major provider of basic welfare services in UK throughout this period, with many hospitals and care services for children and the disabled heavily reliant on voluntary support. Attempts were made to co-ordinate the voluntary sector at local level through the development of Councils for the Voluntary Sector, and Guilds of Help. By 1919 this had become manifest at the national level in the National Council for Social Services, a forum that moved to direct action by becoming involved in community development.

Despite the major role played by the voluntary sector in the provision of social supports at this time, large numbers of elderly were still entering the workhouse. Increasingly, however, these institutions were seeking to segregate both the chronically sick who required medical provision, and the elderly. Both were viewed as 'deserving poor', as opposed to other 'undeserving inmates'. By 1929, the Local Government Act had re-titled the best of the poor law hospitals as public health hospitals, so becoming the responsibility of local authority health committees. As such, they no longer formed part of the poor law system. These hospitals, however, focused almost entirely on the *acute* sick rather than the medical needs of the frail elderly, who more usually experienced chronic ill-health. The remaining workhouses were renamed Public Assistance Institutions (PAIs) but essentially retained the concept of provision for the indigent, and an institutional regime.

By the 1930s, however, there was growing disquiet about the nature of institutional care, and calls for change to the lives of the elderly within these institutions were being voiced. It was argued, that many of the chronically sick elderly, rather than being located in the new municipal hospitals, had in fact been sent to Public Assistance Institutions simply as a means of emptying beds as hospitals sought to upgrade their own medical services (Means and Smith, 1994). With the onset of the Second World War, overcrowding within such institutions became aggravated by the influx of war casualties and the need to create an emergency medical service. Many frail elderly were simply discharged to their own homes, where they received little (if any) care, often being regarded as an added burden by family and relatives caught up in the war effort. The war period also caused problems for the frail elderly as families were split and homes were damaged or destroyed. Growing numbers of elderly individuals who had *no* major health problems were also finding their ability to remain within their own homes reduced, either due to the lack of familial support arising as a consequence of their relocation to other localities, or simply from having lost their homes through bombing raids. The demand for in-patient care increased, and many elderly who would *not* have been described as 'indigent poor' found themselves reliant on Public Assistance Institutions as a consequence of war.

While the voluntary sector played a major role in the provision of [albeit limited] social welfare services in the pre-welfare state period, it is nevertheless possible to see in the first half of the 20th century the beginnings of legislation which, though limited in scope, sought to introduce social provision for some sections of the population outside the system of poor relief (e.g. pensions, school medical services, unemployment and health insurance). Such legislation enshrined the principle of state involvement in the establishment of minimum standards - an involvement which gradually extended to the extent that by the inter-war period, most of the working population was covered by national insurance.

Introducing the welfare state

With the establishment of the National Health Service (NHS) in 1946, the state undertook to provide basic social care. At the same time, Public Assistance Institutions were brought under the same administrative system as that of other hospitals, though there was a growing awareness within central government of the need to address the problem of bed-blocking within hospitals. This problem was seen to arise as a consequence of three factors (Means and Smith, 1985):

- a failure to tackle the needs of acute illness amongst the frail elderly population;
- the need for rehabilitation services; and
- a growing awareness of the inappropriate nature of this kind of institutional care for frail elderly individuals.

Whilst the Poor Law was finally removed from the statute book in 1948, it had nevertheless left a legacy of attitudes and practices redolent of poverty and minimal service. The physical premises of the old workhouses remained the mainstay of local authority residential services for the frail and disabled. Further, while most of these premises had been transferred to the NHS by 1948, their continued usage meant that in fact both the NHS *and* the Local Authorities had inherited the legacy of the Poor Law. A study of residential homes for the frail elderly conducted in the 1950s, for example, illustrated that over 60 percent of those admitted to institutional care were being cared for within the old workhouse buildings (Townsend, 1962).

Research highlighting the poverty of the elderly and the need to reform the system continued to emerge in the post-war period. In the 1960s, studies noted that the main shortcoming of care was not so much the failure to improve the quality of the residential buildings and staff, but a failure to develop community-based alternatives that would reduce the *need* for individuals to enter institutional care (e.g. Townsend and Wedderburn, 1965; Harris, 1968; Seebohm Report: Cm. 3703, 1968). Nevertheless, despite an emerging social criticism of institutional care, concern throughout the 1950s and 1960s (as in the earlier part of the century) still focused largely around the economic question of pensions, rather than with the condition and composition of the elderly population itself. The care needs of the frail elderly continued to be treated largely as a secondary issue.

The contribution of local authorities to the provision of community-based and domiciliary services at this time centred largely on grant-making to voluntary organisations for services such as meals-on-wheels and recreational facilities. Whilst a patchwork of services *did* emerge, development was highly uneven. Harris's (1961) survey of meals-on-wheels services, for example, found that of 453 identified schemes, as many as 40 percent had an insufficiency of volunteers to *deliver* the service, with a further 40 percent of recipients receiving only one meal per week. In addition, it was noted that at least 162 of these schemes closed completely for at least some part of the year, leaving its service recipients with no service during these periods.

Legislative change empowering local authorities to provide domiciliary services was slow to develop. Despite growing evidence of the inability of the voluntarily sector to cope adequately with both the need and demand for such services, prior to 1962, local authorities were restricted to an essentially grant-making role for the provision of care. By the late 1960s, this had resulted in a service that was not only varied in terms of its objectives and responsibilities, but also in terms of a social welfare provision that was spatially differentiated in its stages of development. Waiting lists for day and residential services for the frail elderly, the mentally and physically disabled, along with a shortage of domiciliary services were evident in many areas. Access and availability of such services was clearly spatially differentiated. Local Authorities had no general responsibility for promoting the welfare of the elderly within their locale until 1968, and it was to be 1977 before the National Health Services Act would make homecare a mandatory responsibility, rather than a discretionary one, as had previously been the case. Thus, while the earlier 1948 National Assistance Act had contained a clause empowering local authorities to promote the welfare of those who experienced physical, mental or sensory impairment, local authorities were largely unable to develop their own domiciliary services. This reflected an underlying belief that such services were an additional 'frill' and, as a consequence, could be left to the voluntary services to be developed.

These developments highlight not only the growing separation of the frail elderly from other groups in society, but also the growing involvement of the state in welfare provisioning. Concomitantly, there was a change in the perception of the role of the voluntary sector, from that of a key provider of welfare services to that of supplementary support. With the introduction of the welfare state and the growing public provision of social services, the voluntary sector found itself increasingly directed towards a role viewed as 'supplementary' to that of the statutory provision rather than providing a parallel, but separate, system. For some, the growth in public provision heralded the 'death knell' of the voluntary sector. Such commentators believed it would simply wither away and die in the face of growing statutory provisioning (Wolfenden, 1978). Others (Beveridge, 1948) still viewed the voluntary sector as having a significant role to play in the care of the frail elderly, children, the mentally and physically disabled (those groups that now form the focus of contemporary community-based care initiatives). Emphasis was placed on the *moral* contribution that voluntarism had to play in society; as a consequence, voluntarism continued to be encouraged through local and central government grant-aid.

In the light of increased public provision, some significant changes began to occur within the voluntary sector from the late 1950s onwards. Organisations sought to reorient their services in order to differentiate their contribution to welfare support from that of the statutory sector (for example through providing specialist services not available within the statutory sector), while at the same time there was also a growth of co-ordinating bodies at the national level. This period also saw the emergence of different forms of voluntary organisations, with the burgeoning of groups who operated less as direct providers and more as pressure groups campaigning on behalf of specific groups or issues (for example, Shelter, Carers National, the Disability Income Group).

Restructuring Health and Social Care: The Last Two Decades

While the previous section reveals an early pattern of 'care' for the frail elderly that can be characterised more by its absence than any profound change, neglect for this group was never absolute. At various times, concern about demographic change, or the conditions of care for those in institutional environments raised the profile of these services and led to expressions of intent to change the prevailing situation. As the previous section has highlighted, by the mid-20th century British society was becoming increasingly disillusioned with institutional care, with calls being voiced for the development of community-based alternatives. The rationale for a move toward deinstitutionalised care was threefold:

- there had been a long-standing concern within central government with regard to the high costs of institutional provision (Guillebaud Report, 1956);
- there were growing concerns about the basic standards of institutional care for the mentally and physically disabled - many of whom were elderly (e.g. Robb, 1967); and
- clinical advance and the development of new drugs meant that a growing number of treatments could now be provided outside large institutional environs.

Thus by the mid-1960s, the emphasis on care provision was increasingly being reoriented *away* from institutional to deinstitutionalised care within a community environment. As the Seebohm Report (1968) noted, "greater emphasis has now been laid upon community rather than institutional care" (para. 80). Individuals living in the community, however, need a variety of forms of help across different agencies. Thus the report highlighted the need for more effective co-ordination between social services, housing, health, education and social security, in order to support such policies. This report, however, had also highlighted deficiencies in social care and the need for organisational change in the provision of services. In particular, it recommended the setting up of a social services department within the local authority structure to meet social needs within the community of the frail elderly, the mentally and physically disabled, children and other "neglected flotsam and jetsam of society" (para. 139). It further maintained, "much more ought to be done in the field of prevention, community involvement, the guidance of voluntary workers and in making fuller use of voluntary organisations" (Seebohm, 1968, para. 139).

The reorganisation of local authority social services in 1970, under the Local Authority Social Services Act, gave local authorities the responsibility for the development of social work departments, whose functions were to include that of community care. The Act also gave local authorities a responsibility for establishing a social work committee with responsibilities for (amongst other roles):

- the provision and regulation of residential accommodation for frail elderly and disabled persons;
- welfare services for frail elderly and disabled persons, those suffering mental disorder and the chronically sick - including practical assistance in the home, day centres, visiting and advisory services; and
- assisting housing authorities in relation to cases of homelessness.

Yet despite the findings of the Seebohm Report and the setting up of social service departments to take responsibility for social and welfare services, residential care for the frail elderly continued to predominate over domiciliary care throughout the 1970s. This is attributed in part to a statutory redefinition of community care (Parker, 1990). The [Labour] 1977 consultative document 'The Way Forward' (DHSS, 1977), for example, maintained that 'community care' covered a range of provision from community hospitals, hostels, day hospitals, residential homes, day centres, as well as domiciliary support. The main priority of government during a period characterised as one of 'austerity measures' was to ensure that frail elderly populations were kept out of increasingly expensive general and long-stay hospitals.

By the late 1970s, however, economic recession had shifted the debate *away* from any focus on the perceived need for an overall increase in social care expenditure to a focus on care restructuring and the need to shift priorities from institutional to domiciliary and residential provision (DHSS, 1978). Residential care was seen as a particularly significant means of achieving this - though (as before) it did little to encourage the development of domiciliary care. Changes to the supplementary benefits system in the early 1980s had, in fact, had the unforeseen impact of enabling poorer frail elderly individuals to claim residential care costs, with the result that private residential places mushroomed. Places were seen to rise from 46,900 in 1982, to 161,200 in 1991 (Laing and Buisson, 1992, 156). This development brought government unease, as public spending in this area leapt from some £10 million in 1979, to £1872 million in 1991 (Means and Smith, 1994, 50). In effect, deinstitutionalisation from NHS environs had been replaced by a *re*institutionalisation within largely private and local authority residential and nursing facilities. As such, the pattern of 'deinstitutionalised care' for the frail elderly can be seen to have followed a somewhat different path to that of other community care groups.

Nevertheless, by the mid-1970s and throughout the 1980s, concern over the increasing costs of institutional care, combined with growing concern over the basic standards of care was bringing pressure for change. However, though the NHS Reorganisation Act of 1973 aimed to drive forward deinstitutionalisation policies through the establishment of a new machinery for joint planning between health and local authorities, it failed to make any significant progress. As a consequence, it was followed in 1976 by joint-finance arrangements aimed partly as an incentive towards joint planning. Joint finance was viewed as a mechanism through which social service departments could obtain health authority monies for a time-limited period to establish community-based initiatives as a means of either facilitating the hospital rundown programme, or to provide adequate support mechanisms to individuals to enable them to remain within the community.

The 1977 National Health Services Act, and later Health and Social Services and Social Security Adjudications Act, 1983, also gave health authorities and local social services a duty to co-operate with one another in order to secure and advance the health and welfare of the key groups (including the frail elderly). Broadly similar provision was made in Scotland under the National Health Service Act (Scotland) in 1978. This same Act also empowered both the Secretary of State and local authorities to make grants and loans to voluntary organisations operating in the field of welfare services.

Progress throughout this period, however, was slow. The 1983 document *Care in the Community and Joint Finance* (DHSS), for example, set only a fairly modest increase in available funding, though it aimed to encourage resource transfer monies between health authorities and local authorities. The document further extended the remit of community-based care initiatives to include housing and education projects, and for the first time announced that there should be voluntary sector representation on the Joint Consultative Committees. By the mid-1980s, however, central government was becoming frustrated at the lack of progress in community care.

A number of other reports in the mid-1980s, had also been highly critical of government failure to develop any coherent community care policies (e.g. Social Services Committee Report, 1985; Audit Commission, 1986). The Audit Commission had noted that not only had movement towards community care been slow, but it was also geographically uneven. Further, it pointed out that too many individuals had been released from institutional care only to be reinstitutionalised within private residential or nursing homes, rather than developing into a genuine community-based care. Concern was also being voiced by local authorities and health authorities with regard to the existing joint planning system. The report highlighted the need for strategic planning, including a clarification of those agencies that should take responsibility for which care groups.

Government response to these criticisms was to set up a review of community care headed by Roy Griffiths, the outcome of which, highlighted the failure of community care policies to clarify the responsibilities of social services, health, housing, voluntary and private sectors within the field of community care. The Griffiths Report (1988) recommended that social services take the lead role, under a nominated Minister, whose role would be to define the values and objectives of such care. Local authorities, the report argued, should take the lead role in identifying need, co-ordinating services and regulating voluntary and private sector residential care - the funding subsidy to which should be reformed. Housing was seen as playing only a 'bricks and mortar' role, with health services taking responsibility for medical care, including any input necessary in assessing needs for care packages. It was further argued that such care should be delivered within a mixed economy approach, so placing public, private and voluntary sector provision on an even footing.

Whilst the Griffiths Report was welcomed by social services, who saw themselves elevated to a lead role in community care, the report was not so well received in all quarters. Health professionals and independent residential care services were less enthused about some of its recommendations, with health professionals losing clinical dominance, and care home owners viewing the report as hostile to residential care. The Treasury was also hostile to any ring-fenced funding for community care, that would: (i) make explicit the levels of commitment from central government; and (ii) allow for a clearer identification of when cutbacks were being made (Means and Smith, 1994). Thus, though the 1989 White Paper that emerged the following year took on board most of the Griffiths recommendations, there were two key omissions: firstly, there was no implementation of any ring-fenced funding (with the exception of some specific monies for mental ill-health and substance abuse); and secondly, there was to be no specific Minister for Community Care. Funds were to be channelled through transfers from the social security budget (where they were used to pay residential costs) with local authorities given discretion regarding how much funding they allocated to residential provision, and how much was to be focused on community-based initiatives.

The funding framework for community care, however, has proven problematic. Whilst local authorities and central government have provided grants for the establishment of a wide range of organisations to provide services since 1948, tensions arising from the implementation of community care legislation, and over local government funding, are bringing about changes in the pattern of remaining services. Budgets are allocated to local authorities from central government which, at that time in Scotland, were channelled through the Scottish Office. Most monies, however, were not specifically earmarked for care services - rather they have to be argued for at a local level from general rate support money dispersed by the Scottish Office to each local authority. Within each block grant, there are assumptions about what each individual local authority should spend on its main services (Standing Spending Assessments - SSAs). These SSAs were introduced in 1990/91, and were divided into three blocks - under 18s (35.5 percent of total); the elderly (45.2 percent of total); other adults requiring support (19.3 percent of total) (Harding, 1992). These blocks were calculated in different ways, but relied on population estimates and deprivation factors - some of which were open to challenge in terms of their relevance to what local authorities needed to spend on their social services. That is, they were not built-up from local need, rather they were devices for distributing the overall money which Ministers and the Treasury had made available to fund services through local authorities. Two criticisms in particular, have been levelled at this assessment criteria (Means and Smith, 1994):

- that the overall sums of money were inadequate to meet the objectives for social services being set by the Department of Health; and

- that the SSA weighting variation between local authorities was not justifiable, the net result being, that most local authorities overspend on the SSA for social services.

Thus as government expenditure tightened, local authorities increasingly found themselves facing the option of either 'robbing Peter to pay Paul', or attempting to generate income through the introduction/expansion of charging policies for services.

While the White Paper elevated social services as the lead agency responsible for defining need in collaboration with health and other caring agencies, local authorities were to act predominantly as *enablers* rather than providers of services, so placing an emphasis on a mixed economy approach. Local authorities were to make use, where possible, of non-profit and private care providers where these represented a cost-effective choice. In undertaking this mixed provision, local authorities were recommended to introduce the concept of contracting and service agreements as the main funding mechanism in an 'evolutionary way'. The White Paper became enshrined in legislation in the 1990 NHS and Community Care Act, though difficulties in its execution lead to major delays, to the extent that it was 1993 before the Act was fully implemented.[2]

Summarising the development of social welfare

The above discussion has illustrated how the role of both the state and the voluntary sector in the provision of health and social welfare in both pre- and post-welfare state, has been intimately linked to change and developments in the wider social and structural context. The development of social welfare for the frail elderly can thus be seen as a reflection of three main factors:

- the gradual separation of the elderly from other groups in society;
- the changing role of the voluntary sector versus the state in the provision of social welfare; and
- changes in public attitudes to care provision.

The historical development of local social care services across UK has nevertheless been erratic due firstly, to variations in both their point of origin, and secondly, to variations in the public view of 'deserving' and 'undeserving' individuals - and so their willingness to support and finance certain services. As a consequence, the social and spatial development of these caring services for the frail elderly have emerged within different areas at different times, for different reasons, and to meet specifically defined needs.

The Contemporary Legislative Framework in Scotland

Until the implementation of devolved government through the new Scottish Parliament in May 1999, welfare restructuring in the UK stemmed from change enacted by central government at Westminster, but implemented through a legislative framework of agencies located at the regional and community level. The Scottish Office was the key government agency in Scotland [3] empowered to oversee the implementation of central government policy. However, as indicated in the previous section, due to differences in its legal framework, Scotland has historically required a separate policy amendment to legislation existing elsewhere in Britain (Murphy, 1992). The policy framework thus varies by degree to that existing in England and Wales. Scottish local government, and hence social and housing services, have developed on lines distinct from those of England and Wales.

The 1990 NHS and Community Care Act, for example, notes that local authorities should encourage a mixed economy of care, incorporating public, private and voluntary/non-profit provisioning. To enhance this provision, there has been a legal requirement for local authorities in England and Wales spend 85 percent of their Special Transitional Grant [4] (STG) on the purchase of external care services. The separate Scottish amendment, however, recognised the lower levels of development of voluntary and private sector care services in Scotland. Thus, unlike England and Wales, there has been no legal requirement for Scottish local authorities to adhere to the ruling, rather there was a *recommendation* that full use be made of voluntary and private sector care supports wherever possible.

The 1990 NHS and Community Care Act also made a number of other changes in social services legislation in Scotland. Local Authorities have been required to prepare and publish plans for the provision of community care services in their area. Whilst Scottish health and social work authorities were not *required* to establish joint liaison committees, social work departments were required to work with the appropriate Area Health Boards at the strategic planning level in matters of common interest to clients and patients (Scottish Office, 1993). Further, in undertaking the preparation and publication of care services in their area, local authorities were directed to collaborate with other formal and informal care providers and service. To this end, the legislative framework made provision for the development of joint-planning fora through which Social Services, Health, Housing, the voluntary sector, informal carers and service recipients can access the policy and planning process. Emphasis has been placed on the development of a partnership between local authorities, providers and service recipients (Scottish Office, 1993, para. 10).

Drawing these strands together, care provision in Scotland has been enacted through an organisational hierarchy emanating from central government in Westminster, through to a mix of local private, voluntary and informal sector agencies (figure 3.2). This forms the structure for the caring network involving actors and agents sited within both the formal and informal sectors. [5]

Figure 3.2   The Organisational Hierarchy of Community-based Care in Scotland (1990-1999)

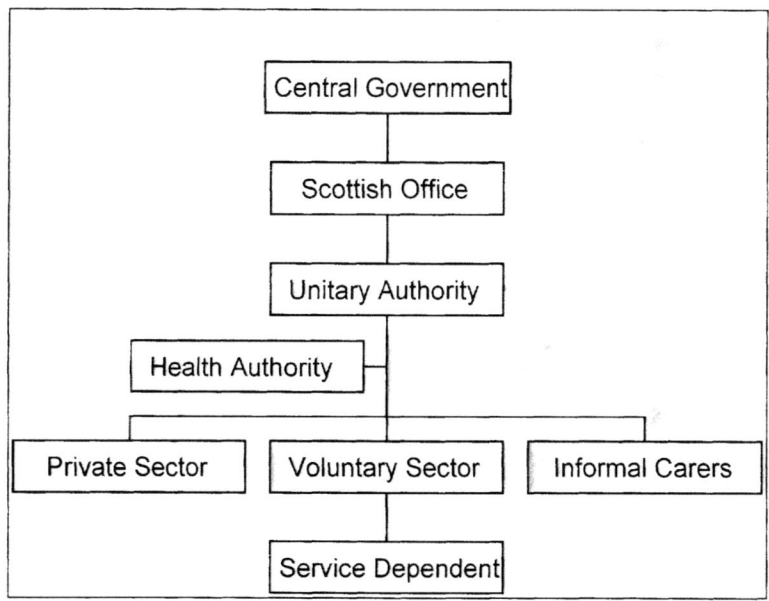

Within this framework, local authorities are allocated the lead role in a partnership seen to comprise local authorities (in particular social services and housing departments), health authorities, voluntary and private sector providers and informal carers. The 1990 NHS and Community Care Act outlined the roles and functions of each of the key agencies involved in the delivery of health and social care within community environments (see table 3.1).

In addition to the re-structuring of social welfare services, local authorities in Scotland have also faced organisational change arising from

Table 3.1   Key Roles of Actors Within the Scottish Framework of Community-based Care (1990-1999)

Agency	Key Roles
Central Government	Determination & implementation of national legislation. Central determination of budgetary allocation to UAs and Health Authorities.
Scottish Office	Allocation of central government budgets to UAs and Health Authorities. Allocation of ring-fenced grants e.g. MISG and Urban Aid. Monitoring of community care plans. Secretary of State for Scotland has overall responsibility for social services, and housing, and Area Health Boards are directly to him/her.
Unitary Authority (UA)	Prime responsibility (in collaboration with health professionals and other agencies as necessary) for community care provision, particularly (i) assessment of individual need; (ii) designing care packages; (iii) securing delivery of service. (role is both as enabler and provider e.g. day and residential care, domiciliary/ homecare and therapeutic aids). Primary role in strategic planning of services and preparation of joint community care plans. Responsibility for inspection and registration of services. Social services to be 'gatekeepers' to social care - responsible (in collaboration with health, housing and other interests) for identification of need and assessment criteria, also purchase services from private and voluntary care providers. Housing - role in provision sheltered housing, groups homes, hostels and housing adaptations.
Health Authority	Community health services e.g. GPs, community nursing and other community health services. Hospital daycare and some residential respite. Key role in strategic planning of care services and development of joint community care plans. Collaboration with local authorities in assessment of need and development of care packages for clients.
Voluntary Sector	Provision of community care support services. Role in planning of care services and joint community care plans. Collaboration with local authorities in assessment of need and development of care packages where relevant. Advocacy and lobbying on behalf of service recipients.
Private Sector	Provision of community care support services purchased privately (by clients) or through UAs. Collaboration with local authorities in assessment of need and development of care packages where relevant. Consultative role in planning of care services and joint community care plans
Informal Carers	Care and support to the service dependent. Collaboration with local authorities in assessment of need and development of care packages where relevant. Consultative role in planning of care services and joint community care plans.

Source: Adapted from Cm. 849 (1989).

local authority restructuring. Under the 1996 Local Authorities (Scotland) Act, the existing two-tier local government was abolished in favour of new single tier unitary authorities. As evident from map 3.1, in the process of restructuring some Scottish local authorities have experienced boundary changes as a number of the larger regional authorities have been disaggregated. The old Strathclyde Region, for example, was disaggregated in favour of twelve smaller unitary authorities. As a consequence of this changeover, some social service departments have found themselves having to restructure their own geographical boundaries, while at the same time coping with a changing organisational role with regard to community-based care.

Summary of 'Caring' Models

Every revolution in care for dependent groups is defined by a new relationship between that group and the society that cares for and interacts with them. Whilst under an exclusionary system of segregation it was easy to 'map' service dependent populations, with the development of deinstitutionalised, community-based systems of care, it is much more difficult to know *where* individuals are located, *what* the patterns of development are, and *how* policy affects those involved. The philosophy of community-based care combined with its translation into a social programme in the UK has, as a consequence, created a new generation of service-dependent who experience unique problems in accessing the system of care. So while dependent individuals experience similar frailties to those of their earlier counterparts (whose care, as illustrated in the previous sections, was largely located within institutional environments) as Bachrach (1989) notes, these individuals are now *situationally* different as a result of service system changes.

Community-based care, which represents the contemporary form of care provision to the frail elderly, is predicated on the assumption that the community will provide the social and tangible supports to ensure the continued optimal functioning of the service-dependent (Cm. 849, 1989). Thus, in the restructuring of care, there is a presumption that the individual will become immersed into the social structure of both the family and community, so connecting the individual to those supports which enable him/her to thrive in such a setting. Such a development however raises questions about the nature and degree of support available to the individual in community-based settings. It is unclear, for example, how services and supports combine for the service recipient - what are the interactions between the system and those providing care, and how these might be

Map 3.1 New Unitary Authorities in Scotland

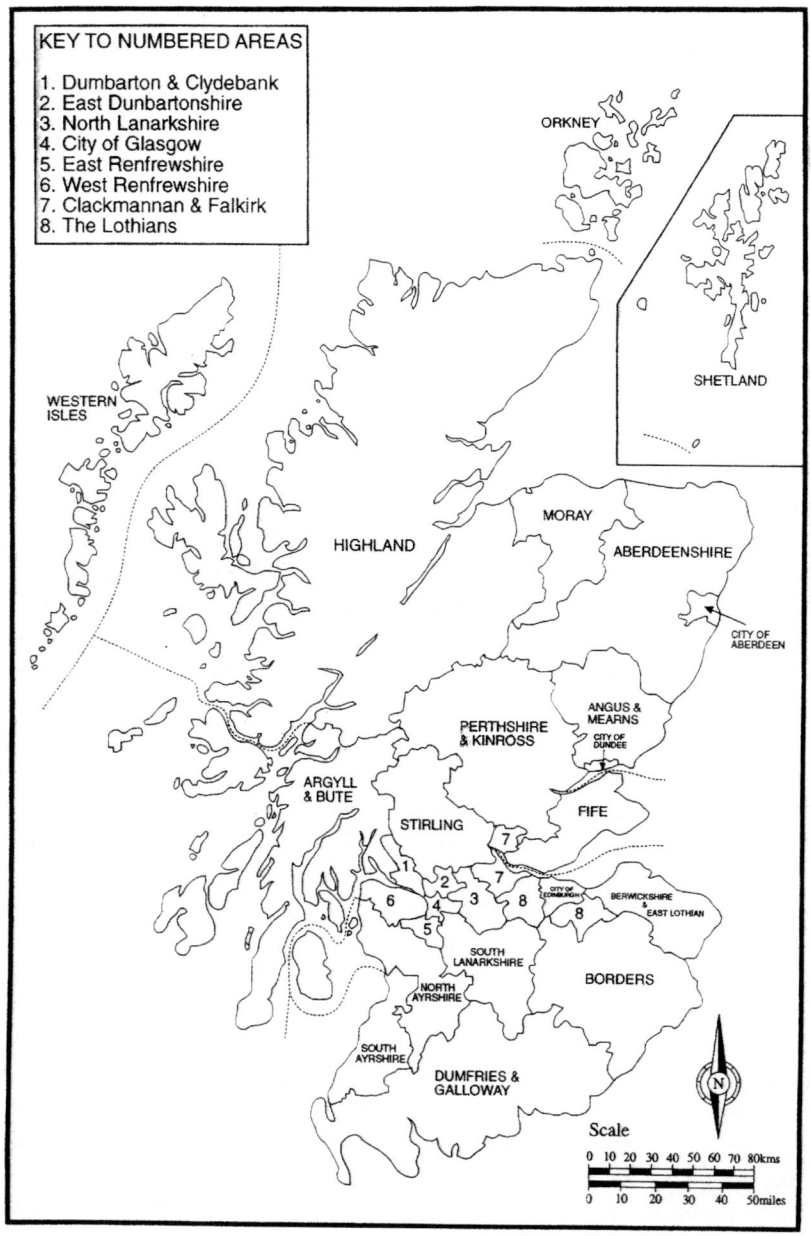

KEY TO NUMBERED AREAS

1. Dumbarton & Clydebank
2. East Dunbartonshire
3. North Lanarkshire
4. City of Glasgow
5. East Renfrewshire
6. West Renfrewshire
7. Clackmannan & Falkirk
8. The Lothians

differentially experienced as a result of an individual's location in space? These factors highlight a need to focus on the interactions between care providers, service-users and their environment.

This marks a move away from the former over-arching focus on a bio-medical approach, to a need to incorporate social models of care. Such models require a consideration not only the determinants and dynamics of service delivery and the resultant outcomes, but also to identify variations within and across communities which may influence the equity of support available to the end-user. Under institutional models of care, the health or illness of the individual has largely been medically defined. That is, illness and disability have been interpreted as physical conditions whose existence can be established through medical diagnosis. Under these models, health and illness have been viewed as objective categories, consequently it is not social meanings which create ill-health, but malfunctions of the body. Access to care and treatment under such models occurs within a framework of biomedical interventionism, with the spotlight resting on the individual (Graham, 1985). In contrast, later care regimes reveal a reorientation in thinking that can be seen to incorporate social constructionist approaches to health and illness. As illustrated in the preceding chapter, the change in emphasis from bio-medical to social models - and hence the impact of socio-cultural influences on health outcomes - is one that has been recognised and incorporated into the research of those working within 'contemporary' strands of medical geography.

'Placing' the Study: The Geographical Context

Despite the passing of legislation at the level of central government, there can be considerable scope within the legislative frame for local variation in the translation of policy into practice (Mohan, 1995; Pinch, 1997). At the level of the unitary authority, policy can be shaped by the political disposition of the democratically elected local government. While this may be fully in-tune with central government policy, this is not always the case. As a result, variations can arise in the ways in which policy is enacted and translated into practice (Curtis, 1989; Rhodes and Marsh, 1992). Similarly, professional working relationships between local authorities, Health Boards, and the voluntary sector can vary. Thus at each tier, and within each locally-embedded network of care, the interpretation of care can be shaped by the range of agents concerned with its implementation. Local policies and professional relationships *within* organisations concerned with community-based health and social care programmes can also have a large effect on the ways in which these programmes are conducted. This places a focus on the policy process, but is also suggestive of the need to focus on: a) place outcomes in practice; and b) the internal dynamics of the framework. Attention is thus directed to how particular locales can constitute the settings within which the structural forces, institutional practices and the everyday routines of agents, interact to produce a concrete manifestation of community care outcomes. Any such narrative is inevitably both geographical and place-specific.

The implementation of recent legislation in UK renewing the emphasis on service delivery within domestic and small community-based locations, combined with the recent creation of new single-tier local government in Scotland, has drawn attention to the need to assess how the social and spatial implications of these changes are impacting at local level. To date, such a focus has been absent. Yet as Kearns (1993) has argued, a central requirement for a geography of health is a need for research that recognises the contingent relations pertaining to individuals and groups at particular locations. The current legislative frame which places a focus on: a) the community; b) local authority tiers of control; and c) the rise in the number of sectors involved, reinforces the need for just such a study.

Given the intensive methods used in this study and their potential for uncovering a rich array of data, it was not the numerical breadth of coverage that was viewed as important in the selection of the study areas, but their potential for uncovering how responses to community-based care and its outcomes have been conceptualised and transformed across space and within places. Though one area would have been sufficient to give a flavour of these outcomes, one objective of the study has been to examine difference as experienced across urban and rural space. Scotland is a region subject to immense variation in its physical geography and demographic profile. It is a region dominated by rural landscapes but urban-based populations. In order to incorporate these factors, the study examined the experience of care restructuring within two local authority areas in Scotland (see map 3.2).

The selection of these areas was based on four criteria:

(i)   *the urban/rural dimension*: the impact of policy manifests itself in very different ways across urban and rural locations - a factor all too often neglected in policy formulation. It was consequently important that these issues should be addressed within the study;

(ii)   *local authority reorganisation*: in addition to health and social care restructuring, local authorities in Scotland have also undergone reorganisation resulting in structural and geographical boundary changes since April 1996. For some authorities this has had little impact, others, however, have experienced profound change;

50

Map 3.2 New Unitary Authorities in Scotland - Highlighting Glasgow City and Dumfries and Galloway

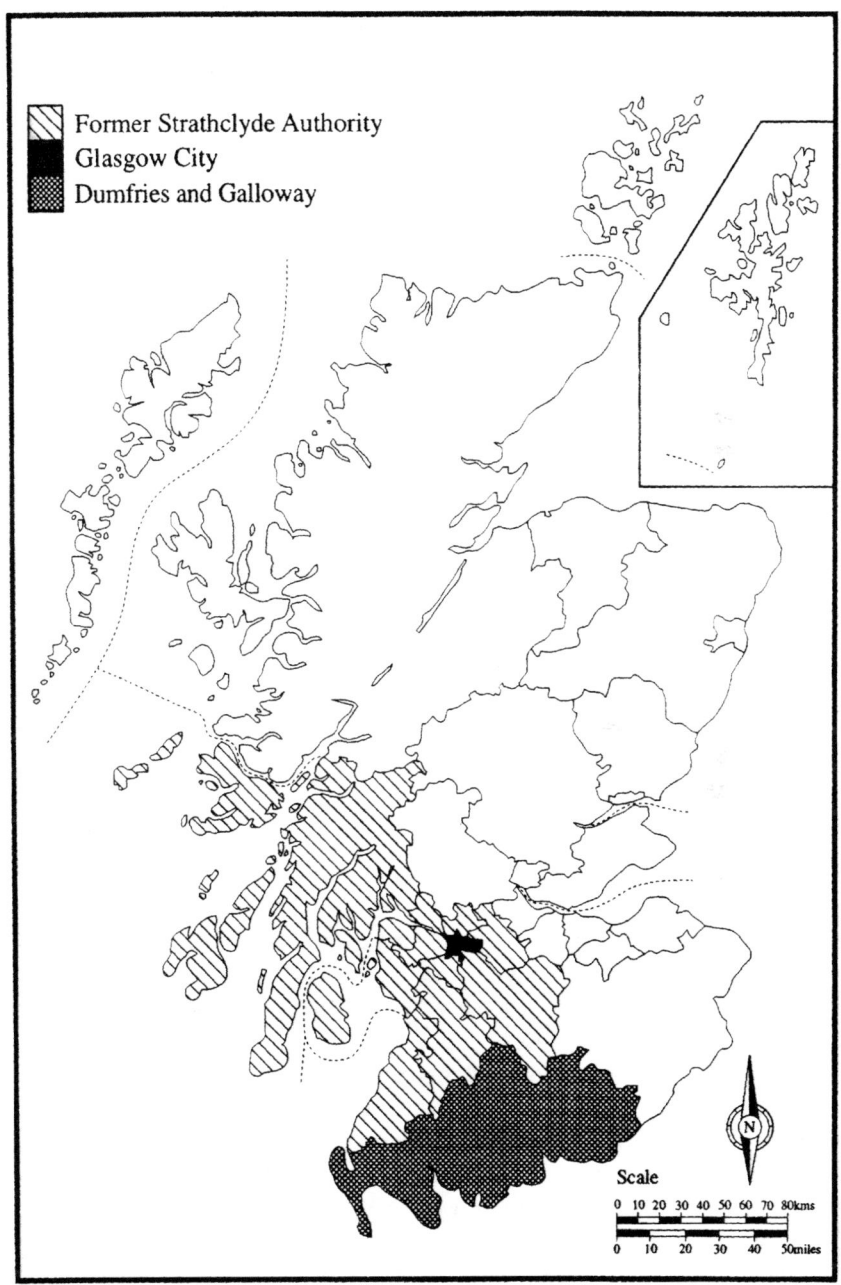

(iii)   *practical field work considerations*: In order to avoid data collection from becoming overly complex, each area should deal with only one local authority and one health authority; and

(iv)   *local demographic variations*: variations in both the socio-political and demographic profile of particular locales are likely to impact differentially on a geography of caring. Differences in age profile between localities may have implications for the feasibility of any community-based service delivery to the frail elderly focused around the encouragement of informal care provision which is sited within the homespace.

The first of the local authorities selected was the largely rural area of Dumfries and Galloway in the south-west of Scotland. This local authority region has a population base of some 147,300, and covers an area of 6,370 sq. km. (GRO Scotland, 1998). The population density of the area is thus 23.2 per sq. km. While local authority restructuring has created changes in *personnel* within this region, there has been no change in the size or boundary of this new Unitary Authority. Local authority and Health Authority boundaries in this area are coterminous. Politically, this is an area that (up until the 1997 general election) has been dominated by Conservative Party representation within central government, and Independent representation at the level of local government. Finally, Dumfries and Galloway is also a region with an ageing population, in-migration of younger retired elderly and out-migration of young people seeking employment opportunities is contributing to a slightly higher proportion of elderly and slightly lower proportion of younger age cohorts than is evident in the general Scottish profile.

The second location is that of the urban centre of Glasgow City - this is the most populous local authority area in Scotland. With a population of 627,000 (Glasgow Unitary Authority, 1996) Glasgow City comprises an area covering just 198 sq. km, and hence has a population density of 3,167 per sq. km. Consequently, there is considerable variations in population density – with implications for service delivery - between the two local authority areas. Glasgow City also forms part of an area that was disaggregated under the 1996 Act, from one large single authority serving the whole of Strathclyde, into twelve smaller, single-tier unitary authorities.

Whilst Glasgow City now forms a new UA, at the time of writing, it nevertheless remains (as prior to reorganisation) within the boundaries of the Greater Glasgow Health Authority. While the Greater Glasgow Health Board serves populations within six different Local Authority jurisdictions, Glasgow City is the major authority and lies fully within the Health Board's geographical boundaries. Politically, Glasgow City is an area that has been dominated by Labour Party representation at both central and local government levels. Finally, as illustrated in figure 3.3, Glasgow City, though around the Scottish average for those cohorts in the 60+ age groups, has a considerably larger population in the young adult groups.

These two localities offered the potential to assess not only urban/rural difference, but how variations in networks of care can arise as a consequence of particular locally-embedded factors.

Notes

[1] It should be noted however, that not all voluntary organisations at this time were influenced by this 'self-help' philosophy. A number of organisations developed to deal with specific issues, such as orphaned children (Barnados), moral welfare (the Salvation Army) and those concerned with such issues as mental and physical disabilities.

[2] e.g. those monies available to local authorities for the 1993/4 period and the following two years, were not known until late 1992 - meaning Local Authorities were expected to outline strategic planning for the first Community Care Plans without knowledge of what funding would actually be available to implement these plans.

[3] At the time of the research - between 1996-1999. The Scottish Office has since been renamed as the Scotland Office with the devolution of power to the Scottish Parliament.

[4] Those monies derived from the transfer of funds from health to social services as institutional services are wound-up in the move to community based care.

[5] Since Scottish devolution in 1999, the Scottish Office has been replaced by the Scottish Executive. The Executive now hold responsibility for overseeing the implementing health and social care policy as directed by the Scottish Parliament (see Epilogue).

4 Constructing the Conceptual Framework

Introduction

The previous chapter has drawn attention to changing societal perceptions of the frail elderly and accompanying variations in emphasis from individual to communal responsibility for their care. Such changes are manifest in the ebb and flow of the importance placed on voluntary, private and statutory care provision. Since the late 1980s in Scotland, however, the organisational hierarchy of care for the frail elderly and other community care groups has been relatively stable. Yet despite the relative stability of the framework, as Wistow et al (1994) have noted, little attention has been given to the *inter*-agency relationships that exist between informal and state providers. Still less attention has been given to any detailed examination of how these relationships vary across space and how this impacts on care outcomes for service-users. One way in which it may be possible to facilitate our understanding of these processes is through the adoption of a conceptual framework that allows for a multi-levelled analysis of the socio-spatial and structural impacts of care restructuring. Such a framework should, in a heuristic way, enable the positioning of actors to be defined (in a legislative sense) and allow interactions between them to be mapped out.

The need to explore the linkages and relationships between a variety of actors operating within different spatial contexts and across multi-levels of the policy process points to the possible utility of a networked approach as a conceptual framework within which to locate the study. At its most simple, a network approach to analysis requires the researcher to follow the network all along its length. It maintains that there is no need to step outside the network, for all the qualities of spatial construction and the configuration of interests will be found within them (Latour, 1991). In this way, space is seen to be bound into networks and any assessment of spatial qualities is an assessment of network relations (Murdoch, 1997).

This chapter is concerned to construct such a framework. In doing so, it is organised around four sections. Firstly, it discusses some of the ways in which existing geographical research has usefully adopted conceptual frameworks that incorporate analyses of spatial and structural factors occurring across a variety of scales. These are explored as a foundation for thinking about ways in which it might be possible to develop a framework of analysis that operates across a number of planes that are both spatial and organisational. Following on from this, the chapter examines some of the key concepts used within networked approaches as a means of understanding the relevance of these interactions and how they might be usefully employed in the analysis of geographical problems. It examines the development of various networked approaches within the social sciences, how these concepts have been used, and how a small group of [largely] economic geographers have sought to incorporate network approaches into geographical thought and analyses. These approaches are drawn upon as a means of facilitating the construction of the 'dependency network' as a framework for exploring how the inter-relationships between actors operating across space and at differing levels of the care process contribute to local variations in care outcomes.

'Placing' the Conceptual Framework

As noted above, one way of contributing to an understanding of how care policy determined at the macro-scale is translated at locality level is through the development of a conceptual framework that aims to elucidate how the provision of supports for frail elderly individuals are mediated by the meso- and micro-situational environments within which they are located. Within this study, the meso-level is taken to comprise activities occurring at the level of local governance, and thus consist of relations occurring at the mid-level tiers of the care hierarchy (figure 3.2). The micro-level is seen to comprise activities occurring at the level of the individual (e.g. within the homespace) and thus refers to the lower levels of the hierarchy.

Commentators such as Dear and Wolch (1987) and Moon (1990) have pointed to the utility of combining an analysis of both the structural and spatial context when examining problems of health and social welfare restructuring. They maintained that while geographies of social welfare need to reflect spatial difference, such analyses also need to take account of the wider economic and socio-political arena within which change is located; an arena which may influence and in turn be influenced by those agents involved in newly emerging processes. Through an analysis of socio-structural and spatial factors relating to deinstitutionalisation within the North American context, Dear and Wolch (1987), for example, were able to reveal factors contributing to the spatial manifestation of the service-dependent ghetto. This geographical outcome was shown to arise as a consequence of the ability of individual actors to both transform, and be transformed by the context itself. Ghetto formation was viewed as the consequence of agents operating within a social context (or structure) which both enabled and constrained. Such work highlights the importance of examining the inter-relationships between long-term structures and the actions of key actors. Thus, Dear and Wolch (1987, 10) maintain, that 'any narrative about landscapes, regions, or locales is necessarily an account of the reciprocal relationship between relatively long-term structural forces and the shorter term routine practices of individual human agents'.

More recently, Allen (1997), in a study of the housing sector and its role in community care drew attention to the failure of researchers to locate their investigations of care policy within what he refers to as a contextual 'world view' (1997, 86). That is, that researchers use either a *prescriptive* top-down framework aimed at minimising the incidence and extent of implementation gaps in policy (Hogwood and Gunn, 1984; Sabatier and Mazmanian, 1981) or a *descriptive* bottom-up framework (e.g. Ham and Hill, 1984; Lipskey, 1980). The former, he contends, is ineffective and lacking in context, whilst the latter, though having useful things to say about the nature of policy and implementation, places an over-arching emphasis on individuals, and thus tends to ignore critical questions relating to structure. This is argued to have led researchers to construct analyses that have mis-represented the meaning and significance of community care policy and the role of housing within it. As a consequence, he calls for an analysis of policy and implementation that seeks to investigate the multi-levels of the policy process, the linkages between them, and the manner in which they interact in order to produce and transform policy materials.

Work in this vein employs the transformative concepts of 'transmission' and 'translation' developed by Callon (1986) and Latour (1986) [concepts discussed below]. Great emphasis is placed on the competence of agents to translate material that is within both temporally and spatially defined sectors of activity. As discussed in chapter two, despite the passing of legislation at the macro-level, the legislative frame allows considerable scope for local variation in the translation of policy into practice. Hence, by conducting micro-situational research within particular locales at particular points in time across a policy sector, events can also be analysed for site-specificity and the extent to which policy material is translated and transformed by agents acting within the implementation process (Duster, 1981; Sibeon, 1991). Such an approach, it is maintained, allows us to transcend specific sites and move between macro-trends in the policy sector to understand the dynamic nature of policy materials. This draws attention to the role of three sets of influences on policy outcomes (Allen, 1997):

- macro-influences which are external and non-specific to the policy context (e.g. ideology);
- macro-influences (or structural properties) which are seen as specific to the policy-sector (e.g. the social construction of the policy sector and policy materials); and
- the 'negotiation context', which is seen to comprise those rules formulated to guide the implementation of particular policies.

By using these distinctions, it may be possible to place policy materials and the activities of actors and agencies (including inter-relationships within agencies) within a "multi-levelled structured context of meaning" (Allen, 1997, 87). Within care restructuring, for example, such an approach would require structural influences to be analysed within those formulated rules specific to the implementation of care policy operating in a mixed market of provision, giving consideration to the ways in which agencies handle community care materials.

The approaches highlighted by both Dear and Wolch (1987) and Allen (1997) are important in that they point research *away* from macro-reductionist, structuralist and functionalist approaches which demonstrate a tendency to divorce agents from their own actions and meanings (e.g. Gough, 1979; Dearlove and Saunders, 1984). This emerges through the inference that agents are merely pre-determined micro-expressions of an over-arching social order. Such approaches can also address criticisms of micro-reductionist approaches which have been argued to assign undue competence to agency by inferring that actions and meanings are agency specific (Giddens, 1984, 1993; Sibeon, 1991).

For a study to achieve integration of the local scene with an analysis of a broader understanding of social, cultural, political and economic forces, there requires to be an 'inclusion of the separate levels of entry into the empirical world, buttressed by a ... strategy of substantive contextualisation' (Duster, 1981, 133). Any such framework needs to take account of the interaction of macro-level political economic structures and constraints; the role of institutions such as the state in translating those structures into policies and programmes; and the activities of knowledgeable and capable human actors and agencies involved in the health and social care system. So by raising the empirical question of how phenomena under investigation are manifest at each of these levels, there is an implicit injunction to examine how they are shaped and reshaped as a consequence of these inter-linkages. From this perspective, such phenomenon are understood as the structured medium and outcome of reflexively (and contingently) produced and reproduced activities of spatially and temporally located actors. These actors

57

are seen to be defined according to a socially constructed context. Within a deinstitutionalised environment of care, new sets of actors can be seen to emerge as a consequence of this changing societal response to the delivery of care.

To examine this process Duster (1981) conceptualises three levels of entry:

- the direct observation of behaviour in a local setting which routinely occurs at the micro-level of analysis;
- the observation and analysis of the administrative, bureaucratic, or organisational unit[s] that are interposed between the local scene and the state; and
- the macro trends or national policy developments.

As alluded to in the work of Dear and Wolch (1987), a fourth factor also needs to be addressed - one that is concerned less with the level of entry and more with a concern to provide a wider (temporal and spatial) contextualisation for the problem under investigation.

These issues are also of methodological significance. They highlight the importance of examining the inter-relationships between actors and agencies operating at different levels of the implementation process as a means of understanding how policy material is translated and transformed by agents acting within site-specific contexts at particular points in time. In this sense, the four issues highlighted above are of inter-related concern to both the conceptual framework discussed within this chapter (and which is derived from the policy framework discussed in chapter three) and to the developing of the research design and methodological framework of the study.

Exploring Networked Approaches to Analysis

To address the need to understand how policy implemented at the macro-level is played out through these multi-levelled contexts, the study looked towards networked approaches. References to the complementary nature of network and institutional analysis can be found in work that stretches back over three decades (e.g. Mitchell, 1969; Rhodes, 1981; Berkowitz, 1988; Hardy et. al, 1990). It has only been in more recent years, however, that the utility of networked approaches as a means of overcoming the conventional dualism between macro- and micro-level analyses have been explored (e.g. Callon, 1986, 1995; Latour, 1986, 1988). While these approaches are largely located within sociology, a small but growing body of researchers have begun to explore their utility for the analysis of geographical research (e.g. Dicken and Thrift, 1992; Murdoch, 1994, 1997a, 1997b; Amin and Thrift, 1995; Murdoch and Marsden, 1995). These geographers have begun to draw attention to the potential of networked approaches as a means of examining the nature of spatial relationships in a manner that negotiates a path between macro- and micro-theory and practice.

A number of terms and concepts are key to understanding networked approaches. It is useful to identify these concepts as a starting point to any discussion regarding the relevance of a network approach to the examination of care restructuring. Their defining features have been summarised in table 4.1.

Contemporary network theorists (e.g. Callon, 1986, 1995; Latour 1986; Law and Hassard, 1999) maintain that the conventional opposition between macro- and micro-analysis is both inappropriate and outdated, developing the concept of *translation chains* as a mechanism through which to establish a continuum between these two extremes. The extension of a network and the diversity of its translations means that the organisation of interaction between the heterogeneous elements of the network is an important strategic matter. This points to the utility of studying the distribution of *actants* within the network and the links between them.

The concept of translation is viewed as offering a broader definition of action - actants have been seen to range across such diverse subjects as scallops within the French fishing industry (Callon, 1986); a pharmaceutical firm aiming to develop a particular drug (Callon, 1995); the politics of anaemia (Mol, 1999); to a chemical with the ability to inhibit a specific action/reaction within another human/non-human entity (Latour, 1987). All these actants are mobilised in statements, instructions or embodied skills. Each new translation is thus viewed as having the ability to modify, transform, contradict or strengthen former translations. As a consequence, each may act to modify or stabilise the actant's universe. Actants' identities and interactions are, thus, seen as being defined by the translation process, with new translations producing a discrepancy in relation to previous ones. Even the most insignificant of actants can produce slightly differing translations. Hence, actants operating at all levels of a network can serve to influence translations and completely new actors can be drawn into the network. This inevitably has implications for the ways in which outcomes are manifest across time and space (Callon, 1995). In this way, the concept of translation does not oppose the local/global or negate agency and passive behaviours. Rather it is viewed as a means of describing the dynamic nature of the network's diversity, interconnectedness and irreversibility.

Table 4.1 Some Key Concepts Within Network Approaches

Concept	Defining features
Translation chain	All operations that link technical devices, statements and human beings. Translation chains are seen to combine a variety of heterogeneous elements, in which human actors, technical devices and *inscriptions*, are brought together and interact with each other. Translation can be inscribed in texts, material substances or skills and instruments, and consist of the negotiations, calculations, or acts of persuasion through which an actor or force takes (or confers on itself) the authority to speak or act on behalf of another actor or force.
Inscription	A device placing the individual within a 'network of writing' e.g. all the registration and documentary accumulation built in to medical examination process, to which the individual is also bound (Foucault, 1979, 191).
Actant	Any entity, human or non-human, endowed with the ability to act.
Prescription	Whatever of a scene is presupposed by its transcribed actors. Using the theme of the traffic light, Latour (1987) draws attention to the way in which its users will watch it from the road and not the side, and that its rhythm will be regular. The result of such an alignment of set-ups is that much action becomes silent, familiar, or incorporated - the 'taken for granted' aspects that become habitualised and institutionalised once created. Prescription is also viewed as representing the moral and ethical dimension of mechanisms.
Pre-enscription	This refers to all work done 'upstream' of the scene, and all those things assimilated by the actant before coming to the scene as a user (Latour, 1988). In this way, pre-enscription can be seen to take cognisance of the wider context within which action occurs.
Symmetry	The actor network approach does not attribute any essential characteristics to an entity, these are seen to emerge as effects once the associations have been 'stitched together'. Human and natural actants are treated impartially and symmetrically, removing humans from the pivotal role as a means of understanding how classifications such as human/non-human, subject/object, nature/society emerge as network effects.

Source: Adapted from Latour, 1988; and Callon, 1995.

A cornerstone of the actor network approach, however, is that of symmetry. Latour (1994) maintained that whilst a single actant within the network may take different shapes and play different roles, it is as entities are enrolled and combined within the network that they gain shape and function. The symmetry that lies at the heart of the actor-network approach thus stems from the belief that 'power' and 'size' are not set in stone. In Murdoch's (1997, 335) words:

> it therefore aims to uncover how associations and networks are built and maintained. Once we understand how size and power are manufactured then we can understand how they can be transformed. But we will only fully recognize the potential for change if we stay within the networks: thus we should never vacate the local and the micro in order to look for 'explanations' at another scale of analysis; neither should we remain trapped in the local and the micro for the networks will undoubtedly travel far from those restricted realms.

The creation and development of networks can be seen to depend upon a set of conditions that either facilitate or constrain the deployment of translations. Other obstacles to the proliferation of translations can lie in the [more or less] explicit arrangements that define the circulation of statements, instruments and embodied skills - for example, rules of confidentiality, exclusive rights to a process, or of particular relevance here, the 'negotiation context'. The mechanisms for designating the actants authorised to speak on behalf of other actants within networks can also influence the character of possible translations. This raises issues about who may be authorised to speak to whom; who may ally with whom; and who speaks on whose behalf. Within the context of care networks, this focuses attention on questions of representation and empowerment, the importance of examining such mechanisms as the joint-planning processes (as discussed in chapter three) and the importance of strategic alliances. Entities are seen to achieve their form as a consequence of the relations within which they are located (Law, 1999). Hence the concept of translation offers a way of examining the inter-relationships within a network, and the ability of actants operating within it to modify, transform or translate materials coming within their orbit.

Geographical Approaches to Network Theory

Network analysis has been evident within geographical thinking and practice for well over three decades. In the mid-1950s, for example, Lösch

(1954) expressed a concern with the form of road networks linking places of varying size and function [later to become a key plank in the development of central place theory]. Whilst other geographers have also explored the utility of these approaches (see for example Haggett, 1967; Chorley and Haggett, 1974) such analyses have, until relatively recently, been largely confined to the examination of transport networks and linkages between locations, or other types of linear patterns including political and administrative boundaries, social contacts and communication (Johnston et al., 1994). Such work focused on the *structure* of the network; that is, the geometrical pattern of linear connections, their mutual relationships, and their links to external controlling forces such as the identification of relationships between the network and other variables including terrain, population density and the economic climate (Haggett, 1967). However, even within these early networked approaches, there was some recognition of the need to make reference to changing social, economic and political climates to gain a fuller understanding of the relationships.

Derived in part from graph theory, early geographical approaches to network analysis focused on three main concepts: the nature of nodes; linkages; and connectedness. Whilst the latter two can perhaps be seen as having been incorporated and further developed within the concept of the translation chain, references to nodes as core sites connected by the linkages (Grigg, 1967, 479) have largely been jettisoned in favour of the notion of *actants* - a concept viewed as offering a greater potential for understanding the influence of both human and non-human action within the network.

Others have sought to use social network theory to as a means of examining geographical problems (see for example, Taylor, 1971; Olssen, 1980; Ley, 1983). Here, networks have been characterised in terms of the linkages between a defined set of persons tied usually by shared values, attitudes and aspirations. The spatial concentration of such networks has been viewed in two ways:

- as a consequence of members of the network choosing to live proximate to others to whom they are linked in order to maximise the potential for contact and interaction; and
- as a means of demonstrating how social networks are subject to the influence of distance decay.

These approaches have developed from sociological perspectives first adopted in the mid-1950s (e.g. Barnes, 1954; Mayer, 1966; Mitchell, 1969). Barnes (1954), for example, used the concept of the social network as a means of describing the order of social relationships in a study of a Norwegian island parish, which, he argued, was insufficiently explained by the socio-structural concepts of territorial location and occupation. As a consequence, he maintained, there was a need to consider 'that part of the total network that is left behind when we remove the groupings and the chains of interaction which belong strictly to the territorial field and the industrial system' (Barnes, 1954, 43). The potential expansiveness of the social network, however, was viewed as requiring both the definition of some point of 'anchorage' or initial starting point for analysis and the designation of a bounded zone beyond which levels of influence are not analytically significant for the social situation being studied (Mitchell, 1969).

Social network theory also has its origins in graph theory. As such, it too perceives the lines which *connect* the points as having a value ascribed to them. Its concern is with the ways in which the links between individuals are constructed and how this mediates outcomes. Such networks as seen as being spatially bounded as both cause and effect; members choose to live proximate to others in their social network, so maximising the potential for social contact and interaction. It is the characteristics of these linkages as a whole that are seen as being of importance in interpreting the social behaviour of the individual involved. Social network theory, as a consequence, focuses less on the individuals within the network and more on the characteristics of the linkages, their relationship to one another and on how the interactional characteristics refer to the nature of the links themselves. Thus, as with the concept of translation, emphasis is placed on the network itself and its characteristics in shaping outcomes.

Arguably, it is in its focus on the linkages at the expense of both the individual and the wider context that such an approach displays weakness. That is, that firstly, it fails to account for embodied social and cultural dimensions that can impact on the individual; and secondly, it fails to incorporate the wider social, political and economic environment within which networks are embedded. Nevertheless, this approach offers some useful tools for understanding the ways in which social relationships operate outwith a focus on occupational and territorial boundedness. In particular it draws attention to the importance of the *direction* of the linkages and the ways in which the characteristics of the linkages themselves can affect outcomes. The social network approach, however, is essentially one that operates at the micro-level. So while it offers a useful framework for examining relationships occurring at this level, it fails to link micro-scale analysis with the wider policy context. Hence, in its level of operation, it offers only a limited ability to uncover the ways in which change operating at the macro- and meso-levels impacts on social processes.

Though network approaches have a strong geographical lineage, these early approaches are of limited utility for undertaking a multi-levelled analysis of the socio-spatial and structural impacts of care restructuring. The emergence of a small but growing corpus of geographical work in recent years, however, has begun to incorporate new sociological approaches to networked theory into its analysis. These works have called for the development of an associationalist geography; a mode of thinking which seeks to negotiate a path between macro- and micro-theory by investigating the links rather than the distinctions. Largely situated within the sub-discipline of economic geography, the focus is on Actor Network approaches derived from the work of Callon (1986, 1995), Latour (1986, 1988) and Law (1986, 1994). Geographers, such as Dicken and Thrift (1992), Cooke and Morgan (1993), Murdoch (1994), and Amin and Thrift (1995) have begun to explore the utility of these approaches as a means of analysing spatial change arising as a consequence of economic and regional transition.

Using Actor Network theory (ANT) these commentators have sought to bring together the social and the material, as a means of overcoming the dualisms that have been of concern to other theorists (e.g. Giddens, 1981; 1984). ANT claims to overcome those problems of dualistic thinking which have tended to polarize theoretical approaches into two incompatible parts, by placing the social and the material at the centre of analysis in a way that sees scale simply as an outcome of the heterogeneous links established between actors. Hence, ANT 'celebrates its powers of 'in-betweenness' and proclaims the end of 'heres' and 'theres'; from now on, it says, we should concentrate on middles, links, chains, networks and associations' (Murdoch, 1997a, 322). Human societies are seen as 'framed interactions' within which social interaction is always bounded and configured, but which can be stabilised and extended over time and space through the use of material tools (Latour, 1994). Human interaction is not seen as purely local, but also constituted, construed and configured by distant actions. The key to understanding this is the role played by resources in stabilising and maintaining past actions in a way which allows them to bear on the localised present (Murdoch, 1997). Networked approaches thus emphasise 'path-dependent evolutionary change' (Amin and Thrift, 1995, 53); that is, it emphasises the degree to which networks constructed in particular contexts for particular purposes are sedimented over time.

In this way, an ANT view of an agency begins not with fully-formed agents, but with an already constituted social space (the network) and demonstrates how agents emerge from a series of trials in which they are continually striving to become actors and gain powers. As with social network theory, action is viewed as the property of associations rather than human agents (i.e. it is the character of the *network* that shapes action). Thus, in principle, non-humans have the potential to act arising from the network relations within which they are enmeshed.

To illustrate the importance of incorporating both humans and non-humans into the framework of analysis, Latour[1] (1988) used the analogy of the hinge. As a mechanism for enabling the construction of the door, he demonstrated the hinge's utility for maintaining the wall within which it is located in a reversible state - so enabling access to a specific area without having to resort to continually knocking down and rebuilding the wall each time an individual wishes to enter/leave a particular space. He further drew attention to the way in which specific *types* of hinges can serve to both enable and constrain. The hydraulic door-closer, for example, in enabling the door to be closed, excludes unwanted elements - such as drafts - without the need for the presence of a human actor to facilitate this action. However, for certain humans, for example the very small and the very old, the energy required to open such doors may discriminate against them. In this way, such mechanisms can also be seen to impose constraints. Latour (1988, 299) thus argued that "the hinged door allows a selection of what gets in and what gets out so as to locally increase order or information". Such action is seen to be, in part, determined by the wider context within which the action occurs, leading people to a gradient of aligned set-ups that endow actors with the pre-enscribed competences to find its users a necessary path (e.g. the door).

Translation within the network involves a complex series of negotiations in which identities are fought over, roles are ascribed and power relations fixed - the identities of the actors and actants are determined *within* the network in relation to one another (Law, 1992). Forms of domination and control are established within multiple and complex associations, where power lies not in the properties of actors but in the relations established between them (Latour, 1986). The alliances of networks can be contested at any moment. Any identities these entities hold before enrolment within the network, can be redefined by the network builders as new sets of relations are established. While such relations may be only provisional, even if they fail they may alter the shape of the social and non-human constituents in what can be irreversible ways (Murdoch, 1997a).

Such theorists, however, are primarily interested in *how* these categories emerge from the processes of network building itself rather than the ways in which network building can impact on emerging outcomes. The incorporation of Actor Network approaches within geographical work has thus sought to investigate the means by which associations come into existence, and how the roles and functions of subjects and objects, actors and intermediaries are attributed and stabilised. Both Cooke and Morgan (1993) and Dicken and Thrift (1992) used associationalist approaches to examine inter- and intra-firm associations within business enterprise in the geographical structure of economic activity. For them, geographical industrialisation is seen not only in terms of changing industry trajectories, but also in terms of dynamic webs of power relationships. While such webs of power and influence are tied to particular places, they are also seen to *transcend* place, thus networks become a vital subject for geographical research. Though this is not in itself a new idea, it is a powerful and flexible way of capturing the dynamic complexity of inter-dependent production systems together with their resource circuits. In particular, it points to the relevance of exploring the inter-relationships within and between firms, and the need to examine power and contractual relationships between actants and strategic alliances and collaborations that can occur within and between sectors and actants within the network.

ANT acknowledges the differential embeddedness of networks within particular places, however, in its adherence to the notion of symmetry it appears to assume that the emergence of these associations occurs from some point in time and space which is essentially represented as a level playing field. As a result, it has thus been subjected to criticisms about whether the notion that symmetry must always be maintained, and whether it is realistic to propose that impartiality can always be maintained in studying the causes and effects of network attributes. Questions have been raised, for example, with regard to the authority of actor-network theorists to speak for non-humans in their analyses. Such reliance on a human-centred account of the behaviour of such non-human actants, it is argued, belies the symmetry ANT ascribes to human/non-human agents (Collins and Yearley, 1992).

Geographers in particular have demonstrated the *asymmetry* of power between networks and interdependencies that are underpinned by inequalities within and between networks. In examining the role of business enterprise in the geographical structure of economic activity, inter- and intra-firm structures have been shown to comprise diverse networks that arise as the outcome of differential transactional relationships within and between firms, with differing degrees of power and influence (Dicken and Thrift, 1992; Amin and Thrift, 1995). Some of the networks of power and influence are seen to be based on their ability to deploy corporate power, whether in the form of strongly asymmetrical dominance of the large over the small, or the more symmetrical power relationship involved in strategic alliances between two or more relatively equal partners that constitutes a new form of diplomacy between firms. Geographers working within this vein maintain that the network represents a new form of relation in which 'the power and control exerted by large firms vis-à-vis smaller ones is moderated in its execution but is by no means transcended' (Cooke and Morgan, 1993, 562).

In its unwillingness to attribute any essential characteristics or status to entities *within* the network as it is being formed, ANT also ignores the role of both motivations and intentionality [intrinsically human characteristics] that drives actants to build associations and networks in the first place (Pickering, 1992). It assumes, for example, an almost passive submission of human actants within the process of shaping the network (e.g. it ignores those who opt out of the network rather that submit to the designs of the network builders). Thus for network approaches to examine issues of distribution, there needs to be a shift in focus to acknowledge and encompass issues of marginality and the ways in which some forms of exclusion are reinforced by the network (Murdoch, 1997b). Hence, there is a need to examine how standardised networks can act to 'screen out' those actants who do not fit standardised patterns. This further raises the issue of whether non-humans actants are as malleable as human actants - given that the latter are products of society.

Governance, policy and network approaches

Network theorists tend to focus on intermediate forms of governance as a means of best illustrating the power of networks and the information they carry (Amin and Thrift, 1995). Such approaches view the boundaries between state and civil society as being fluid. Thus, as the institutions of state and civil society become increasingly blurred, the role of the state is seen to become redefined. Within care restructuring, for example, while the state is seen to maintain its functions as the purchaser of services and provider and regulator of resources, it becomes involved in fostering new trans-boundary organisations via funding, regulation and the transmission of new ideas. In the process of doing so, however, the state is also forced to redefine its *own* practices, so coming to mimic more closely these new forms of association by demands from newly formed decentralised associations (many of which were formerly in the state sector). As it cannot be assumed that such networks are a guarantor of social and political democracy, this points towards 'progressive' and 'regressive' coalitions, whereby progressive coalitions are defined by their participatory mode of governance (Amin and Thrift, 1995, 59).

Within care restructuring, the local state has been seen to be legislatively assigned an enabling role aimed at fostering the involvement of voluntary and private sector providers. New associations are formed as the informal sector is increasingly drawn into the network and taking an increasing share of that part of the caring role previously the domain of the public sector. Wolch (1990, xvi) has referred to the changing status of the informal sector as contributing to the emergence of a 'shadow state', 'a para state apparatus comprised of multiple voluntary sector organizations, administered outside of traditional democratic politics and charged with major service responsibilities previously shouldered by the public sector, yet remaining within the purview of state control.' This points to the emergence of new political spaces that operate between the state and civil society (Brown, 1997). It also raises questions with regard to the symmetry or asymmetry of power relationships within a network of associations concerned with care restructuring, and the ways in which care policy is translated within the network in the light of these developments.

An alternative network approach used to examine the links between the meso- and macro- levels of interest has been that of policy network analysis. Used largely by political theorists (e.g. Rhodes, 1981, 1986, 1988; Marsh and Rhodes, 1992; Nyland, 1985; John and Cole, 1995), this approach has focused mainly on the UK environment, and has been defined by its key proponents as a meso-level approach that focuses on the inter-linkages between central government and sub-central political and governmental agencies (Rhodes, 1981; Marsh and Rhodes, 1992). This approach has been used in two ways:

- to emphasise the structural relations between institutions, organisations and companies [rather than the interpersonal relations evident within social network theories]; and
- as a means of focusing on the existence of networks *within* policy sectors operating at central and sub-central levels of government.

The policy network approach considers central-local relations based on a number of propositions that include: resource interdependency; the need to exchange resources to achieve goals; the process of exchange, strategies employed within the rules of the game to regulate the process of exchange; external constraints on organisational decision-making; the influence of dominant coalitions within organisations; and the relative power potential of interacting organisations (Rhodes and Marsh, 1992, 10-11). Central and local actors are seen to manoeuvre within a complex game in which they seek for advantage in deploying the resources they control as a means of: firstly, maximising their influence over outcomes; and, secondly, avoiding becoming dependent on other 'players'. Organisational resources, however, are seen as creating only the *potential* for the exercise of power - whether that potential is realised depends on the effective deployment of resources, the rules of the game and the choice of strategies.

Rhodes (1981, 1988) has elaborated on the policy network approach maintaining that networks have different structures of dependencies that vary along four key dimensions:

- the constellation of interests - in which the interests of actors within the network can vary by function, territory, client group, and common expertise (or a combination of these factors);
- membership - which differs in terms of the balance between public, non-profit and private sectors, and between administrative and professional elites, providers and clients;
- interdependence - where relationships within the network vary in their degree and type of resource dependence and their degree of horizontal articulation; and
- the distribution of resources - where actors within the network control different types and amounts of resources, and where variations in distribution can impact on the pattern of vertical and horizontal interdependence.

This approach has been employed by Hardy et al. (1990) to analyse the implementation of community care policy in the UK. Using this approach to study community-care services for individuals with mental handicaps, they were able to explore centre-periphery relations in health and social care as a means of examining the implementation gap between policy and reality. They noted, for example, that implementation failures resulted not simply from clinical determinants (e.g. the dominance of professionalised values and interests and clinical autonomy) but were also due to the inherently limited power of the centre, where sub-central units do not perform merely as the obliging agents of central government. This analysis offers some useful insights into the ways in which policy implemented at the macro-level is mediated by actors and agencies at the meso-level. Nevertheless, it does not extend *beyond* this point. The study examined only those relations occurring between the macro- and the meso-levels, so failing to account for relationships occurring between the meso- and micro-levels. No account, for example, was given of the ways in which care providers (increasingly the informal sector) translate - and become transformed by - care outcomes. Further, it failed to account for micro-situational influences on the network. Given the importance placed on concepts of empowerment and the inclusion of informal carers and service users in decision-making structures within the community care process, any examination of policy outcomes that does not extend beyond the macro-meso level can be only partial. As a consequence, it is argued, that before offering conclusions with regard to *why* this 'implementation gap' exists, there is also a need to consider the micro-situational environment within which policy is translated.

So, while the policy network approach is useful in that it looks at the translation process as it occurs within a network of hierarchical inter-relationships, to date those working within this approach have done so only in relation to actors operating between the meso- and macro-levels of the network. This, however, appears to be less a structural problem with the analytic framework and more a lack of attention by researchers working within this approach to the role of the micro-level of inter-personal behaviour in translating outcomes. Nevertheless, by operating within a framework whose emphasis is largely on associations operating within the organisational and structural planes of the network, the policy network approach is seen to be largely aspatial. As such, it fails to take account of the many local contexts within which policy implemented at the macro-level is mediated and transformed. Consequently, while emphasising variations in the wider political and economic environment within which networks are formed and operate (e.g. Rhodes and Marsh, 1992), little emphasis is placed on the way in which spatial and temporal variations can act to influence the character of the network.

While the policy network approach has proved largely aspatial in its analysis, geographers have also begun to explore the potential of network perspectives as a means of integrating political action into the spatial study of social change. This a vastly under-researched area of geographical enquiry. In one study, Murdoch and Marsden (1995) have highlighted the potential of such an approach for examining how socio-political change within localities can arise from a variety of different associations, or networks of relations, operating across varied scales and distances. Using the minerals industry as a window through which to examine the relationship between economic and political change within the mineral planning process, they illustrated not only how national-local networks are constituted, but some of the ways in which associations are made as actors pursue particular goals, and the relative powers of such associations as they come into conflict. In doing so, they concluded that as certain actors win out over others, so they are likely to increase their access to resources and assets ensuring their future success. In this way, Murdoch and Marsden (1995) have highlighted the potential for analysing political outcomes in various local spheres, through examining the links between actors operating at different spatial scales, and the terms upon which the links are constituted. By focusing on the inter-relationships between local and non-local actants, it may thus be possible to identify the means by which actors formulate goals and seek to achieve them.

Towards the Construction of a Conceptual Framework

As the previous section has illustrated, to construct a framework that enhances our understanding of the ways in which policy enacted at the macro-scale is manifest at locality level, we need to 'climb through the layers' and take cognisance of the ways in which policy is mediated and translated within such a multi-levelled context (Duster, 1981). As suggested in the work of both Dear and Wolch (1987) and Murdoch and Marsden (1995) any such framework is at one and the same time, both place specific and place transcending. While acknowledging the wider context within which change occurs, it is also necessary to identify how variations within and across communities arise, as a means of contributing to our understanding of the interactions between the system, those providing care, and the ways in which care outcomes may be differentially experienced across space and place.

The previous sections of this chapter have illustrated that though the incorporation of networked approaches into geographical analyses have offered some useful insights into social, economic and political change, they also have limitations. Social and policy networked approaches, for example, have both offered only a limited attempt to overcome the dualisms between macro- and micro-analysis. While ANT claims to overcome the problems of dualistic thinking, it too has limitations. Firstly, it has been criticised for failing to acknowledge the role of both motivations and intentionality that drives actors to build associations in the first place (Pickering, 1992). Secondly, debate surrounds the claims made for symmetry within the network (Collins and Yearley, 1992; Amin and Thrift, 1995). And, thirdly, ANT fails to account for the ways in which networks can act to 'screen out' actants who do not fit standardised patterns (Murdoch, 1997). These are important issues that need to be addressed if we are to understand the impact of policy change at locality level.

Despite these clear limitations, there is also considerable potential for development of a networked approach that is of relevance to this study. Two key factors are of particular import:

- the geographical dimension to network analysis - whose relationships can be seen to be both locally embedded and transcending place;
- the organisational dimension (i.e. the ways in which control and/or co-ordination *between* elements in the translation chain are exercised).

A number of additional factors are also worthy of note. The concept of translation within ANT offers a potential means of overcoming the conventional dualism between macro- and micro-levels of analysis by providing a mechanism for establishing a continuum between the two extremes. Scale within this approach is seen simply as the outcome of the heterogeneous links between actors, i.e. it focuses on how things are 'stitched together'. This offers a means of exploring how policy is translated and transformed and how translations can act to facilitate or constrain actants across various spatial scales. Power, however, is seen to lie not with actors but in the relationships established between them, so placing a focus on the need to examine the inter-relationships between actants and the nature of these relationships. In this way, network approaches highlight the importance of the characteristics of the network itself.

Each of the four key dimensions identified by Rhodes (1981, 1988) in relation to the policy network approach can also be seen to have resonance for care restructuring. In particular, this approach highlights a pattern of resource interdependency between actants within the network that can be both vertical and horizontal, and thus it is not bound by the symmetry of ANT. Network formation within this approach can be seen to comprise a constellation of interests that varies across public, voluntary and private sectors, and also between administrative, professional, provider and clients. Within care restructuring, for example, a cluster of interests is evident that varies by both function (e.g. enabler/provider), territory (e.g. their locus of operation at national, regional and/or local level) and client group (from provider to service recipient). The legislative frame discussed in chapter three (and illustrated in figure 3.2) also reflects a hierarchy of interests that vary across public, private and informal sectors, and who have differential access and control to varying types of resources, yet whose members are subject to some degree of interdependence.

Networked approaches also offer a number of useful tools for analysis. The relations binding actors and entities will vary, however, by using the concept of translation networks can be investigated as sets of power relations. Translation offers a mechanism for examining the differential ability of actants involved in community-based care to translate material within their temporally and spatially defined sector of activity. As Cooke and Morgan (1993) noted, transactions in network modes of allocation do not occur through discrete exchanges or administrative decree, but through networks of actors or institutions engaged in reciprocal, preferential, and mutually supportive actions. Two forms of transactions are of particular relevance to this study are subcontracting and strategic alliances. Such alliances can occur in the inter-relationships within and between statutory and informal agencies involved in health and social care and sub-contracting to the informal sector. Thus, rather than considering structural change as the determinant, it may be more useful to view change as the result of a co-evaluation of entities, actors and networks.

Further, by pointing to the ways in which translation is seen to be inscribed in skills, texts, negotiations, and/or acts of persuasion etc., through which an actant takes upon itself the authority to speak for others, we are also drawn to the *nature* of these actants; that is, how and where they undertake different roles, and possess, mobilise and manipulate their role-specific knowledge in the service of implementing policy (Berger and Luckmann, 1966). Since non-professional actants (e.g. the informal sector, carers and service-users) have access to differing technical knowledge-bases of relevance to the implementation and mobilisation of power, this may also be seen as influencing their perceptions of the policy debate, and their conduct within negotiations (see for example, Clapham and Smith, 1990; Prior, 1993). However, this also leads us to consider those issues of motivation and intentionality that drive actors to form associations in the first place, while at the same time, alerting us to the need to consider how and why some actants are excluded from the network. Consequently, in developing a conceptual framework, the emphasis should not be placed *exclusively* on the characteristics of the linkages between actants located within the network, but also on the characteristics of the actants themselves. The benefit of such an approach, is that whilst it allows us to see the paths of transition as determined by the networks, it does not deny the role of agency. In other words, it allows for the incorporation of internal motivational characteristics of actants that may influence them to act in non-standardised patterns.

As discussed above, to examine the ways in which policy is translated by actants operating within locally-embedded networks of care, it is necessary to consider the temporal and socio-spatial context within which change occurs. Duster (1981,113), for example, highlighted both the theoretical and the empirical usefulness of considering the 'intermediate rungs' on the ladder of hierarchy when considering macro- and micro-issues. This carries with it the implicit notion that direct observation of a local setting is insufficient to understand the social forces that help explain the social behaviour observed. While one kind of explanation can be taken from the people in the scene (based on their stated motives and interests), actors are themselves often unaware of historical, demographic and other factors that can better account for occurrences than stated motives. It is only by focusing on the congruence between needs, aspirations, capabilities and resources, and the opportunities characteristic of the environment (i.e. the 'fit' of the actor with communities and facilities, within a temporal and spatial context), that we can begin to understand the interaction of structural, environmental and individual characteristics. Thus, there is a need to incorporate a demographic, and/or historical analyses of a particular local scene as a way of placing *context* around the scene, and providing grounding.

Pathways of Dependency

Drawing upon networked approaches, and in an attempt to understand the connections between the new forms of care and the local environment within which such care is being provided, this research adopted the notion of the 'dependency network' as an analytical tool. This was designed as a means of elucidating the ways in which structural forces, institutional practices, and the everyday routines of knowledgeable and capable actors and agencies involved in the health and social care system can impact on the translation chain to produce community care outcomes.

The dependency network has been constructed around the legislative structure summarised in figure 3.2. This structure involves all those formal and informal actors and agencies that nationally-defined legislation has outlined as having an integral role to play in the formation and implementation of policies and services at local and national level. This forms the frame for the analytical purposes of the study. Thus the network does not imply a *territorial* bounding. Rather it illustrates how, by exploring the network from within, it may be possible to weave a path through those multi-levelled contexts of the policy process that are both locally embedded, and place transcending. Space, in this context, is seen to be more akin to Castells' (1996) concept of a 'space of flows'.

Given the potential expansiveness of the network, some bounding is required for practical reasons. It is acknowledged, however, that any such bounding of the dependency network (whether territorial, political, economic or ideological) is an artificial construction. The influence of external forces such as the political and economic influences of the EU and the global economy, for example, cannot be ignored. Nor can the network ignore change stemming from any ideological shift that can occur as the result of a change in government at the national scale. Thus, in its construction, the network is also cognizant of the wider context within which change occurs reorientation (e.g. from policy translations based on collectivist ideals to those based on a residualist agenda and vice versa). With its focus on the meso- and micro-level, in this research, the wider context is acknowledged but is not subjected to detailed analysis. The key point is that the organisational structure of community-based health and social care provision helps to illuminate a pathway of the varying levels of

74

articulation that permit a connection between the local and community activity in the specific scene under investigation, and macro-level decision-making at state level. As network theory suggests, this presents one way (though by no means the only way) of integrating macro- and micro-social theory and observation, in a way that will allow us to 'map' the ways in which the new system operates.

Building upon the organisational structure, the dependency network incorporates all those actants concerned with the provision of community-based care that are sited within both formal and informal sectors of care - including statutory, voluntary and private sector actants, informal carers and service users. While the network of care provision is relatively stable, legislative change has nevertheless effected a change in the inter-relationships between those actants charged with providing care, and the associations between them. As a consequence, new associations are forming as actors come to take on an increasing share of the caring role, and changes are occurring in the balance of power relationships within the network. It is in the elevation of the role of certain groups within this network of health and social care provision, and how this manifests itself within place-specific environments, that we are perhaps most likely to be able to understand how restructuring is impacting on those concerned with the provision of care and support to dependent populations. This points to the relevance of exploring the inter-relationships between actors concerned with the implementation of care, the need to examine power and contractual relationships, strategic alliances, and collaborations that may occur within and between actants located within the dependency network.

The dependency network is conceptualised as embodying that network of interests concerned with care restructuring affecting dependent populations. The linkages (as highlighted in figure 4.1) represent the translation chains through which policy can implemented. The process of implementation alerts us to the inter-relationships that occur between interests [or actants] within the overall structure, and thus those [formal] opportunities for interaction that exist within the network. It is recognised, however, that such inter-relationships can be either formal - as overtly defined by figure 3.2 - or informal (so allowing for the incorporation of motivations and intentionality of actants within the network). Figure 4.1 offers only an illustration of the former, with actants referring only to those legislatively defined bodies given a 'role' by the state within care restructuring. Actants within the network manoeuvre within a series of complex negotiations, alliances and collaborations in which they seek to deploy resources in ways that might include: (i) maximising their influence over outcomes; and (ii) minimising their dependency on other actants. These interactions not only act to modify former translations, but can also be seen to impact on the internal structure, culture and actions of other actants within an actant's sphere of influence. In this way, the network recognises the need to address the nature and characteristics of actants themselves.

The development of the network is seen to depend on sets of conditions that can serve to facilitate or constrain the deployment of translations. Obstacles to the proliferation of translations can lie in those explicit arrangements that define the circulation of resources, the negotiation context, and mechanisms for designating an actants authorisation to speak on behalf of the network. The joint-planning framework, for example, can be seen to form part of the negotiation context through which actants become authorised to speak on behalf of other actants within the network. This also focuses attention on the need to explore issues of representation, empowerment, marginality and the ways in which the network can serve to exclude.

The ability to affect translation is dependent on the level of influence and power that an actant may be able to exert in relation to any other. Further, as illustrated by figure 4.1, there are a number of possible pathways within which translations can occur as factors of change [in this case, care policy and inscriptions surrounding its implementation] pass along the translation chain, from one actant's sphere of influence/action to another, and along pathways which may be either [or both] hierarchical and horizontal. Any such variation in the pathway taken is likely to create differentiated translations and impacts on the role and nature of actants involved. The conceptual image of actants formed in 'journeying' from one point to another is thus translated by those perceptions gained through the particular inter-relationships formed and the pathway through which translations occur before reaching a specific destination. The relative importance of an actant within the network is determined by the number of pathways with which it is inter-linked - so widening its possible sphere of influence - and consequently the translations occurring along a particular pathway. The more influential the actant through which factors of change flow, the greater its ability to translate material. Pathways of dependency are consequently envisaged as comprising the numerous and varied combinations of routes through which actants are linked both hierarchically and/or horizontally within the network. The degree of influence over change in any one specific political, social or economic arena that a particular actant will be able to exert on *other* actants linked within these translation chains will be determined by three factors:

- the location of that actant within the overall network;
- the number and importance of those pathways into which it is linked; and

76

Figure 4.1 The Dependency Network

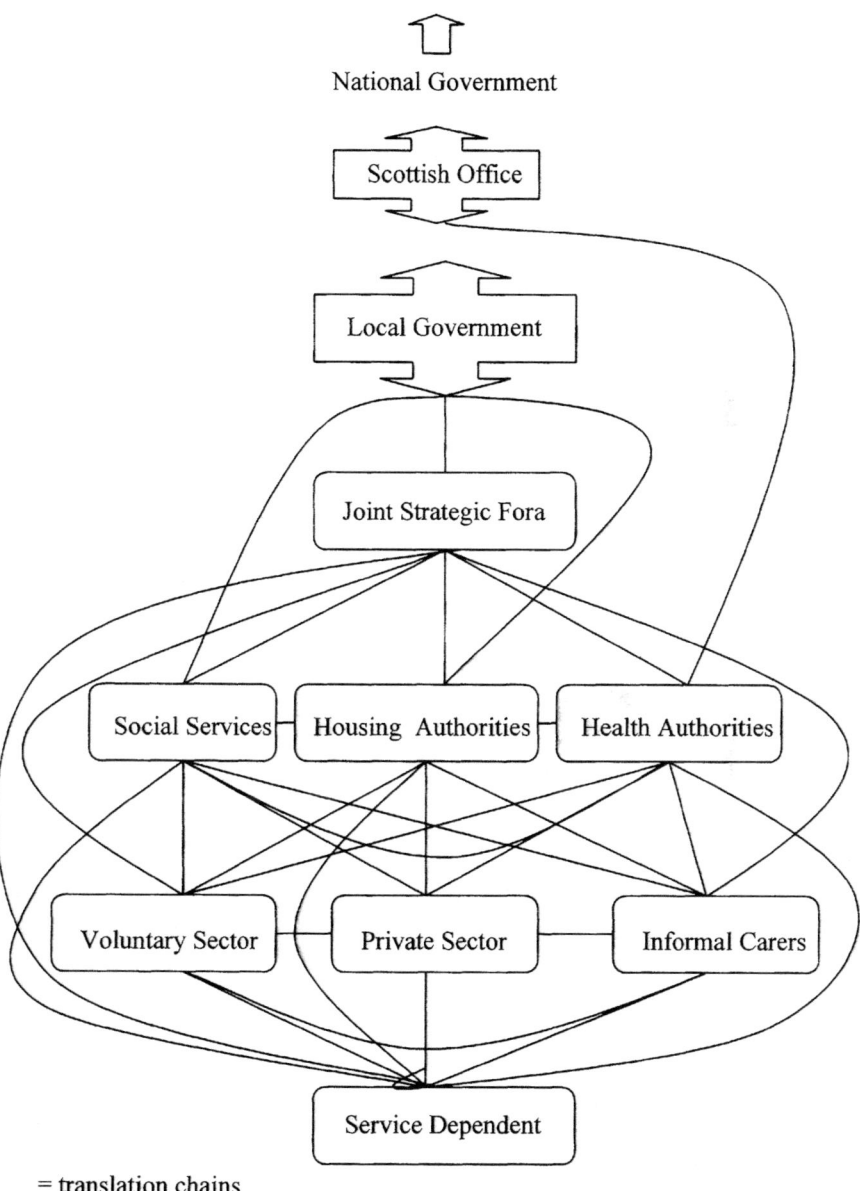

= translation chains

- the historical development of an individual actant within the particular framework in which it is situated.

Importantly, this framework is conceptualised as being both fluid and dynamic, and thus is not bound by any formal rigidity. It may be subject to variation, appraisal and reappraisal over both time and space. Consequently the degree of power and influence any one particular actant exerts along any given pathway can fluctuate, weakening the relative influence of one actant along the route, whilst elevating that of another or creating new ones. Community care legislation, for example, may be argued to have elevated the power of local authorities in this particular network, whilst weakening that of local health authorities. However whilst this may be *legislatively* the case, the degree to which local authorities have been *successful* in exerting this lead role over local health authorities has been demonstrated to vary between locales (see for example Hardy et. al., 1990). As Rhodes and Marsh (1992) also illustrate, sub-central units do not necessarily act as the obliging agents of central government. Thus while the legislative frame forms the basis of the network, given the nature of actants, there is no guarantee that translations enacted within the network will occur as per government expectations. This highlights a distinction between the formal network (illustrated in figure 4.1) and the actual character of translations, which take place within it.

The term 'dependency network' has been adopted here to reflect an explicit awareness of power relationships. By that, I mean that the service recipient is dependent on a tiered hierarchy from above that assumes national government to be the source of power. This implies the existence of asymmetry within the network. However, as noted previously, while this is legislatively the case, there is a need to examine the reality of how this is being played out on the ground. Further, while the legislative frame itself implies an explicit asymmetry, it also points to an undefined symmetry *between* tiers (for example, between the voluntary sector, the private sector and informal carers). Thus the study does not assume asymmetry, rather it aims to tease out the inter-relationships within the dependency network to assess the extent to which symmetry (as evident within horizontal sets of relationships) or asymmetry (as evident within hierarchical relationships) may exist. For as Latour (1986) points out, power lies not just in the properties of actants, but in the relationships established between them.

Such organisational networks, however, can be differentially embedded within particular places. As a consequence, different translations within the network and different sets of inter-relationships can evolve within different socio-cultural contexts. Further, not all environments are receptive to all innovations, and thus, different patterns of inequality can arise *between* places (Murdoch, 1994). The ability to alter and modify such innovatory change may thus require a level of resource that is unequally dispersed. In terms of the dependency network, this may be evident in the differential ability of locales to enrol voluntary, private and informal health and social care resources based on variations in the physical, socio-economic and demographic profile of an area. By conducting micro-situational research within particular sites at particular times, across the policy sector, occurrences can be analysed for their 'site specificity', and therefore, the extent to which policy material is being transmitted/transformed by agents acting within the implementation process (Sibeon, 1991; Duster, 1981).

Concluding Comments

As this chapter has argued, while action by central government is important and serves as a guideline for interpreting both the spirit and intent of the law, it is only by climbing through the various layers to get to ground level - where policy is turned into practice - that it is possible to make the connections between theorising and community care and the many local scenes within which it is practised. Developments at the micro-level cannot be anticipated at the macro-scale. Consequently, until empirical patterns are uncovered locally, it is difficult to see how even a well-intentioned legislative body can create policy that serves the interests of such diverse community responses to programmes.

   To understand the ways in which the new system of care operates, the framework must allow for the determination of how legislation enacted at the national (macro) level is translated into a social programme at the local (meso) level, and what this means for the end recipient [at the micro level]. It is thus important that we remain aware of the need to understand how we get from the client/provider exchange in service provision, to national legislation on an issue and an understanding of the wider activity surrounding the topic. Such a framework needs to incorporate and take cognisance of the multi-levelled contexts within which care policy is mediated and its outcomes experienced. By adopting a networked approach that allows for such a multi-levelled analysis of the ways in which care policy is translated and care outcomes are manifest, the book aims to facilitate an understanding of how the inter-relationships between actants operating within the dependency network contribute to socio-spatial variations in the experience of care restructuring.

   As noted, the dependency network (figure 4.1) shows only those groups of actants given a role by the state and who actively inter-relate within the care process. It does not illustrate the shifting positions within the care process i.e. the actual position of actants on the ground. Further, by incorporating elements of those networked approaches to geographical analyses, attention is focused on the need to examine power relations within inter-dependent systems through such processes as a) sub-contracting; b) strategic alliances; c) inter-collaborations; d) inter-dependencies; and inter-organisational influences. The question of symmetry or asymmetry also highlights the need to explore issues of partnership, representation and empowerment as experienced by actants operating within the dependency network, and the need to explore the ways in which the network can act to enable or constrain, and how it can act to 'screen out' those actants who do not fit the standardised pattern of the network. These issues are intimately linked to the research design and the development of a methodological framework through which these issues can be examined. This is explored within the following chapter.

While initially such a framework operates at a level of abstraction, it is as categories and properties emerge from the empirical analysis, develop in abstraction and become related, that the accumulating interrelations will develop to form an integrated central theoretical framework. In this way, there emerges a 'dialectical interplay' between the concrete and the abstract, leading to the development of concepts as the world comes to be understood (Murdoch, 1994). Understanding such concrete realities involves a shift from superficial categories to an accounting which is complex, composed of underlying real mechanisms, and connecting them to the actual empirical components of the research. While such evidence may not necessarily be accurate beyond a doubt (nor is it in studies concerned only with accuracy) nevertheless, the concept is undoubtedly a relevant theoretical abstraction about developments in the area studied. In the course of enquiry, these concrete outcomes come into increasingly complex articulation with the underlying concepts. Thus "theoretical argument moves between hypothetico-deductive and experimental phases so there is a continual, dialectical transformation of concepts" (Murdoch, 1994, 164). Such a theoretical enterprise is thus conceived of as open and in continual dialectical interplay with concrete reality. These interrelationships are drawn together within the second part of the book.

Note

[1] This particular article was written under the pseudonym of Jim Johnson.

5 Landscapes of Care: Issues of Design and Implementation

Introduction

The preceding chapters have not only drawn attention to a number of the issues involved in care restructuring, but have also contributed to the development of a conceptual framework aimed at enhancing our understanding of the ways in which care restructuring is being played out at meso- and micro-level.

The adoption of a networked approach pointed to a number of issues that needed to be considered in developing a methodological framework through which the aims of the research could be explored - highlighting the inter-linkages between the conceptual and methodological frameworks. Of particular relevance are those differing levels of entry to the examination of the process of care restructuring discussed in the previous chapter, that is:

- the direct observation of behaviour in a local setting which routinely occurs for the micro-level of the analysis;
- an observation and analysis of the administrative, bureaucratic, or organisational unit/s that are interposed between the local scene and the state; and
- the wider spatio-temporal contextualisation within which the issue under investigation is located.

These concerns have methodological significance, in that they draw attention to the importance of examining the distribution of actants within the implementation process and the inter-relationships between them as a means of understanding how policy material is translated and transformed by agents acting within site-specific contexts at particular points in time.

A networked approach also directs the study to the need for anchorage, that is, a window through which to examine change as experienced within the network. This study has taken the voluntary sector as the lens through which the dependency network is explored. Given the elevation of its role in the provision of community-based care, the voluntary sector now constitutes an agency of some significance in care restructuring. Thus change within the network is likely to have had a significant impact on the voluntary caring experience.

Attention is also drawn to the need to define the (non-territorial) boundedness of the network. Within care restructuring this is determined by the organisational structure which forms the basis of the dependency network, and which also serves to define the key actants investigated within the study (as illustrated in figure 3.1). Finally, by pointing to the local embeddedness of networks, the conceptual framework has provided a further rationale for examining change as manifest within different settings.

In a study which takes as its locus change as identified at the meso- and micro-levels, the *explanation* of such change is seen as of greater significance than a surface identification of spatial patterns. Local government reorganisation, differing priorities and patterns of spending within and between health and social services at locality level, and differing degrees of independence and autonomy experienced by locally-based voluntary organisations from their national body, illustrate the need to understand change as it is impacting on organisations at branch or local level. Qualitative approaches are particularly suitable for developing an understanding of how the organisational responses to a problem have been conceptualised, and the ways in which policy formulation may be transformed in the implementation by actors and agencies who are geographically distant (Rist, 1994). They are further well suited to uncovering causal relationships, in that they can look both directly and longitudinally at local processes underlying a temporal series of events and conditions, and demonstrate how these can lead to specific outcomes. Huberman and Miles (1994, 434) neatly described this process as one in which "In effect we get inside the black box; we can understand not just that a particular thing happened, but how and why it happened."

Emphasis on the identification of a 'spatial patterning' of health related issues has, in the past, led to a predominance of quantitative methodology in medical geography. It has been argued, however, that this frequently leaves major problems unaddressed at the local level, presenting a reductionist analysis in which locality plays little real part (Jones and Moon, 1993). Patterns can be found, but not explained. Conversely, qualitative methodology is associated with an interpretative epistemology, which looks not so much at outcomes, as is the case with the quantitative paradigm, as 'meanings'. The task for qualitative research is viewed as one of uncovering the meaning of social events and processes based on understanding the lived experience of human society. As McCracken (1988, 17) puts it, "qualitative work does not survey the terrain, it mines it".

Each sector within this study, however, is different, so bringing its own sets of issues and problems. These factors lead to the development of a pathway of methods in which a blend of strategies that address the specific requirement for investigating each sector was adopted. So, while recognising the benefits of reaching a wider sample of respondents through the use of extensive methods, the problematic identified by Jones and Moon (1993) has also been acknowledged and addressed. These issues are further explored below.

The research has further assumed that the effects of restructuring cannot be adequately explored through a 'snapshot' approach - the interactions and effects of changes in care systems occur slowly. Such complex processes demand adequate time for exploration, with the interactions between people, policy and place demanding a longitudinal, in-depth approach. Consequently, the study called for the long-term engagement in the social world of the informal sector within the two locations within which the study was undertaken. This approach also aimed to overcome some of the more obvious problems associated with retrospective reconstruction, enabling respondents to provide accounts of their experiences over several points in time, rather than relying on a single static representation. So, while it is commonly assumed that there should be a correspondence between epistemology, theory and method, as Brannen (1992) notes, it is unusual for epistemology or theory to be the sole determinant of method. The research strategy was designed as a consequence of the above factors. Where appropriate, the study also incorporated quantitatively gathered data. This allowed not only for the identification of groups or individuals for research purposes, but had the further advantage of highlighting issues for further investigation.

It is worth noting, however, that though the study has primarily adopted an intensive research strategy, the intention has not been to present this as superior to, or in competition with, alternative extensive methods. Rather it is an acknowledgement that different data produce different kinds of evidence, and that different approaches lend themselves to different research problems. As Wolcott (1995, 163) maintains, "Every way of knowing has its place. Science cannot proceed without controlled experimentation, but neither science nor controlled experimentation can reveal all we seek to understand about ourselves and our fellow humans". The adoption of the methods used within this study were based on the perception that they represented the most appropriate strategy for achieving the defined objectives of this particular research project.

The remainder of this chapter has been designed around three main components:

- research design and implementation;
- issues of principle in intensive research; and
- methods of analysis.

It should be noted, however, that the design and order of these sections within the overall chapter are not reflective of the degree of importance attached to the relevant sections. Rather it is seen as an aid to the reader, in that it recognises the need to highlight issues relating to the particular (in terms of the development of a 'pathway' of methods) before moving on to issues which are of equal importance to the overall design of the research. Issues of validity and reliability, subjectivity and bias, positionality and ethics are seen as integral to the whole of the research design. The ways in which these issues are addressed within the research project, however, are best understood from a informed position in relations to the research design and its implementation.

Research Design and Implementation

The aims of this study have been threefold:

- to explore the process of change within the network via the inter-relationships between key actants operating within it;
- to consider the roles of these key actants and their experience/views of care restructuring; and
- to examine the social and spatial impact of care restructuring on actants within the network.

The section that follows is specifically concerned with the research design and implementation rather than the methodological issues which are dealt with elsewhere in this chapter. This is constructed as a straightforward chronological account which narrates the sequential unfolding of the research methods employed in the gathering of empirical data. Following a discussion on the key actors involved in care restructuring, and a brief summary of the research design, the section is built around four sub-sections related to the key actors identified below.

Key actors

As discussed in chapter four, there are a number of key actors and agencies whose experience of the restructuring process needs to be explored if we are to understand how the restructuring process is being played out at local level. In particular this involves four sets of key players:

- locally based voluntary and non-profit organisations;
- informal carers;
- the private sector; and
- the statutory sector.

In undertaking a longitudinal approach to analysis, the research sought to combine interviews with key actors from all those groups outlined above, with the exception of the private sector (the rationale for which is discussed below). Access to, and the characteristics displayed by, each of these groups, however, varies significantly. As a consequence, it was necessary to innovate and specifically tailor the research design to maximise data collection opportunities from within each group. So, for example, as good secondary sources (e.g. community care plans, committee and annual reports) were available for the statutory sector, it was not deemed necessary to undertake serial interviews with this group. This publicly available documentation provided good background data on the statutory sector and its working relationships with other organisations, making it possible to identify recorded policy and planning issues relevant to the research. Data collection within this sector consisted of a series of semi-structured interviews with key informants from the Social Services, Health Authorities and Housing Authorities within each of the study areas. The voluntary sector, however, is a heterogeneous group and, as such, there was less cohesive secondary material available. In order to address this diversity, a postal survey was undertaken in order to supplement available secondary material and gain some contextual data on this sector. At the time of undertaking the study, the voluntary sector had been affected not only by care restructuring, but also by the more recent changeover to single tier local authorities. The view was thus taken, that repeat semi-structured interviews would facilitate the uncovering of the impact of these changes over time.

Informal carers are also a key group for any successful implementation of care that focuses on the domestic sphere. Secondary data for this sector, however, originates largely from within statutory or voluntary sector reports that have their own agenda. Further, many carers do not recognise the 'provider' role that they play. As a consequence, it was necessary to devise a research strategy that uncovered the ways in which informal carers impact upon the dependency network. This required an

85

increased depth of data, which the use of focus groups, serial interviews and diary techniques were designed to achieve.

The fourth group referred to - the private sector - is also touched upon here. It was never intended that this sector would form a major element of this project, nevertheless, the private sector is a significant player in the overall caring process. As a consequence, the project was designed to give a 'feel' for the ways in which the private sector may be changing as a result of care restructuring. As the intention was only to gain a generalised view of the private sector's response to care restructuring, this was undertaken through a postal questionnaire.

It should also be noted at this point, that while it had initially been envisaged that both carers and cared-for would participate in the serial interview process, there were practical problems of communication. A significant number of those frail elderly being cared-for were experiencing the effects of Alzheimers, dementias, or strokes, the nature of these illnesses/disabilities meant they were either unable to communicate verbally, or were only able to do so through their carer - raising issues of representation. While it is acknowledged that the cared-for are an integral and important part of the care process, the objective of this study was to explore change as experienced by providers of care. As a consequence, it was decided at an early stage to focus on informal carers, leaving the issue of the cared-for to be dealt with in other [future] research.

Summary of research design

The innovative nature of this research design lies in its pursuit of a 'funneled' approach to method. That is, it has sought to develop a blend of methods that increased both the breadth and depth of data gathered as appropriate. This incorporated the use of surveys, focus groups, serial and semi-structured interviewing and carer-diaries as the principle sources of information. The approach adopted for each of the key groups considered within the project, is summarised below in table 5.1.

This approach aimed to increase the 'thickness' of description (Geertz, 1973) as a means of deepening our understanding of the complex ways in which health and social care is differentially mediated and accessed within local environments. In doing so, the objective was to uncover the social processes and relationships of power that lay beneath geographical patterns. The overall research framework was thus designed as a means of facilitating access to the complex relationships embedded in local networks of care, helping to elucidate how care provision is mediated, who gets what, where and why, and also who is excluded.

Table 5.1 Summary of Methods

Method	Voluntary Sector	Informal Carers	Statutory Sector	Private Sector
Postal Questionnaire	Yes	No	No	Yes
Focus Groups	No	Yes	No	No
In-depth Interview	Yes	Yes	Yes	No
Serial Interviews	Yes	Yes	No	No
Diaries	No	Yes	No	No

The remainder of this section considers, more specifically, how the research strategy was applied to each of the key groups in turn.

The voluntary sector

As noted above, to examine change as experienced within the voluntary sector, the study used both questionnaires and in-depth semi-structured interviews. Preliminary research into the voluntary sector was initiated through a small pilot study consisting of exploratory interviews with the directors/co-ordinators of a five voluntary agencies known to have branches operating in both study areas. The aim was to determine some of the key issues impacting on voluntary organisations in the current political and economic climate. The issues raised in the course of these interviews combined with a review of the literature formed a foundation for the construction of a mail-questionnaire. This was aimed: firstly, at gaining a profile of those voluntary organisations operating within the two selected areas; secondly, at exploring how health and social care restructuring may be impacting on the culture and service provisioning of these organisations; and thirdly, at examining their inter-relationships with other agencies within the dependency network.

Questions focused on four main areas:

- the profile of the local organisation and its volunteers;
- services and recipients of services;
- funding issues; and
- relationships with other actants within the network.

Some difficulties were encountered in attempting to identify all relevant organisations within the study areas due to a lack of any comprehensive list of local branches/organisations. The local authority in Glasgow City kept no listing of voluntary organisations operating within their jurisdiction and that obtained from the local authority in Dumfries and Galloway was out of date. The Council for Voluntary Organisations was able to provide some listings, but again these were not comprehensive and tended to consist of national bodies and omitting many smaller, locally-based organisations. Local libraries, telephone directories, directories of voluntary organisations and 'snow-balling' were used to supplement these lists. To the best of available knowledge at the time of research, the final listing represented a total sample of *all* identifiable voluntary organisations within the two study areas that had some involvement in campaigning, supporting, or direct provision of care to frail elderly populations and their carers.

The questionnaire was administered between May and June 1996, and sent to the directors or local organisers of all identified organisations. This amounted to a total of 108 organisations, 72 of whom were located in Glasgow City, with the remaining 36 situated in Dumfries and Galloway. The questionnaire also included a request for a follow-up interview, with the intention of conducting repeat interviews with a number of organisations over the period of study. Non-respondents to the questionnaire were prompted initially by a postal reminder, followed by a telephone call to all remaining non-respondents. This had the dual purpose of (i) further prompting a response, and (ii) eliciting *reasons* for non-response. This raised the final response rate from 62.5 percent to 71 percent, representing a response of 69 percent from Dumfries and Galloway and 72 percent from Glasgow City. With the exception of 4 percent of the sample who were not contactable by telephone, some rationale for non-response was obtained from all those who did not return their questionnaire. A further 4 percent agreed to respond following the telephone call, but failed to do so. Of the remaining 21percent of organisations from whom no response was elicited, 6 percent said they had sent their questionnaires to their national or regional office (so rendering them void for the purposes of the study), 5 percent quoted time constraints or lack of staff, 4 percent had been subject to rationalisation (thus three local organisations had been amalgamated into one regional branch), 4 percent felt that the questionnaire was not relevant to their organisation, and 2 percent were in the process of closing down due to lack of funding.

Despite the positive response rate, it should be noted that for the purposes of this study, the data derived from the informal sector questionnaires is viewed solely as contextual, relying on numerical material and illustrative quotes. Given the heterogeneity of the voluntary sector, the data served the purpose of providing some cohesive contextual information not available through other sources. The numerical data is not presented in any statistical sense its purpose, rather, being to highlight similarities experienced in the restructuring process.

One third of all those organisations to whom the questionnaire was sent agreed to participate in the longitudinal interview process. Thus respondents from forty voluntary organisations were involved in this stage of the research process - amounting to a total of twelve from Dumfries and Galloway, and twenty-eight from Glasgow. Initial interviews were conducted between June and September of 1996, with follow-up interviews completed during the following year, by which time it was anticipated that changes arising from the 1990 Act (which did not become fully operational until 1993) and the introduction of single-tier local authorities in 1996, might be expected.

The pilot interviews, questionnaire responses, together with background secondary material, formed the framework for the construction of a semi-structured interview schedule. Unlike the standardised interview, the semi-structured interview has no specific question order, rather there was a prepared interview schedule of themes or topics, that was broken down into component elements and initially set in some appropriate order. In the interview process, however, it was found that in answering one question, respondents frequently also answered another, or opened up new avenues for questioning, thus the schedule was not strictly adhered to. As a consequence, it was necessary to work through the materials in a flexible way, while simultaneously noting the time and coverage of the schedule. This flexibility, however, is seen as a strength, rather than a weakness of this approach. For as Moyser (1988,116) maintains, the 'purposive interaction' of the semi-structured interview can uncover a rich array of personal insights and commentary that can flow from respondents where an unstandardised, flexible or variable agenda format is adopted as opposed to the statistical rigour of a more standardised approach.

The aim of the initial interview was threefold:

- to identify the main factors of change affecting voluntary organisations within the two study areas;
- to identify how different organisations were being affected by these changes and the implications for future voluntary service provisioning; and
- to examine the links between voluntary organisations and other actants within the network.

The follow-up interviews were undertaken in summer 1997, approximately one year from the initial interview. The aim here, was firstly, to revisit issues arising from the initial interviews; and secondly, to examine changes that may have occurred in the intervening period. Each interview was of approximately one hours duration, and was taped and transcribed ready for later analysis.

While the interviews were clearly shaped by the prior knowledge of the researcher (and thus the researcher must be seen as a positioned subject) the initial questionnaire served a further purpose in that it provided a useful aid in the attempt to overcome any in-built bias that may have arisen in the course of the pilot interview process. It also allowed for a degree of neutrality within the interview process - the interview schedules being shaped by the responses of the voluntary sector itself. The semi-structured nature of the interviews also allowed for the incorporation of additional issues raised by voluntary sector respondents, permitting the researcher to uncover new clues and new dimensions to a problem, and to obtain accurate, inclusive accounts from respondents based on their everyday experiences. Given the varying degrees of autonomy, independence, flexibility and creativity demonstrated by actors within this sector, this element of freedom in the expression of their experiences was viewed as fundamental to identifying the underlying processes and possible outcomes.

Such interaction allowed for the recording of everyday life, and permitted the researcher to obtain vivid, accurate, inclusive accounts from respondents based on their everyday experiences (Burgess, 1982). The adoption of such a non-standardised approach was viewed as particularly appropriate where the researcher wished the respondent to define situations, problems, and issues etc.

Informal carers

Following the completion of this stage of the research project, the decision was taken to continue with the informal sector during the second stage, before approaching the statutory sector. The rationale for this was based on the recognition that the research material obtained from within the voluntary sector represented only one facet of change within the informal sector - albeit an important one. Any approach made to statutory bodies at this point in the research might imply a confrontational approach due to the weighting of information gained. Though this is certainly a valid mode of approach, this project was less concerned with a critical analysis of the statutory sector and more with illuminating the processes involved in change, how they may be coloured by actors or agencies within the dependency network, and the impact on care outcomes. As confrontation was unlikely to prove a fruitful approach in the attempt to uncover these issues, the decision was taken to gain a wider view of the informal sector. Hence, an exploration of the ways in which informal carers have experienced care restructuring formed the next stage in the project.

The method adopted was one of initial focus groups, followed by semi-structured serial interviews with selected respondents, returning repeatedly to the same individuals. Four visits were scheduled with each respondent over a one year period. The aim was to build up a relationship with the individual which would allow for the gradual uncovering of the ways in which the informal carer both contributes to care provision, and the ways in which they interact with other actants within the dependency network. The potential 'depth' of serial interviewing has two major attractions for the intensive researcher:

- it can (in part at least) allow for the dismantling of the hierarchy of knowledge between researcher and researched which is often at work in questionnaires and 'initial' interviews, and where both parties cannot be said to participate in the construction of knowledge on an equal footing; and
- serial interviews can enable research encounters in which there is sufficient time, space and trust, to plumb the depths of people's taken-for-granted lifeworlds in order to study actions and feelings, which if ever exposed in the initial interview, might be difficult for either party to enunciate or reflect upon in any sustained or detailed fashion (Rowles, 1986).

The serial interview has the added advantage of allowing the researcher to gain greater understanding of the subject of scrutiny and gather information at a more leisurely pace. In this way, the aim was to build up a sufficient degree of familiarity with the research subjects to allow them to speak freely about the issues which concerned them, and allowing explanations of the taken-for-granted routinisations of people's everyday lives to be constructed. As illustrated in the work of geographers such as Rowles (1978) and Seamon (1979), and also the more theoretical work of Giddens (1984, 1993) and Thrift (1983), the vast bulk of knowledgeability which lies behind people's daily actions does not operate at a level of 'discursive consciousness' (i.e. where everything must be consciously put into words before being perceived, felt or done). Instead, it operates at a more routinised 'practical consciousness' in which people make elaborate manoeuvres through many complex environments without giving them much thought (Seamon 1979). This research strategy provided additional information regarding motives, understanding and outlooks which helped to explain actions and constraints on respondents and the policy process and implementation that are not readily found within secondary sources.

The content of the interviews was loosely based on a schedule of topics drawn up in advance, and designed to reflect the study objectives; that is, to explore the changing role of informal care and how carers experience care restructuring within the network. Each topic was tailored to achieve some kind of balance between the general issues with which the researcher was concerned and the more idiosyncratic biographical and everyday contexts in which these will become embedded and interpreted throughout the course of the participants' lives. Three main sets of issues were explored:

- factors influencing the social support networks of informal carers;
- socio-spatial variations in access and the availability of voluntary and statutory care supports; and
- the opportunities available to informal carers to influence the caring process.

In this way, the study sought to make sense of how the researched has lived his/her life within the context of the issues with which the project is concerned through their life histories. The importance of this approach to life history work, where a broad knowledge of events and institutional structures are likely to have had an impact on a person's lifecourse has been highlighted by Miles and Crush (1993). In theory, each carer was to be interviewed on a three-monthly basis over a one year period, in order to facilitate an understanding of their changing experiences over time. In practice, however, the frailty of the 'cared-for' meant that in a number of instances, follow-up interviews were curtailed, either due to the declining health - and hence the institutionalisation - of the 'cared-for' within nursing/residential care, or by death. This is discussed in more detail below.

Finding caring households

In intensive approaches, the researcher is often unable to control the sampling process (Wolcott, 1995). Any attempt at systematic sampling within this part of the project was rendered impossible due to the difficulties of accessing informal carers for whom there is no complete formal record. Even if such records existed, they would be the subject of client confidentiality. Further, many carers do not formally identify themselves as such, seeing themselves rather as 'looking after mum or dad', a spouse, or other close kin. This was entirely predictable. As a consequence, it was evident from the outset, that the identification of carers would have to be established by informal means, removing the possibility of gaining any comprehensive record of such individuals in the study areas. All other means of accessing carers are partial, i.e. carers are frequently invisible, due to their lack of external symbols and the fact that they do not always access formal or informal services. However, within this type of approach, generalisation is not an issue. There is no attempt to identify the 'typical', for as Wolcott (1995) argues, there is no such thing as the 'typical' person; each case is unique, yet not so unique that we cannot learn from it and apply its lessons more generally. The question is rather one of how the informant fits into the larger scheme of things - as Agar (1980, 75) comments, "an isolated observation cannot be understood unless you understand its relationships to other aspects of the situation in which it occurred".

The next logical step was to work with voluntary and statutory support organisations that dealt directly with carers and their dependants. Here, the nature of the gatekeeper was crucial. The voluntary or statutory co-ordinators of the support groups explained the nature of the research to the carers prior to the carer agreeing to a personal visit within their own home, or the carer agreeing to attend a focus group on a pre-agreed date. In the first of these cases, a further screening process occurred as co-ordinators approached those carers whom *they* thought would be willing and able to participate. In the latter case, the process was more self-selective on the part of the carer - though inevitably this excluded carers who did not participate in carers' support groups.

With the co-operation of a number of these agencies, six focus groups were set up across the two study areas during the summer of 1996. The timing of these focus groups was largely dependent on the date of the monthly support group meetings. This required the focus groups to be set up at least two months in advance to allow for carers to be forewarned of the event, and to give them the opportunity to 'opt out' if they so desired. Around seventy carers attended in total. The aim was to generate groups of between eight to ten people. However, in reality, attendance numbers were controlled by a number of factors outside the researcher's control, especially distance, weather and interest. Group size varied from between four in very rural areas, to over twenty in one urban setting. The largest group, however, proved impractical for the purposes of any meaningful discourse and was consequently divided into smaller groups.

The focus groups were used as a methodological tool that helped to frame the in-depth interview schedule (in a very loose way). Those participating in the focus groups were prompted to give a general accounting of their lives as carers, the formal and informal supports available to them, how they accessed supports, and what opportunities were open to them to feed into the planning process. Those who participated in the focus groups, or who linked into the support groups in some other way, were further asked if they would be willing to participate in the serial interview process. By setting out clearly at the outset what the researcher wanted to discuss, why this would require a series of meetings, and the amount of time it would be necessary to set aside for this, clear parameters to the research encounter were laid out. This had the advantage of:

- apprising potential participants of the level of commitment to the research that would be required of them;
- facilitating an easier withdrawal from the relationship once the interviews were completed; and
- allowing for the construction of a set amount of intensive data with which to work.

Whilst a high percentage of volunteer participants were accessed through the focus groups, not all were suitable subjects for the purposes of this project. A number of individuals no longer cared directly for their dependent, either because the cared-for had been relocated to a nursing home, or because they had recently died. At the final stage, twelve individuals were selected to participate - six from each area. This reflected a key aim of the study - that there may be a distinction between the experience of caring within urban and rural locales. In selecting six carers from each area, it also allowed for the possibility that some respondents may, for a variety of reasons, choose not to continue with the research process. Indeed, as a result of the increasing frailty of those being cared-for throughout the period of study, three carers discontinued their participation in the longitudinal phase of the study part-way through. In two instances this occurred as a consequence of the cared-for being transferred from home-based to nursing-home care. Here, the respondents ceased to be the primary carers, hence, for the purposes of this study, any further interview would serve no useful purpose. Additionally, given the change in circumstances, the individuals concerned were reluctant to continue with the interview process. In one further instance, the cared-for died. This was always a possibility in a study of this nature, as these events too represent the reality of the caring experience. The possibility of such an event occurring had been anticipated in the research design and built in to the sampling process. Thus the final analysis was based on a complete set of serial interviews with nine carers, a set of three interviews with one carer, and two interviews with the remaining two. The profile of carers participating in the in-depth study is illustrated in table 5.2 below.

As the carer profile illustrates, only 25 percent of those participating in the in-depth part of the study were male. This does not purport to reflect the wider balance of caring between the genders. Rather it reflects a balance of those carers accessing support services known to this study at the time of interview. The group further illustrates a mix of age groups, kinship and employment status.

Table 5.2   Carer Profile - Glasgow (G) and Dumfries and Galloway (DG)

Carer	Male/ female	Age	Employment Status	Dependant
DG - 1	F	37	non-employed	mother
DG - 2	f	early 40s	non-employed	father & daughter
DG - 3	f	mid-30s	mature student	mother & brother
DG - 4	f	70	retired	husband
DG - 5*	f	mid-60s	retired	husband
DG - 6*	m	early 70s	retired	wife
G - 1	f	early 40s	employed p/t	mother-in-law
G - 2*	f	early 50s	employed p/t	mother
G - 3	f	57	non-employed	mother & aunt
G - 4	f	68	retired	husband
G - 5	m	28	employed p/t	grandparents
G - 6	m	late 70s	retired	wife

* Denotes carers who did not participate in the full intensive study.

The intensive part of this stage in the research process sought to uncover the formal and informal supports available to carers who were differentially located in space. It also sought to uncover how carers accessed information about services and how links developed with voluntary and statutory agencies. The 1990 NHS and Community Care Act makes assumptions about informal care networks that a number of commentators have argued may be non-existent (e.g. Nissel, 1980; McDowell, 1992). Consequently the burden of caring may fall unequally on the shoulders of one individual - these issues are explored in chapter seven.

Though the interviews aimed to illuminate the ways in which the restructuring process was impacting on the lives of carers within community settings, such individuals often undertake a very heavy burden of caring without formalising those 'services' that they provide within their own thoughts. As a consequence, these roles and experiences may not be vocalised in an interview setting. In order to facilitate the uncovering of some of these factors, carers were asked during the second interview to complete a diary detailing their day-to-day lives over a one month period. The quantity and quality of data provided in the diary method is both significantly different to that available through questionnaire and interview approaches, and offers a more comprehensive picture of an individual's activities (Thornton et al, 1997). Of the ten participants still remaining at this point in the research process, eight agreed to undertake this task. Each respondent was given a diary with a set of points to consider when completing each entry (see table 5.3).

Carers face many pressures in undertaking their caring duties, consequently free time is a precious commodity not to be 'misused'. As a consequence, carers were given the proviso, that if in the completion of the diary they felt physically or mentally unable to make an entry on any given day, they should address their omission by entering a few lines of explanation on the following day. For those that completed the diary, this proviso proved unnecessary. However, given the considerable effort required on the part of the respondent for this type of data collection, only six carers completed the diaries. This completion rate was not wholly unexpected. Those diaries that were returned were well completed and offered some revealing insights into the lives of carers that were not identified by the other methods used.

Though the research design was never intended to achieve a representative sample in the statistical sense, or to generate numerical information, the particularities of the selection procedure need to be acknowledged. It is important to note that it included only those carers known to either the voluntary sector and/or statutory sector. There was no way to access those many carers with whom they have no contact, either in terms of information and support, or more formal service provision. As a result, those who participated in the research process may well be those who are more capable of actively seeking outside help. The carers participating in the study were reasonably articulate, understood what was occurring and heeded the advice of those involved in the caring network. The inability to access those individuals who do not formally identify themselves as carers had implications for the theoretical framework outlined in chapter three. The inability to identify carers who do not access formal or informal supports meant it was necessary to revise figure 4.1 to include *two* groups of carers (see figure 5.1); one whose existence is known, but whom we are unable to access (type a), and one, whom it is possible to formally identify as being located within the dependency network (type b).

Table 5.3 Carers' Diaries - Points for Consideration

1.	What interaction have you had with people from voluntary or private organisations, the statutory sector, (social services, GP, community nursing, occupational therapy etc.) – how beneficial was this to you/your relative?
2.	What respite have you received - from whom, for how long (i.e. days or hours)?
3.	What free time is available to you on a day to day basis?
4.	What restrictions on your time occurred due to your caring role i.e. are you able to go out? Are there restrictions on the distance/time you can go out, due to the need for you to be within the home at certain times?
5.	Who undertakes the caring role when you do go out (friend, relation, member of statutory or voluntary organisation) - or is no relief necessary?
6.	Have you been able to go outside the home with the person you care for? What transport was available to you? i.e. your own car, friend's/relative's care, public transport, taxi etc.
7.	What alterations have you made to your social life as a result of your caring role?
8.	(If employed) Have there been interruptions to your working life due to your caring role? i.e. your in/ability to work certain hours, accept training etc.
9.	Where have you gained information about help/entitlements as a carer? How easy/difficult was it to get? How were you treated?
10.	Other factors not listed that may form part of your daily life as a carer.

Figure 5.1 Revised Dependency Network

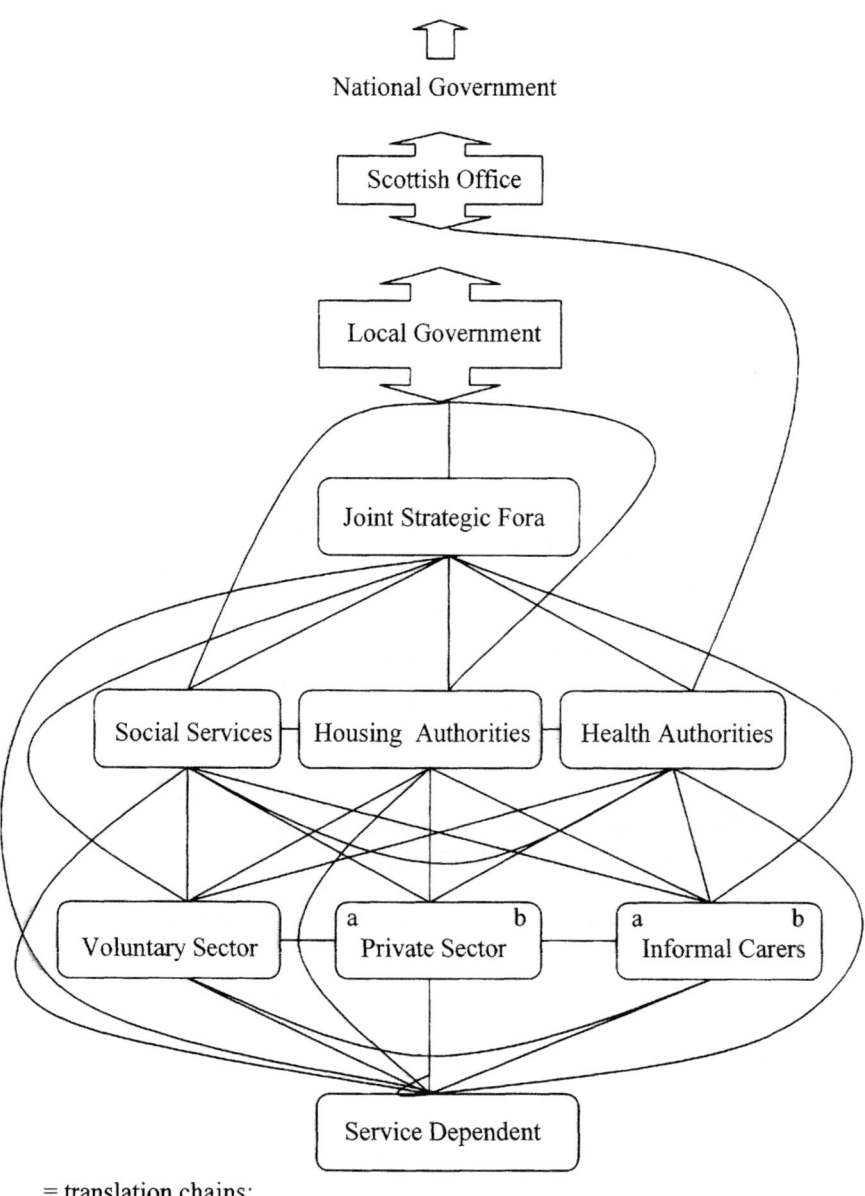

__ = translation chains;
a = actants whose existence is known, but whom we are unable to access;
b = actants whom it is possible to formally identify as located within the
     dependency network.

The private sector

The private sector is also a key player in the process of restructuring community-based care for the frail elderly. As previous studies have noted (Parker, 1990; Filinson, 1998), this sector has been particularly prominent in the provision of nursing homes and residential respite care, and there is also evidence of an increase in the growth of private sector domiciliary care. This is potentially a huge area of study, and one that represents an alternative route through which factors of change may be influenced within the dependency network. However, in order not to compromise the depth of this study, the decision was taken not to pursue this particular pathway in any great depth. Hence, though the role of the private sector has been considered, it does not form an integral part of the study, rather it is viewed as a project for further exploration at some future stage.

Nevertheless, in order to give a 'flavour' of the ways in which the private sector may impact, and be impacted upon, by care restructuring, a questionnaire was constructed around the key themes of the research. This was sent to all nursing homes and domiciliary care providers within the two study areas between February and April of 1997. The aim was to develop a contextual understanding of private sector care provision to frail elderly populations. Questions focused on gaining an insight into three main areas of private sector care provision:

- a profile of relevant private sector organisations operating within the two areas;
- the role of the private sector within the framework of this study; and
- their links with other formal and informal agencies.

Private sector providers were identified through lists of approved providers held by local authorities, telephone directories and local advertising. This amounted to a total of 111 organisations, of which, eighty-four were located in Glasgow City, with the remaining twenty-seven situated in Dumfries and Galloway. An overall response rate of 63 percent was achieved, representing a return rate of 78 percent in Dumfries and Galloway and 58 percent in Glasgow City. In a further five percent of cases, respondents were found to form part of another organisation within the same area to whom a questionnaire has also been sent, in these cases one response was returned on behalf of all the relevant agencies. A further 1 percent of agencies were no longer operational. Allowing for the latter two explanations, an overall response rate of 67 percent was achieved. A further

17 percent agreed to return questionnaires at the time of the follow-up telephone call, but failed to do so.

The response rate for private sector organisations in Glasgow was considerably lower than both that of respondents in Dumfries and Galloway, and that of the voluntary sector in both areas. No definitive accounting can be given for this, although it is speculated that this may be a consequence of private sector reluctance to give out company information in an environment of increased competition in Glasgow for a declining number of local authority referrals. Some respondents, for example, though replying, took the precaution of removing the identifying code. No interviews were undertaken with this sector for the reasons discussed above.

While the research design was aimed at accessing all visible private sector residential and domiciliary care providers, it should also be noted at this point that there exists a high level of private sector domiciliary provision that is purchased at the level of the individual. There are no current figures available for the scale of this private sector provision, many of who form part of the black economy. It has been estimated, however, that figures for private provision at the level of the individual account for somewhere in the region of 4 - 7 percent of private sector provision in the UK as a whole (Parker, 1990, 322). There is no immediate way of accessing these individuals. The inability to identify this group meant that, as with carers, it was necessary to revise further figure 4.1 to include two groups of private sector providers (see figure 5.1). The first group (type a), representing those private providers whose existence is known, but who cannot be immediately accessed, while the second group (type b) is seen to consist of those formal and organised private sector providers whose existence is known and who form part of the dependency network.

The statutory sector

The final stage of the research involved a consideration of the statutory sector. The nature of the relationship between the formal and informal sectors formed an integral part of the study, in that it attempted to understand how and why actors/agencies respond in particular ways, and the subsequent impact on change effected within the dependency network.

Community care legislation identifies the key role played by three distinct statutory agencies within the process of health and social care delivery to community-based groups within a Local Authority area:

- the Social Services;
- the Health Authority; and

- the Housing Department.

Interviews were arranged with key actors from each of these agencies within the two unitary authority areas. As discussed above, however, the availability of considerable secondary source material - in terms of policy documentation, community care plans, research reports, committee and annual reports - meant that much contextual data was openly available. It was felt, therefore, that a single, in-depth interview with a range of actors from the identified statutory agencies would be sufficient to gain that data not readily available through secondary sources. Interviews were, thus, undertaken with key figures from the relevant housing department, the health authority, social work committee (the political arm of local social services department) and from the central office of the social services department. Unlike health and housing, however, social service departments within the unitary authority area are divided into separate districts, each with their own budgets and a degree of autonomy from the centre. As a consequence, additional interviews were undertaken with a key figure from each of the districts (three in Glasgow City, and four in Dumfries and Galloway). Fifteen semi-structured interviews were conducted in total, each was of approximately one hour in duration, and each was taped and transcribed ready for later analysis. Interview schedules focused around five themes:

- policy formulation and communication;
- links and relationships with other statutory actants and the informal sector;
- issues surrounding the purchase and provision of services;
- the impact of key individuals; and
- rural/urban issues.

The objective was to uncover how statutory actants at local level translate nationally defined policy, variations in its interpretation and implementation, and the ways in which they may influence and be influenced by other actants working within the dependency network.

Issues of Validity and Reliability

The strength of any study lies in its validity. Whilst the quest for validity is not unique to qualitative research, it does manifest itself in different ways to more extensive methods. Validity in qualitative work is dominated by an approach that emphasises the meaning of events and situations, rather than the quantitative focus on causes and output (Finch, 1986). Nevertheless, when carefully administered, qualitative research can offer greater accuracy and validity than comparable standardised methods, in that they allow for a more comparative and detailed elucidation of the interplay between strategy, history and circumstances (Schoenberger, 1991). In this sense, the method can greatly amplify and complement information derived from more conventional approaches. Further, as Marshall and Rossman (1989) note, in-depth description showing the complexities of variables and interactions will be so embedded in the data derived from the setting, that within the parameters of that setting and the theoretical framework used, the research will be valid.

Nevertheless, the ultimate test of any piece of research, lies in exposing the methods to scrutiny - laying out the stages of the research, what data was used at each stage and how inferences were drawn from them - so that the reader can make his/her own judgements about the degree of confidence that can be placed in the conclusions. This chapter represents one such stage, in that it lays out the methods used within this research to scrutiny. The more detailed issues of data usage and inference are to be found within the substantive chapters that make up the remainder of the book.

As noted above, ethnographic methods require a different set of principles through which truth claims can be validated (Cook and Crang, 1995). Within this study, a number of checks were employed to address this. Firstly, the concept of *theoretical sampling* was employed. This involved the means by which the researcher decided who should be approached to participate in the study, gaining selective access to appropriate respondents and encouraging them to inform the researcher about the issues under investigation from their various perspectives. As noted above, the voluntary sector sample included all those organisations that indicated a willingness to participate in the interview process. While this points to a self-selecting sampling process, as chapter six reveals, this did not act to alter the profile of voluntary actants. Further, as previously noted, it was not the sheer number, typicality or representativeness of people approached within this study that was important, but the rich and detailed nature of the data uncovered.

A second key principal adopted within the study was a concern that the data gathering process should reach a point *of theoretical saturation*. As Burgess (1992) notes, researching the lives of every member of every interest group is both impractical and unnecessary because there usually comes a point in the research process where the range of arguments which *can* be made concerning a particular matter *have* been made (i.e. the point of theoretical saturation). This occurs when accounts told begin to have the same ring about them. Though some level of theoretical saturation *was* reached in investigating the voluntary sector, the decision to continue to interview all willing participants was based on the knowledge that each interview revealed some new insights into the voluntary experience of care restructuring. With regard to informal carers, a point of theoretical saturation was reached following the third interview. The decision to continue with the final set of interviews was more a matter of research integrity and withdrawal from the project than the belief that it would uncover any new data.

Thirdly, the study has sought to engage with the concept of *theoretical reasoning*. That is, that validity of interpretation is seen to depend on the cogency of the reasoning employed. In intensive approaches, the relationship between theoretical constructs and empirical observation must also be validated. This is usually seen in terms of empirical indicators and theoretical concepts, i.e. does the indicator really measure the concept that it is intended to measure? The veracity of this text must be judged by whether or not the work engages with the reader, providing insights that help to organise his/her own observations, or compels the individual to re-examine long-held truths about our life world (Vidich and Lyman, 1994).

Subjectivity and Bias

Intensive methods are often criticised on the grounds that they lay themselves open to 'subjective' or 'biased' data. The presence of the researcher may distort the social setting under study, and/or influence the responses of the researched. While it is inevitably true that both researcher and researched influence, and are influenced by, the situation, it is argued that the extent of this intervention is not problematic as long as it is clearly acknowledged within the research. For as Mead (1927, 164) commented, "one cannot exist as a self without the universal, the group, that makes the self possible". The self, moreover, he argued, continuously shifts and changes with the social situation, as such, it is the product of a complex set of social relationships. Nevertheless, the researcher cannot take for granted that truth claims are absolute, rather he/she is engaged in a struggle to produce inter-subjective truths and to understand why so many versions of events are produced. As a consequence, it is the ways in which people make sense of the events around them and render these 'true' in their own terms that is most revealing about how individuals' lives engage with the larger social, cultural, economic and political processes. Narrative responses told in the research encounter are not simply a means of mirroring the world, but represent a means through which it is constructed, understood, and acted upon. In Haastrup's (1992) terms, the informant's response is an externalisation of their inner (cultural) experience. Intensive research is, as a consequence, concerned with much more than recording the voices of 'others', it is writing a culture that is not just an empirical entity but also has an analytical implication.

Qualitative research is by its very nature subjective. The researcher can never lay claim to being a neutral channel of communication (Pearson, 1993). However, rather than seeing this as a drawback to the engagement with such methodologies (in that it cannot draw the valid 'objective' conclusions offered by quantitative techniques), following Cook and Crang (1995), it is maintained that it is not necessary to assume an abstract advantage in order to study social and cultural processes. The approaches used here offer the possibility of allowing the researcher to uncover the ways in which local cultures reproduce and transform more global 'structures'. Hence, "through the largely taken for granted routinisation of their/our day-to-day lives, people can be seen to reproduce and transform processes that extend far beyond the conscious spheres of their/our actions" (Cook and Crang, 1995, 10).

While subjectivity, in itself, is not viewed as a problem, it is nevertheless an issue that needs to be recognised and harnessed. Hence, the purposes and assumptions of the researcher need to be made explicit and used judiciously to give meaning and focus to the study. To address the issue of possible researcher bias, the study incorporated a number of control mechanisms into the research design as follows:

- following the process of data gathering, all questionnaire data and interview transcriptions were offered and subjected to the scrutiny of fellow researchers and suggested by Marshall and Rossman (1989);
- the study sought respondent validation of the data (Rowles, 1978; Fountain, 1993; Silverman, 1993). It is recognised, here, that some techniques have more potential for the introduction of the researcher subjectivity and bias than others. The analysis of interview transcripts, for example, may offer more opportunity for the introduction of researcher subjectivity and bias than the closed responses of a questionnaire. In the attempt to reduce such bias within this study, the opportunity was offered, and arrangements made, for the draft analysis of interview transcripts to be returned to respondents for validation of the researcher's interpretation of their comments and critical comment, prior to the writing of the final draft. While this approach was applied to respondents within the informal sector, respondents from the statutory sector were unwilling to participate in this process - a factor stemming largely from constraints on their time. Due to the abundant availability

of secondary data sources with which much of the data could be cross-checked, this was not seen as problematic for this project;
- in the process of data analysis, the data was subjected to a constant rechecking of the data in order to uncover the most common or insidious biases. The researcher also sought, where relevant, to test for alternative hypotheses (Huberman and Miles, 1994); and
- during the sort and code process, the data was checked for negative instances. Where these occurred, they have been examined and acknowledged in the substantive chapters of that follow.

Whilst these controls were adopted within this project as mechanisms for checking the worst excesses of bias, the process of forming links between ideas in the researcher's mind and what he/she has observed, is dialectical. Ideas inform observation and vice versa, with the prime motivational force in the process being the researcher (Wolcott, 1995). Objectivity is thus an elusive quality. In any qualitative research, the dialogue has an inevitable bias resulting from the unsolicited questioning of the researcher, which will of necessity shape the response, the researcher is then in the position of "interpreting these interpretations" (Schoenberger, 1991, 183). The knowledge generated in the course of the research is unavoidably filtered through the processes by which people make sense of their own experiences. The resultant text, as Haastrup (1992) argues, must inevitably consist of contextualised truths.

Positionality

As a mature, female researcher with some experience of informal caring, the issue of positionality should be acknowledged as being one which places myself, as the researcher, as having an element of insider status - a position which gave some initial insight into the research issues. However, all qualitative researchers are positioned subjects whose position is defined not only by age, gender, race and outsider status, but also by the researcher's lived experiences, which enables or inhibits particular kinds of insights. Behind each method of research is the personal equation supplied to the setting by both researcher and researched, hence, all observations are made within a mediated framework of symbols, cultural meanings and the life histories of observer and observed (Vidich and Lyman, 1994). Positionality rather than being viewed problematic, therefore, is simply an issue that needs to be acknowledged and disclosed for the benefit of the reader. What is of primary importance is to "bridge the distance between the experiences of actors and audiences" (Pearson, 1993, xviii).

Ethical Issues

It is also appropriate at this point to discuss the ethical issues and considerations raised in the course of this research. Primarily this has been concerned with two main issues: firstly, the question of confidentiality; and secondly, the issue of exit strategies when working with vulnerable groups. The issue of confidentiality was concerned with the disclosure of personal information or viewpoints, and the use to which they are put. While it may be common practice for researchers to assure informants that the raw data will be seen by themselves alone, as Finch (1986) has noted, though the identity of the informant can be removed, the small-scale of a qualitative study of this nature tends to make individuals more identifiable. Further, the unexpected turns characteristic of semi-structured interviews, may have led informants to go beyond tacit agreements about what to reveal. This has particular implications for the dissemination of information to a wider audience where there may be a hostile reaction to critical comments. In this study, this has been of particular relevance to elite informants from within the statutory sector, many of whom disclosed information only with the assurance of anonymity.

While Moyser (1988) has argued that those holding public office are legitimately open to scrutiny, in this study, information was given on the assurance of confidentiality - an assurance that has been upheld. Given the period of uncertainty experienced by many of those working within the local authorities (due to restructuring) a number of respondents from the statutory sector were only willing to divulge information in the knowledge that confidentiality was assured. It should be noted, however, that while every effort has been taken to maintain confidentiality, unlike mass data, it is far more difficult to use information about elite individuals in such a way that they are not identifiable by the profile of comment and background information contained within the data.

The second ethical issue was concerned undertaking research with vulnerable groups such as informal carers. This relates to the place of power and ethics. Finch (1986) draws attention to the fact that where research concerns powerless groups, privacy and protection are paramount. Here, for example, some informal carers raised particular concerns about possible identification by members of the statutory sector - in particular Social Services – which, they felt, *may* result in a loss of services. The challenge as a researcher was thus one of honouring guarantees of confidentiality entered into with respondents and rendering the data sufficiently anonymous, without losing much of its intrinsic value. Two main strategies were used as a means of surmounting the challenge of respondent confidentiality:

- all respondents were rendered anonymous and pseudonyms attributed to quotes or vignettes highlighted within the research; and
- in the process of respondent validation, informal carers were given the opportunity to request the re-wording of any material they believed may have adversely identified them. Each respondent was sent a draft copy of chapter six. Though carers acknowledged receipt of these drafts, none requested any amendment to the text.

In undertaking research with vulnerable groups, it is also important to identify a clear exit strategy at the outset, so individuals are aware of the commitment and time they can anticipate will be required of them, and that there is a clearly defined end-point to the study. As discussed above, informal carers were informed at the focus groups about what would be required and the broad themes they could expect to discuss should they choose to participate in the in-depth stage of the research. Thus, despite the fact that it became evident that a point of theoretical saturation had been reached by the third of the serial interviews, the decision to continue with the final meetings was viewed in the light of an ethical commitment made on the part of the researcher to the researched.

Two further concerns expressed by both the voluntary sector and informal carers were:

i) that as a researcher, I was not connected in any way with the statutory sector; and
ii) that the research was 'independently' funded.

It is worth noting here, that as mentioned above, when undertaking research of this nature, there is an ethical commitment to the researched. Agreement to participate is often motivated by the belief that by doing so, the individual is, in some small way, helping to develop new policies or approaches to the research problem that will be of future benefit to others. The commitment and goodwill of such individuals is crucial to the research process. It is thus of immense importance, that participants' expectations (particularly amongst vulnerable groups) are not raised unrealistically, and that the outcomes of the research are fed back to participants in some way. Within this study, each participant was apprised of the nature and purpose of the research, and each was sent a draft of the relevant chapters, both for comment and information. Participants were informed, that further information on issues arising from the study would be made available on application to the author.

Issues of Analysis

Though a variety of qualitative data analysis packages are now available for the computerised analysis of raw data, as a number of geographers have noted (e.g. Crang et al., 1997; Hinchcliffe et al., 1997), each programme brings with it its own in-built bias to analysis and knowledge construction. Consequently such packages cannot be uncritically adopted and any application of data analysis packages needs to address these issues. However, it is equally possible to undertake this sorting and analysis process manually, using more traditional cut and sort methods (Cook and Crang, 1995). Litva and Eyles (1996) also demonstrated how the adoption of a simple word processing package can aid this manual process without succumbing to the additional bias of data analysis packages. This was the approach adopted within this study.

The quantitative data acquired from questionnaire responses was coded and analysed using the Access software programme. As previously noted, however, this data was tabulated with the intention of providing a general indication of the voluntary and private sector 'profile', and as such, the evidence has been viewed merely as contextual. The primary data has been qualitative in nature, largely based on in-depth interviewing with key informants as discussed above. The use of diaries was a additional means of extrapolating caring issues and experiences amongst a group of respondents that are less familiar with vocalising their role as a care provider. All qualitative responses were analysed in the same code and sort manner utilised in analysing the interview transcripts as detailed below, so facilitating the interpretation of data between sectors.

All primary materials (field notes, transcripts, open-ended questionnaire data etc.) were analysed initially using a process of coding. While a grounded theory approach would maintain that no significant themes should be sought at this stage (Strauss, 1987), in practice, because of the ways in which the research materials were constructed and the ways in which the project became inspired at various stages by specific ideas about what was important at the time, it was acknowledged that the text could not be confronted so innocently. Loose themes arising from the pilot interviews and literature review, for example, were inevitably embedded within the construction of the questionnaire. This, in turn played a role in shaping respondents' expectations of the interview process and, as a consequence, had an impact on responses. Further, as Cook and Crang (1995) note, it is virtually impossible for the researcher to banish all his/her prior thoughts from the analysis, since his/her research will have been based around a theory-driven selection of participants.

While the coding process was inevitably shaped, in part, by the in-built biases discussed above, the semi-structured nature of the interview and diary processes allowed for the introduction of ideas, views and themes initiated by respondents themselves, so allowing for some degree of openness. Following the initial coding process, the data was sorted into similar events, themes, actions and sentiments.

As materials became sorted and connected, there inevitably emerged some things which appeared either not to fit together, or to contradict each other within the codes. At this point, it was necessary to use the *iterative* process (Cook and Crang, 1995). While, in large part, the placement of these materials was found to have arisen as a result of mis-filing or erroneous grouping, it was also the case that on some occasions it was necessary to go back and reclassify other instances in which the code was used. In some instances, however, contradictions did occur. This was not viewed as problematic. Such contradictions are part of normal human inconsistency between two conflicting sources, and indeed, may be crucial to the understanding of a particular theme. These issues are addressed within the interpretation of the data in the following chapters. The emerging groups became the 'dimensions' of the analysis, each one relating to some key issue.

It was also necessary to resist the temptation to set up the analysis as an omniscient view. This was done by a process of constant cross-referring between abstractions and the contexts that gave rise to them. Additionally, given the differing settings within which the participating actors were located, it was unlikely that any single account of events would emerge. Rather, as anticipated, there were multiple competing versions. It was by shuttling back and forth between these competing versions that it was possible to begin to perceive how participants produced and reproduced the world through their lived experiences. Thus, the process of analysis has not been viewed as developing a definitive account, rather it has been viewed as one means of trying to understand the inter-relations of multiple versions of reality, and in doing so, it serves to stress the interconnectivities between actants located within the dependency network.

Though, as this chapter has revealed, some problems did arise in the course of undertaking the field research, as Burgess (1984) notes, there is a need for research strategies to be flexible, and for researchers to select a range of methods suitable to the problem under investigation. The research design was thus not simply the end process, but was ongoing, and as illustrated, formed the basis for the next stage of enquiry. The interview and negotiation process themselves formed part of the research data. The actual process of transcript analysis and the building of links between data and theory thus represents only one part of the research methodology.

The remaining chapters of the book represent the outcome of the sort and code process discussed above. Three issues are of relevance to understanding the structure of the analysis that follows:

- the voluntary sector is the lens through which the network is explored;
- the research has been concerned to explore the relationships between actants within the network; and
- the research has been concerned to examine the implications of change in care provision.

In this way, the analysis offered in chapters six to nine emphasises both the interconnectivities (Cook and Crang, 1995) between actants as well as the different 'realities' of care provision as expressed by actants from different sectors within the network. As a consequence, these chapters cannot be seen as separate entities, rather chapter nine seeks to weave together the threads of the issues emerging from the discussion in chapters five to eight, drawing together the interconnectivities between actants as discussed in the individual chapters. In this chapter I also address the temporal and spatial dimensions of the study. These are referred to in the individual chapters but drawn together within chapter nine.

While the material presented in the following chapters aims to maximise the voices of those participating in the research process, the final presentation of data makes no attempt to reflect the views of *all* respondents. Rather the aim has been to reflect the balance and range of opinion, and to highlight emerging patterns using a selection of detailed case study material. Although ultimately each case study is unique, it nevertheless provides a way of looking at the processes involved in the restructuring process.

6 A Geography of Care Restructuring: The Voluntary Experience

Introduction

This chapter serves to illustrate how restructuring is being played out through the voluntary sector - *one* of those sets of actors and agencies that form part of the dependency network outlined in chapter five. The chapter examines the collective experiences of those voluntary/non-profit organisations concerned with health and social care provisioning to the frail elderly within Dumfries and Galloway and Glasgow City. The aim, here, is to examine how the forces of change arising from care restructuring are experienced by voluntary sector actors and agents within localised contexts, and how restructuring, combined with social and spatial variations within and between locales, can impact on voluntary care provisioning. In doing so, attention is drawn to some of the ways in which the dependency network becomes differentially mediated by the local environment within which it is embedded.

The chapter has been constructed in two main parts. The first part is concerned with the context within which the voluntary sector needs to be examined, whilst the remainder of the chapter discusses the substantive issues arising from the data analysis. Particular instances from the interview material and other information gathering tools have been presented illustratively throughout the text in order to illuminate key points raised by the analysis.

As noted in the previous chapter, the voluntary sector has been taken as the key entry point to the dependency network and is thus pivotal to the analysis. The construction of the material offered within each of the subsequent chapters, while containing primary information, is seen as of a lesser order. This has been a matter of choice. The voluntary sector was purposively selected as a significant example of the way in which the network can influence agencies located within it. In recognising its importance, however, it was necessary to investigate the influence of other agencies *within* the network. The subsequent chapters are thus concerned to consider the inter-relationships of other actants with the voluntary sector. It is worth noting, at this point, that it would be equally possible to adopt other actants as entry points if desired.

Exploring the Changing Context of Voluntary Care Provision

As noted in chapter three, the UK legislative framework has aimed to reinforce the changing locus of care provision for frail elderly populations from institutional to community-based alternatives. Policy is directed toward shifting provision away from the statutory sector, and attempting to [re]locate provision within the private and informal sectors. Whilst local authorities are allocated the lead role, legislation also promotes the need for a multi-agency approach, elevating the independent sector through a renewed emphasis on private and voluntary provisioning (Cm. 849, 1989). This elevation of the informal sector in health and social care provisioning in the 1990s has implications for both local voluntary organisations, and for those in receipt of their services. In addition, the introduction of new single tier local government in Scotland in 1996 caused many local authorities to experience both geographical and organisational change. These developments have also created changes in the relationships between local authorities and the voluntary sector at local level; issues which are explored both in this chapter and in chapter nine.

Although there is significant diversity within the voluntary sector, a range of techniques were employed to gain insights into the impact of change in care provision and the associations with other actants in the dependency network. Five main themes have emerged from the analysis:

- funding and resource issues;
- organisational change;
- changing relationships within and between organisations;
- the social and spatial dimensions of change; and
- change over time.

Each of these themes is explored within this chapter, and is further addressed from the perspective of other actants in the subsequent chapters. The geographical dimensions are considered more explicitly in chapter ten.

The analysis offered here does not claim to be a definitive account, but rather offers a means through which to understand the inter-relations of multiple versions of reality - so serving to stress interconnectivities operating in the network (Cook and Crang, 1995). This is of particular import given the highly complex and diverse nature of the voluntary/non-profit sector.

Characterising the Voluntary Sector

Though the voluntary sector is a diverse group, it is useful to have a working definition for the purposes of the study. Within the British context, voluntary organisations have been defined as "self-governing associations of people who have joined together to take action for public benefit. They are not created by statute, or established for financial gain. They are founded on voluntary effort, but may employ paid staff and may have income from statutory sources. Some, by no means all, are charities. They address a wide range of issues through direct service, advocacy, self-help and mutual aid, and campaigning" (Taylor 1992, p.171). These characteristics are closely aligned to the "narrow voluntary sector" [1] as referred to by such voluntary bodies as the Scottish Council for the Voluntary Sector (SCVS) (1997) in Scotland. Both Glasgow City Council and Dumfries and Galloway Unitary Authority have also outlined their own working definitions within committee reports (Glasgow City Council, 1997; Dumfries and Galloway Social Services Committee Report, 1996). Both refer to independent non-profit organisations that share a purpose of common benefit of a social or economic nature, which may have paid or voluntary workers, are managed by voluntary management committees, and who do not depend on statute for their existence or purpose. It is also worth noting at this point, that the term 'voluntary sector' is a term used generically in Britain to refer to what in other national settings may more frequently be referred to as the 'non-profit' or 'non-governmental' sector.

While defined and conceived of as a sector, voluntary organisations are not homogenous. The sector is characterised by diversity in sources of funding, services, size, internal structure and autonomy. Organisations range across a spectrum from non-profit making bodies with paid employees answerable to a voluntary committee, to those whom are philanthropic in the purest sense. Services offered can be seen to range from tangible provision such as domiciliary-based respite and personal care; visiting and befriending schemes; practical home support (e.g. meals provision, cleaning and home maintenance tasks, provision of practical aids); daycare and day-centres; transport schemes for the elderly/disabled; to non-tangible services such as support, advice, information and campaigning groups; and 'umbrella' [2] organisations. Voluntary organisations operating at the local level can also be differentiated by their size and organisational structure: i.e. those who are locally-based and independent of any hierarchical structure;

those who are locally-based but affiliated to a national body; and those who are essentially 'satellite' organisations answerable to a national body. The main funding sources, services and organisational structure of those voluntary organisations participating within this study are illustrated in table 6.1.

The chaotic nature of the voluntary sector makes it a highly complex arena within which to attempt any form of analysis. However, to understand how change is impacting on, and being mediated within this sector, it is necessary to attempt to weave a path through this disorder. The ability of voluntary organisations to act, and constraints to action, are in large part linked to the resources they are able to command, and the source and mechanisms through which these resources are accessed. Though resources can be in cash or kind, most require some level of financial resource if they are to provide a regular service. Respondents were thus asked in the questionnaire, to give their *main* source of income. The primary sources of revenue for voluntary organisations within this study were found to come from four main sources:

- central government funding (e.g. Urban Aid and Mental Illness Specific Grant (MISG) allocated through the Scottish Office);
- the local authority (either through mainline grant funding or through contracts/service agreements);
- funding from the head office of a national organisation; and
- donations and fund-raising.

As noted in chapter three, community care legislation recommends a change in funding mechanisms for the purchase of voluntary care provision from the previous predominance of grant aid to contracting and service agreements. Thus, based on the funding mechanisms referred to above, the study has employed a simplistic but useful threefold typology as an initial tool with which to portray the voluntary sector and to elucidate how voluntary organisations are experiencing change from within the network.

The threefold typology is as follows:

- organisations funded predominantly through contract/service agreement;
- organisations funded predominantly through grants from local or central government; and
- independently resourced bodies (incorporating donations/bequests, fund-raised monies, or funding allocated from a central budget).

Table 6.1 Profile of Participating Voluntary Organisations by Funding Structure

Code	Funding Structure	Service Provision	Size
DG3	Contract/service agreement	Domiciliary services	N
DG13*	Contract/service agreement	Domiciliary services	N
DG14*	Contract/service agreement	Domiciliary services	N
DG26	Contract/service agreement	Domiciliary services	N
DG27	Contract/service agreement	Domiciliary services	N
G5	Contract/service agreement	Support Groups, Advice/advocacy	N
G14*	Contract/service agreement	Domiciliary services	N
G37*	Contract/service agreement	Domiciliary services	N
DG2*	Contract /service agreement, LA Grant, Budget from National Org.	Domiciliary services, Social Provision	N
DG6	Contract/service agreement, LA Grant	'Umbrella' Support services, Advice advocacy	N
DG12*	Contract/service agreement, LA Grant	Daycare	L
DG9	Contract/service agreement, LA Grant	'Umbrella' Support services, Advice/advocacy	N
G1*	Contract/service agreement, Central Govt. Grant (MISG), Fundraising/Donations	Domiciliary services, Daycare, Support Groups, Advice/advocacy	N
G7*	Contract/service agreement, LA Grant, Fundraising/Donations	Domiciliary services	N
G15*	Contract/service agreement, Central Govt. Grant (MISG)	Domiciliary services, Daycare, Support Groups, Advice/advocacy	N
G18*	Contract/service agreement, LA Grant, Fundraising/Donations	'Umbrella' Support services, Advice/advocacy, Research	R
G19*	Contract/service agreement, Fundraising/Donations	Daycare, Domiciliary services, Advice/advocacy	N
G20*	Contract/service agreement, Central Govt. Grant (MISG),	Domiciliary services, Daycare, Support Groups, advice/advocacy	N

Code	Funding Structure	Service Provision	Size
G22*	Contract/service agreement, Central Govt. Grant (Urban Aid)	Equipment, Advice/advocacy, Befriending	L
G27	Contract/service agreement, Central Govt. Grant (Urban Aid)	Advice/advocacy, Campaigning	L
G28*	Contract/service agreement / Fundraising/Grant from National Org.	Training, Residential respite, Advice.	N
G36*	Contract/service agreement, LA Grant	Daycare	L
G39*	Contract/service agreement, LA Grant, Fundraising/Donations	Domiciliary service, Advice/advocacy	N
G41	Contract/service agreement, LA Grant	Domiciliary service, Advice/advocacy	N
G42*	Contract/service agreement, Central Govt. Grant (MISG), Fundraising/Donations	Domiciliary services	N
G46*	Contract/service agreement, Central Govt. Grant (Urban Aid)	Domiciliary services, Daycare	L
G54*	Contract/service agreement, LA Grant	Campaigning/advocacy	L
G58	Contract/service agreement, LA Grant	Daycare	L
G60	Contract/service agreement, Central Govt. Grant (Urban Aid)	Domiciliary services, Daycare	L
G61*	Contract/service agreement, LA Grant	Domiciliary services, Daycare	L
G70*	Contracting, LA Grant, Fundraising/Donations	Domiciliary services	L
G72	Contract/service agreement, LA Grant, Fundraising/Donations	Equipment, befriending & support	N

DG30*	# LA Grant	Daycentre	L
G23	# LA Grant	Advice/advocacy	L
G25*	# LA Grant	Advice/advocacy, Campaigning, Research	R
G47	# LA Grant	Domiciliary services	L
DG1	LA Grant	Daycentre	L

Code	Funding Structure	Service Provision	Size
DG11*	LA Grant	'Umbrella' support services, Information, Advice/advocacy	N
DG20*	LA Grant	Support Groups, Advice/advocacy, Information, Campaigning	N
DG35*	LA Grant	Daycentre	L
DG36	LA Grant	Advice/information, advocacy, Campaigning	N
G8	LA Grant	Advice/advocacy, Campaigning	R
G13	LA Grant	Daycentre	L
G32	LA Grant	Advice and Information	N
G50*	LA Grant	Social care, advice and information	R
G62	LA Grant	Careline, safety	L
DG32	LA Grant, Fundraising/Donations	Social care	L
G55	LA Grant, Fundraising/Donations	Befriending	L
G64	LA Grant, Fundraising/Donations	Daycare	L
DG19*	# Central Government Grant (MISG)	Domiciliary services, Support Groups, Advice/advocacy	N
DG24	Central Government Grant, budget from national org.	Training	N
DG31	Central Government Grant	Social provision, Financial aid	L
G4*	# Central Government Grant (Urban Aid)	Domiciliary services	N
G10	Central Government Grant	Advice/advocacy, Campaigning	N
G24	Central Government Grant (Urban Aid)	Daycentre	L
G26*	Central Government Grant (Urban Aid)	Befriending, Volunteer recruitment for daycare services	N
G30	Central Government Grant	Daycare	L
G44	Central Government Grant	Campaigning/advocacy, Research	L
G51*	Central Government Grant (Urban Aid)	Social Provision, Advocacy	L

Code	Funding Structure	Service Provision	Size
DG4*	Fundraising/Donations	Social Provision	L
DG8*	Fundraising/Donations	Transport	L
DG10	Fundraising/Donations	'Umbrella' support services, Advice/advocacy	N
DG25	Fundraising/Donations	Advice/advocacy, Social Provision	L
DG29	Fundraising/Donations	Social Provision	L
DG34*	Fundraising/Donations	Social Provision	L
G9	Fundraising/Donations	Transport, Equipment	N
G12	Fundraising/Donations	Transport, Equipment	N
G17*	Fundraising/Donations	Advice/advocacy, Information, Financial aid, Research	L
G35*	Fundraising/Donations	Social Provision, Advice/advocacy	N
G40	Fundraising/Donations	Daycare, equipment, Advice/advocacy, Campaigning	N
G53*	Fundraising/Donations	Campaigning/advocacy	N
G57	Fundraising/Donations	Financial Aid	N
G68*	Fundraising/Donations	Social Provision, Advice/information	L
G6	Rents, Fundraising/Donations	Housing services	R
G65*	Budget from National Org.	Support groups, Advice/advocacy	R
G69	Budget from National Org.	Social provision, Advice/advocacy	L

* Organisation participating in the interview process.
# contract being negotiated at time of research.
N = National; R = Regional; L = Local (organisational structure).

However, as evident in table 6.1, voluntary sector income comes from a mixed pot of funding, that can incorporate a variety of grants, contracts and fund-raised resources. Reference to the 'predominance' of a particular funding source is an acknowledgement of these differing sources, hence any such typology has its limitations. Yet, as the table reveals, the bulk of voluntary organisations in this study accessed funding through the statutory sector (albeit through different agencies of the state and through different mechanisms). As a consequence, though voluntary organisations can obtain their funding from a variety of sources, the predominance of statutory funding means that the ways in which statutory bodies both translate legislation, and transfer resources to care providers within locally-embedded networks, is likely to impact on how locally-based voluntary organisations are able to mediate care. Such a typology thus offers a useful starting point through which to explore the ways in which change within the network may be impacting on the voluntary sector.

The Influence of Funding Sources and Funding Mechanisms

The 1990 NHS and Community Care Act, while placing greater emphasis on the role of voluntary organisations, also advocates a move away from traditional grant aid, in favour of contracting or service agreements for the provision of specified services. Contracting is viewed as a means of increasing competition and accountability amongst service providers, resulting in lower costs, and greater choice, for service users. Many voluntary sector activities in Scotland are now covered by these contractual or semi-contractual arrangements (SCVS, 1997). For those voluntary organisations with an area of expertise that statutory purchasers want, contracting may present the opportunity to exert considerable influence on the shape of the final contract, which once made, is likely to be renewed (Kramer and Grossman, 1987). Voluntary sector response to this new contract regime, however, has been mixed. While some have grasped the opportunities and adopted the language and working practices of the marketplace, others have voiced concern over the direction that contracting takes the voluntary sector in and the implications for voluntary sector values and independence.

Though only 11 percent of respondents within this study cited contracts as their *sole* source of income, 47 percent were either currently in receipt of contracts or in the negotiation process. Comparatively, this represents a figure of 40 percent in Dumfries and Galloway, and 50 percent in Glasgow City. In Dumfries and Galloway, however, where the local authority is introducing contracting for *all* organisations with an annual turnover of £10,000 or more, this figure is likely to increase. 96 percent of the social work department's budget for 1996/97, for example, went to just 40 organisations (across *all* voluntary organisations) throughout the region (Dumfries and Galloway, 1996). This left smaller organisations able to compete for just 4 percent of the grant budget. This apparent increase in contracting as a funding mechanism for the voluntary sector is one which accords with the more general UK profile (SCVS, 1997).

Contracted funding falls broadly into two categories:

(i)   *block contracting* (sometimes referred to as cost and volume) in which the organisation is paid a specified sum (generally allocated in lump sums at set intervals throughout the financial year). This sum covers core costs and a specified amount of service provision over the year; and

(ii)   *spot contracting* in which voluntary organisations have no core budget and no guaranteed amount of purchased service. The contract comprises an agreed unit cost for service provision (including some allowance for core costs) which the local authority will then purchase on a 'spot' basis as and when required.

While these represent the two main contracting mechanisms, a number of organisations are also in receipt of some combination of the two. This occurs mainly where organisations are in receipt of contracts from two different local authorities, or in some instances, where different social work districts *within* the same local authority adopt different contracting mechanisms.

Organisations who favoured contracting as a funding mechanism pointed to three main advantages:

(i) contracts clarified the boundaries of both service provision and purchase, in that organisations had a legally binding agreement detailing exactly what service was being purchased and the rate for that service:

G7 I: *You said you felt the awarding of contracts would increase the security of funding, could you explain that?*

R: *Well it* [contracting] *lets people know where we stand. I mean, if I enter into a contract with* [the local authority] *to do meals, right? I enter into a contract with them and say, 'right, I am going to do meals for you. I will provide the volunteers and I will deliver them for you. Your side of the contract is, you will give me the transport and see to the utensils, you'll see to the equipment. Then I **know** what I've got to do and **they** know what they've got to do.*

120

I: *Right, so that's clarifying?*

R: *It is. It draws the lines of demarcation, you know, and there's no grey areas.*

* I = interviewer; R = respondent; G7 = code; (1) or (2) denotes sequence of interviews; bold text indicates respondent's emphasis.

(ii) contracting was viewed as offering opportunities to increase the amount of services provided, with most contracting organisations noting [in the first year of interview] an increase in services purchased by the local authority:

G15(2): *Contracting has crept up and up ... we just wouldn't have been able to develop without it. So it's been very positive in that respect.*

Notably, however, in the second year of interview, Glasgow-based organisations with spot contracts reported a considerable decline in purchased services;

(iii) the need to compete and negotiate for contracts encouraged more professional working practices within the voluntary sector. Organisations, for example, spoke of tightening up what in the past have been fairly haphazard or *ad hoc* administrative systems:

G7: *And I came into this office last July and I have two wee ladies down in the bowels of this office, and I knew they did social transport work - I was frightened to ask **how** they did it! Over the months, I discovered that they had been running a scheme for Glasgow and surrounding district, we got 31p per mile from the social work department and I found they give the **driver** the 31p they get, which means its costing **me** for phones and things! And one of them works from home a lot and she **never** puts in a bill! I've worked it all out, so now we have put a contract forward to the Social Work Department, and they will get invoiced at 53p per mile.*

Thus voluntary organisations in favour of contracting felt that it provided a legal demarcation of the service provided for a set unit cost. As that unit cost increased, organisations maintained that contracts gave them an opportunity to re-negotiate the terms. It is noteworthy, however, that those holding such views were largely organisations that had the support of legal and administrative departments at the national level. For smaller organisations without the legal and administrative back-up of the wider organisation, the negotiation process can be a much more difficult and time consuming exercise (issues that will be discussed in more detail later in this chapter).

Organisations with block contracts highlighted the added security such funding offered, but for those with *spot* contracts this security was tenuous. In particular, organisations commented on the difficulties of covering the basic costs of the organisational infrastructure with no core funding. Without the profit-based reserves available to private sector providers, voluntary organisations have only their fund-raised resources to fall back on. Increased administration and the bureaucracy associated with the contracting process, however, has had an adverse impact on the ability of two-thirds of participating voluntary organisations to devote time to fund-raising. This, combined with the slow payment record of the social work department (in both areas) had at times proved highly problematic to them. So while spot contracting has clear advantages for statutory sector purchasers, in that it offers increased flexibility in their allocation of resources, it fails to take account of the non-profit status of voluntary organisations, many of whom have no overdraft facility and no reserves to fall back on:

DG14: *At the moment, we get our quarterly core funding at the beginning of the quarter, and you're invoiced work then is done in arrears. The **difficulty** is, that like all charities, we don't have overdraft facilitates ... and that's the problem that we have at the moment, because we're **now** doing so much spot funding, that by the last month in the quarter, you've actual **used** you're core funding, and there's nothing to pay the bills with, and they haven't paid their invoice, and you're in difficulties! I actually wrote to them and told them they were in breach of contract because they were so far in arrears in their payment of everybody.*

Organisations also noted that the advantages of added security and clarification of contracting were gained at a loss of independence and flexibility. By imposing the requirement for a client's needs to be assessed by social services, voluntary organisations argued that their ability to respond quickly to changes in a service recipient's circumstances had been inhibited. It was also noted, that the problematic created by fluctuating income inherent within spot-contracting, meant that organisations were working *reactively* to situations, inhibiting the development of services and proactive planning:

G15: *The issues around for us and contracting - you can see them both as an opportunity **and** as a constraint. There is an opportunity to provide more services to those who desperately need it. Sometimes they tend to be a bit complicated administratively, em, because as I say, with spot contracts you are not dealing with a set number of hours, but with a flexible number of hours being provided. So you've got that constant change to adapt to. And one of our major concerns was around being **trapped** into only providing a service once a community care assessment had been done. Because in a lot of areas in Glasgow where we are working, that can take three months or more! There's such a backlog in the system. And we've always kind of had **pride** in the fact that we could respond to people very quickly, so we were very concerned about being **trapped** into a system that meant we couldn't respond when people really needed us. So mostly so far we've been able to manage to negotiate a **compromise**, whereby we'll still be able to respond to people - and possibly still offer a service, even though a community care assessment hasn't been done. ... Em, its perhaps a vulnerable situation, in terms of, strictly speaking, we could be in providing a service and then later on they [social work department] go in and do a community care assessment, and there is the **possibility** then they would turn round and say, 'you're not the service that's required'.*

Yet independence has been one of the key features of the voluntary sector that has enabled it to respond to need in flexible, imaginative and innovative ways. Given that progressive ill-health is often a feature for individuals in receipt of community-based care, this flexibility is an important element of provision if the voluntary sector is to retain its ability to respond to constantly changing needs:

G54: *... em, the voluntary sector is so **crucial,** it provides so many services that the statutory sector **couldn't** provide - not just through lack of funding, but because as a whole I think we're more **independent** ... What I think the voluntary sector is free of, is the bureaucratic approach to things, you know? Its much more creative and imaginative - like saying, 'well this is our goal, lets look at the paths to suit, to get to that place', em, rather than 'what are the obstacles along the way?' There's still an optimism and **'oomph'** there that I think the statutory sector tends to sap from people.*

Organisations have argued that it is their ability to undertake multiple tasks [born of the insecure environment within which they operate] rather than the more singular approach prevalent amongst workers in the statutory sector that encourages an imaginative approach to problems. The need to conform to administrative and bureaucratic procedures imposed by statutory funders, however, is they claim, impacting on their ability to mediate care provision.

Tangible v non-tangible services

Of those voluntary organisations who did *not* have contracts or funding from donations or fund-raised sources (37.5 percent), over three-quarters were providers of services linked either to the *social* rather than the care needs of the frail elderly (e.g. daycentres, lunch clubs, befriending and transport schemes), or non-tangible services such as advocacy, representation and campaigning. However, as non-contracting organisations have commented, there are difficulties inherent in trying to both price and quantify non-tangible services in a format that is suited to a formal contract:

DG20 (2): *This service agreement thing is all cut and dried - it says we provide a service for x amount of people, who - if say its a sitting service - are using so many hours. I can't **say** that, because I don't **know** - I can't turn around and say x amount of people have used our service - there's nothing tangible that says what we do. And I think, yes, I think organisations **like** ourselves **are** getting [pause] having more problems, because the social work/health board, want a contract, they want it in black and white what we do, **how** we are going to do it, and what the end result it - almost like an audit. It's very difficult to **do** that with supporting organisations.*

As the above excerpt illustrates, the 'contract culture' appears to favour certain *types* of activity, for example service provision, over others such as campaigning, advocacy and research. 61 percent of respondents felt that this was the case, with some organisations increasingly moving toward the provision of services to individuals alongside their traditional representation and campaigning roles. As a result, concern has been raised that voluntary organisations will find themselves compromised through a gradual process of diversion into those areas amenable to service agreements. Though in the second year of interview some providers of non-tangible services in Glasgow commented that the local authority was beginning to recognise the difficulties they faced within the contract culture, recognition is not universal. The same organisations have commented that outwith Glasgow, there is still a failure by a number of local authorities within the former Strathclyde region to recognise this dilemma. Within Dumfries and Galloway the local authority continued to fund non-tangible service providers, but some organisations noted an increasing emphasis on funding directed at larger over smaller organisations.

While these issues are of little import for organisations funded solely through fund-raising/donations, it does have implications for those voluntary organisations who are in receipt of local government grants and are thus located within the dependency network. If contracting is to become the major source of funding to voluntary organisations concerned with frail elderly and their carers, the implication is, that funding will increasingly be directed toward those providing care services in kind. 81 percent of those in receipt of contracts within this study are providers of such tangible services as day or respite care, meals-on wheels, personal hygiene and tuck-in services. However, as noted above, this appears to be to the detriment of the social, campaigning and advocacy needs of service users.

Central government funding

Central government supports the voluntary sector with both direct and indirect grants through the Scottish Office. Most direct grants of relevance to this study are made through the Urban Programme (30 percent of which comes from the local authority) and the Mental Illness Specific Grant (MISG). Funding is also allocated indirectly through the Social Work (Scotland) Act 1968 Section 10 grant - which is distributed through the local authority. Within this study, 29 percent of responding voluntary organisations in Glasgow City were in receipt of Scottish Office funding, with only 12 percent in Dumfries and Galloway (due largely to the fact that the area did not qualify for Urban Programme monies).

As a source of funding, voluntary organisations viewed Urban Aid as preferable to that of contracting, in that it offered greater organisational flexibility. Though schemes were monitored and evaluated by a local authority supervisory officer (to ensure they were acting in response to an expressed need within the community), providing they met evaluation standards, funding was guaranteed for at least four years (and often extended to seven). Such security of funding allows organisations to plan proactively to meet community needs, rather than reactively, where funding is short-term and insecure. Urban Aid also offered the opportunity for further funding where organisations could prove additional need in the area. One further benefit of Urban Aid was that where an organisation ran more than one service, this funding could serve as an (unofficial) temporary bolster during short periods of funding difficulties (in particular, organisations quoted difficulties arising from long delays in local authority payment for purchased services).

The main constraint of Urban Aid as a funding mechanism was that it placed geographical limitations on voluntary provisioning. Such funds were targeted at specified Areas of Priority Treatment (APTs), consequently, though an organisation may perceive a need outwith the APT boundaries, funding regulations meant they were unable to respond to that need without an alternative source of funding:

G22 (2): *... when we first started, we started on Urban Aid, which means your geographical area is rather small, and you're not **allowed** to go outwith that area. When our funding went onto mainline, your area can actually expand into the area of, like, the social work department itself, which is a wider area. The **other** difference that happened this year was, Milton area up until [pause] within the last one or two years - I'm not exactly sure - was an APT area. When the new council come in, there's been new rules and regulations come in, and Milton was taken out of that APT area. Basically it was taken out of that criteria not because of deprivation, but because of the population - they then went to PPA areas right? And they had to have a certain population of about 10,000 people, em, to be eligible for that. Milton was put in, but the Scottish Office came back and said that we don't have the population size, and we lost that.*

I: *So what size of population are you within Milton?*

R: *Milton is round about 6,500 [pause] but the **deprivation** didn't go away, it didn't stop being a deprived area! And the population didn't go away! But the criteria changed, and that also altered - which **also** altered the type of services and the type of money and the type of various things that can come **into** the area. Because a **lot** of the things that started and originated in the area, started through Urban Aid. To **still** get Urban Aid, you have to **now** be in a PPA, but in the past, it was APT! And 'cos that has stopped, there is no place to get extra money! Which means the area has lessened again, in services that can come in to the area, because there's no place to get the money to get the services to come in!*

The above excerpt illustrates how voluntary care provisioning can arise more as a consequence of policy initiatives than as a response to identified need. Since 1996, the Scottish Office contribution to Urban

Programme funding for the voluntary sector has declined. In 1997, this was replaced by a new structure of council-led partnerships with the voluntary sector, private sector and public sector, with 60 percent of the value of the Scottish Office element of this funding being assigned to voluntary sector service delivery (SCVS, 1997, 21). APT areas within which voluntary organisations were previously eligible to apply for Urban Aid have been subject to restructuring in favour of a new scheme based on PPAs (Priority Partnership Areas). Urban Programme monies have now been split, with two-thirds being dedicated to fifteen PPAs across Scotland, with only the final third remaining as Urban Programme monies. Further, criteria for PPA status varies from that of the Urban Programme, and as a consequence, some organisations are now excluded from this particular source of funding. For others, however, the outcome of the restructuring of the Urban Programme has been more positive:

G54(2): *We had come to the end of our first four years funding, and I mean the whole Urban Programme was reorganised. We've gone from APTs to PPAs, so we're [pause] very, very fortunate that the area we cover has two PPAs - one in the East End and one in Castlemilk - without that we would really be struggling.*

As noted above, Scottish Office funding for organisations within this study was also obtained through MISG. This is a ring-fenced grant accessible to voluntary organisations whose focus is on the provision of services in the sphere of mental ill-health. Within this study its importance has been for organisations that provide care and support to elderly individuals with Alzheimers, dementias and their carers. While this grant is not geographically bounded (as with Urban Aid) it is socially/medically bounded in its specific focus.

As with Urban Aid, voluntary organisations in receipt of MISG are subject to monitoring and evaluation by supervisors from the Local Authority, but again, organisations noted that these grants allowed for a degree of flexibility not available within alternative contracted funding mechanisms. Furthermore, organisations within the dependency network who are in receipt of core grants of this nature retained their ability to make their own assessments regarding individuals to whom their services should be directed. In this way they are able to retain a degree of independence from local authority definitions of need, and maintain some point of access to care for individuals who fall outwith these statutory definitions. [3]

As voluntary care provision has expanded over time, many organisations have developed a mix of funding based on a core of Urban Aid/MISG, combined with spot contracting for additional services purchased from the social services' community care budgets. Organisations noted that the availability of secure core funding enhanced their ability to develop additional services and to run them more efficiently, and more cost effectively, due to the existing core infrastructure of both people and systems. Their ability to access funding from more than one geographical area (e.g. PPAs, social work districts or local authority areas) was an added benefit, in that it facilitated their ability to access matched or partial funding from other sources. Some, for example, noted it enhanced their ability to access EU monies and that it encouraged other social work areas to contribute a percentage of funding towards their service:

G54(2): *So instead of having one core funder, we now have funding from the East End Partnership Area, and we're still negotiating money from the Castlemilk Partnership Area, and we also cover Rutherglen and Cambuslang, so we get money from South Lanarkshire Council. We have three main core funders now, and it has its pros and cons [pause] in some ways, you know, you're not dependent on any **one** funder, although the East End is the majority 'shareholder' if you like ... I think what it **does** do, is because we are attracting money in from different areas, that it **does** make us a more attractive proposition for somebody. So the East End are saying, yes they **are** willing to fund their share because we are attracting money in from other areas ... Particularly now, because we've attracted National Lottery funding for a period, we can say, you know, 'pay your 80 percent and you'll get two workers free!' In having more funders, it **does** make it easier for you to say to other people, 'we have this track record, and we **already** have x number of partners who see us as a valuable and quality service', we are more attractive to them because we are attracting other funding sources.*

The additional 'attractiveness' of voluntary organisations with multiple sources of funding was not the sole benefit of diversified funding. Diversification was also seen to reduce an organisation's dependence on a single funding body, offering greater financial security and flexibility. It further reduced the degree of influence that any single funding body within the network may be able to exert on an organisation's structure, culture and ethos. As such, a number of organisations who have felt increasingly controlled by their statutory funders have made positive plans to reduce this dependency through funding diversification. Diversification is not without its constraints, however. Organisations have found themselves serving 'multiple masters' each with slightly differing priorities, administrative and working practices. This can make for complex working arrangements.

Nevertheless, those organisations that seem best able to retain independence from their statutory funders appear to be those with diversified funding sources.

Fund-raising

A further important source of funding for voluntary organisations was income derived from independent sources such as fund-raising and donations. For organisations that were increasingly resourced through contracting mechanisms, such independent resources provided the only source of income that enabled them to retain the ability to deliver services to individuals who fall outwith statutory criteria of need. The unpredictability of fund-raised income, however, inhibits an organisation's ability to provide a regular service (e.g. regular domiciliary-based respite) thus, its use within these organisations was largely confined to emergency provision or the purchase of new equipment. Further, such organisations also noted that the increased bureaucracy and administration inherent within contracting as a funding mechanism, and the increased time allocated to the constant search for funding, reduced the amount of time available to organisations to fund-raise - a factor noted by 66 percent of those with contracts. Yet as one organiser commented:

DG1: *It's still very important to fund-raise because it's the only way we can help all those currently on our books. But it can be difficult, the amount of time we spend servicing the social work contract leaves us no time to fund-raise - so we're becoming a service provider via social work, but we're still a charitable organisation - it's a difficult situation.*

As the excerpt below illustrates, however, reliance on fund-raised resources as a main source of income was adopted as a deliberate tactic by some organisations. Respondents maintained they had purposively steered away from government funding opportunities in order to retain their autonomy from the statutory sector. Such organisations are thus seen to be deliberately opting out of a network of care in which they perceive power relationships to be unequal, and which, in their view, are likely to have an adverse impact on their autonomy:

DG8: *... if they* [the local authority] *did give us a larger amount of money, there would be some 'quid pro quo' - they would expect a larger amount of say in the running* [pause] *'the piper calls the tune' - and as an organisation, we prefer to be governed by our own lot. We have a management committee of fifteen, who meet every month ... the*

129

meetings go fairly quickly and amicably, and that way of running things I think is ideal.

I: *So you prefer to keep your independent status?*

R: *I don't think we want anybody else to compromise our independence - and if **that** was the cost of getting more money from the local authority, that would be too high a price to pay.*

Organisations also commented on geographical variations in their ability to fund-raise, and the territoriality of philanthropic giving. As Wolpert (1977) noted, philanthropic giving is proportionately higher in growth areas, thus it is unlikely to result in any real redistributive effect. In areas of high unemployment/less affluent locales, and in very rural areas, organisations highlighted the difficulties encountered in fund-raising (for example, the logistical difficulties of selling raffle tickets - a traditional form of fund-raising - to those located in rural areas) and the greater ease with which they were able to fund-raise for a targeted item (e.g. a new mini-bus, new equipment etc.) as opposed to funding for the general day-to-day provision of a service. Others noted that their location in areas of high unemployment also imposed constraints on entry charges to traditional forms of fund-raising events such as craft fairs and car-boot sales.

Lottery funding

Continued cuts in statutory sector funding and an increased emphasis on crisis management and 'life and limb' services at the expense of preventative and social welfare provision, has caused organisations to explore alternative sources of funding. In the second year of interview, for example, organisations noted an increased reliance on national lottery funding as a potential source of income:

G18(2): *More and more organisations, voluntary organisations are relying on lottery funding. Organisations you know, that before the **last** round of cuts would probably **not** have applied to the lottery, that had the normally reliable statutory funding, em, they're now having to look at **all** sources of funding, and em, we've noticed the rise in the number of voluntary organisations who come in here to use our computer package - Funder Finder - because there's obviously more and more voluntary organisations chasing **money,** and its not necessarily statutory money.*

While a number of organisations had been successful in their lottery bids, these had largely been for such items as new transport facilities, building renovation and repairs. The criteria for lottery funding stipulates that bids will only be considered for new/specific services, and thus the lottery cannot be viewed as a source of supplementary income for services currently being provided by voluntary organisations. One organisation, however, did note its success in obtaining funding for a new short-term project (funding being provided for a three year period only), and thus while it may not prove suitable as a source of funding for long-term projects, it could provide an alternative source of finance for pilot projects that contracting, as a funding mechanism, appears to inhibit.

Issues of Organisational Size

As suggested earlier in this chapter, one of the issues raised by voluntary organisations participating within this study was the way in which their ability to compete for resources, and to successfully negotiate with their statutory funders was linked to organisational size. Organisations operating at the local level can, for example, be characterised as:

- locally-based independent organisations;
- locally autonomous organisations affiliated to a national body; or
- locally-based 'satellite' organisations, answerable to a national body.

The level of autonomy held from any higher tier of the organisation clearly has a internal impact on the way in which an organisation can mediate care within locally-embedded dependency networks.

Voluntary organisations held the perception that the statutory sector preferred to work with large organisations, who were viewed as both 'speaking the same language' and having a more professional approach to service provision, than that of their smaller counterparts. Further, where local organisations formed part of a national body, they were perceived as less of a 'risk', in that their services have been proven elsewhere in the country. While there are obvious advantages for statutory purchasers in this approach, it fails to recognise the autonomy of many local organisations from their national body, and can serve to stifle the innovatory potential evident within many smaller organisations (again a key component government sought to harness in its elevation of the voluntary sector). Furthermore, as voluntary organisations increased in size, they developed more complex systems and administrative structures, and thus ran the risk of taking on some of the very bureaucratic features of the statutory sector that as small organisations they prided themselves on avoiding:

> **G18 R:** *There's a tendency here in the west* [of Scotland] *for **both** health and social work to do business with **big** voluntary agencies - national voluntary agencies. They speak the same language. In a way, some of those voluntary organisations are like big businesses themselves, but they're not necessarily the ones that are closest to the people they are **serving**. And I think health and social work find it much more difficult to speak or deal with smaller voluntary organisations where there may in fact be less **formal** expertise, but they deliver the service very well, and much less bureaucratically, but there's a suspicion in health and social work about efficiency and effectiveness.*

Though 'umbrella' organisations aimed to represent the views of smaller organisations, not all voluntary organisations are affiliated to these representational bodies and not all 'umbrella' organisations had adequate mechanisms for the dissemination of information to/from these organisations. Some organisations, for example, noted that where intermediary organisations undertook a 'brokering' role on their behalf, they were not always consulted about the negotiation process. Rather, they were presented with a 'fait accompli' based on the assumption by both the local authority and the intermediary organisation that this was a satisfactory outcome:

> **DG30 I:** *When you first started on the service agreement, did you participate in the drawing up of the agreement?*
>
> **R:** *No, it was* [intermediary organisation] *they dealt with.*
>
> **I:** *Right. And did* [intermediary organisation] *come back and discuss it with you?*
>
> **R:** *No. They just sent the service agreement from Dumfries, and said that this was the service agreement that you're going to adhere to.*
>
> **I:** *So you had no say in whether you thought this was good, bad or indifferent?*
>
> **R:** *No. We never had any opportunity to comment.*

One consequence of such action between statutory and intermediary bodies was that despite the fact that smaller voluntary organisations were often the source of much innovatory and imaginative service provision, they can become increasingly isolated from decision-making processes.

It has further been suggested that increased competition for revenue amongst the voluntary sector can work to the disadvantage of smaller, less financially secure organisations (Kramer, 1986). Where organisations are increasingly competing for resources provided on the basis on their provision, the larger, better established and more professionally organised associations may win out over smaller ones. Where provider status is reliant on public grants and contracts, for example, this inevitably brings with it such things as bureaucratic oversight, monitoring and evaluation, as well as fiscal and management problems that can be difficult for small organisations to deal with. As one larger organisation noted, they themselves find it difficult to keep up with the level of activity required to 'keep ahead of the game' in terms of policy making, performance indicators, quality standards and evaluation, but for small organisations who lack the level of (human and non-human) supports necessary to undertake these tasks, competing for resources is extremely difficult:

G25 R: *Yes, em, I think it favours large organisations, who are obviously able to contract ... I think that's showing and proving to be that that's the way it will go. That it will become like business, and big organisations will swallow up small organisations. I think all those sorts of aspects are there.*

In the second year of interview, for example, one organisation commented on the formation of an association of voluntary sector community care providers (located in Edinburgh) during the previous year, membership of which was based on size of turnover. If such associations continue to develop on the basis of size, at its most extreme, voluntary provision could become manifest in an oligarchical scenario in which smaller organisations would be squeezed out due to their inability to meet the required criteria:

G18(2) R: *To join, you have to have a turnover of a certain figure - I can't remember what it is, but its a very **considerable** figure. So there are signs that the large nationals are [pause] organising themselves in a way that they were not organising themselves before. Personally, I think its a bit of a cartel, which will only go to **squeeze out** some of the smaller providers ... I haven't noticed a **galloping** towards swallowing them up, but what I have noticed, is em [pause] more reaction from* *big* UK-wide organisations, who hitherto have not operated in Scotland, showing an interest in expanding in Scotland.

Such action illustrates how the dependency network can be transformed not only by agencies operating within different sectors, but also by actors operating within the *same* sector, who actively seek ways to influence how resources are mediated. As discussed in chapter four, this highlights the importance of exploring not just the network itself, but also the characteristics of the actants within the network and how these can act to transform the shape of the network.

Placing the Voluntary Sector Within the New Unitary Authorities

A core element within this study has been the influence of place in voluntary service provisioning, and the ways in which such provisioning can be influenced by locally embedded dependency networks. As noted in chapter three, to examine these issues, there was a deliberate attempt to select study areas that illustrated geographical difference within the Scottish environment. Variations between Glasgow City and Dumfries and Galloway are characterised by:

- socio-spatial difference;
- political make-up;
- the degree of coterminosity between the local authority and the health authority; and
- the degree of disaggregation experienced under local authority restructuring.

The disaggregation of the larger tier of local government, and the introduction of new single-tier unitary authorities in Scotland from April 1996, has had an impact: firstly, on those organisations that have now found themselves straddling the boundaries between local authorities; and secondly, on some larger organisations who formerly served the whole of the region. Within this study, these changes have had a particular impact on voluntary organisations operating within Glasgow City. In Strathclyde, one relatively easily accessed funding body has been split into twelve new single-tier authorities. As a result, some voluntary organisations found themselves covering more than one of the new local authority areas. This has required such organisations to monitor planning and policy changes that may affect the groups they represent in up to twelve different authorities. As voluntary organisations work [largely] on the basis of minimum

134

administration and bureaucracy and maximum grassroots level working, this can be costly, both in terms of human and financial resources:

G28 R: *We were told on a **Thursday** that we had to copy everything to the twelve authorities that were going to make up Strathclyde, and it had to be in by the Friday! ... and **each** local authority wanted to know the number of people with* [illness] *and the impact it would have in their area. So we were having to do statistical analysis on the hoof, **all** to send off, whereas **before**, you could send it to the region, **one** person and **one** committee dealt with it. Now what happened, was that Argyll and Clyde - who is probably one of the **smallest** that we could impact upon - **gave** us the grant, Glasgow didn't! So what we were **looking** for the grant for, we can't go ahead with! And we got this money from Argyll and Clyde, and from Inverclyde, and I can't remember the third one, em, I think it might have been North Lanarkshire ... em, **they've all** given us the money, but the big boys **haven't**.*

Such action can contribute to the growth of geographical inequity in provision, as gaps appear in a service that was formerly uniformly funded across the region. Any reorientation of local authority priorities is thus reflected in a shifting pattern of distribution of voluntary organisation resources. One national organisation operating fifty four local authority supported schemes throughout Scotland, for example, noted the closure of its operation in two locations due to the withdrawal of financial support by the new local authorities. Despite the obvious support for the work of this organisation throughout the rest of Scotland, the service in these locales was not seen as a priority. Whilst this may be reflective of a temporal dimension to the voluntary profile of a region as such factors change over time in response to shifting needs, preferences, and resources, it can also contribute to inequalities in service provision as different local authorities stress different priorities, leading to the uneven expansion of voluntary organisations across space and between places. Such action has implications for service-users as such gaps give rise to differential access for individuals with the same or similar needs.

The rise in gaps in service provision, however, was also seen to depend on the nature of services provided:

G25(2) I: *So with regard to the services that you give, if you are getting 100 percent of funding from one area, and a far lower percentage elsewhere, are you still able to promote incentives and initiatives across the region?*

R: *Yeah, well we've taken a fairly pragmatic view about it. I mean ... a couple of authorities only gave us token payments, but we didn't stop working in those areas. If there was opportunities for doing work in a particular area, then the amount of actual authority funding they were giving us didn't particularly reflect on how much work we were able to offer in that area ... because of the **nature** of our work, its not as if we were providing, you know, a certain amount of hours of respite to particular areas. You know, its more about [pause] if somebody phones up from one of those areas - a carers' group - wanting a speaker to go out, or some advice or information, then what can you do on the phone? You can't turn them down and say, 'no, you don't fund us', or what have you ... So its, you know, because of the nature of the services, its not as black and white, I suppose, as it could be.*

So while the picture is fairly clear for those who are direct service providers, those providing non-tangible services (e.g. advice and information) noted, that where possible, they have continued to work in an area despite receiving only token payments from the local authority. A further consequence of disaggregation has been that in the search for funding, some organisations have become increasingly resource, rather than needs led. This has not been a uniform development, however; others, while acknowledging the danger of such a consequence occurring, have sought to retain a clear sense of identity and purpose in order to avoid being transformed in this way:

G25(2) R: *...The danger would be that you would alter what you were saying and what you're doing to try and secure funding, and I think that would take away **totally** from what the organisation **is**. And I think we've always been quite strong, you know? 'We're **this**, and this is what we **do**, and we won't move in to service provision, and we won't do this, and we won't do that'. And I don't think that's altered significantly.*

A further issue that has arisen for organisations operating at the regional scale, is that disaggregation has affected their ability to operate in a targeted manner. Where previously they had been able to channel resources to particular areas in turn, the new local authorities now request precise information with regard to where their funding has been channeled. This requires such organisations to rethink their mode of operation, and some are actively seeking ways in which to reorient their own geographical boundaries to enhance their ability to influence the local authority.

Expressed fears about the problems of trans-boundary working however have [for the most part] not materialised. The problems of 'serving two masters' have largely been administrative, though organisations have had to come to terms with an increased diversity in the structures operating within differing local authorities. Some local authorities, for example, have opted for a corporate approach, whilst others have sought to retain the old committee structures. Organisations have also noted a lack of conformity in the *internal* structuring of local authority departments (e.g. the social work departments) across the former Strathclyde region. Such diversity hampers pathways of communication as organisations struggle to keep pace with internal change - and thus the relevant contacts - within differing local authorities.

Despite these issues, rather than proving problematic for many organisations operating on the periphery of Glasgow City, disaggregation has, in fact, provided an opportunity to expand into new geographical areas and explore potential new sources of funding. Glasgow City was experiencing severe budgetary problems during the period of research (Sinclair, 1997), disaggregation had clearly been beneficial for some organisations, enabling them to replace funding lost through subsequent budgetary cuts. By the second year of interview, for example, a substantial number of peripherally located organisations had experienced a considerable degree of spatial reorientation in the delivery of their services *away* from Glasgow City toward alternative local authorities. While this ensures the survival of the organisation, it does, however, raise questions about the knock-on effect for service-users located within these peripheral areas:

G37(2) R: *I'm actually thinking **myself** about moving to East Dunbartonshire - I mean why **not**? We're getting **more** referrals from them than we are from **any** of the areas in Glasgow! And although the Partick Area Team* [social work department] *didn't want us moving out of Partick - or moving out of the catchment area - because they felt that Anniesland had so **much,** at the same time, they haven't given us any support to maintain us in there.*

Intra-authority variations

The discussion above has focused attention on the ways in which variations in voluntary provisioning can arise between unitary authority areas. The substantive material, however, also revealed that the picture is more complex than simply one of increased *trans*-authority variations. As noted in chapter three, Social Services Departments have the lead role in the implementation of community-based care, social services departments, however, divide their area of jurisdiction into districts (and within districts, areas), each with their own budgetary allocation (see maps 6.1 and 6.2).

Whilst devolved budgets are aimed at allowing for a greater degree of local autonomy (nominally taking choices closer to the local community), variations in the availability and accessibility of service provision *within* local authority areas can mean that individuals with the same or similar levels of disability or impairment experience differential access to provision as a consequence of the particular social work district or area within which they reside:

G70(2) R: *They stopped, yes, they withdrew referrals from* **Govan,** *but we were given so many more referrals from* **Pollock.** *They behave completely **differently**, there doesn't seem to be any dialogue between* [social services] *area managers - I mean the way they approach things ... nobody's really aware of what's happening at different areas, I mean different areas seem to operate differently, so there's no kind of conformity, I think. So although we were getting less referrals* [from Govan], *we were getting **many** more from them* [Pollock], *so it more than made up for it.*

Differential provisioning between areas within Glasgow was also highlighted by voluntary organisations operating in the areas of Easterhouse and Woodside. Both areas had Urban Programme status until 1998, however, with the introduction of PPAs, Woodside lost its Urban Programme status. Easterhouse, however, having had both Urban Programme and PPA status, has had substantial local authority and Scottish Office resources diverted into the area. At the time of the first interview, care provision within the area was described as plentiful. As a consequence, respondents noted, that if an organisation was unable to cover the need of a particular client in that area, it was possible to refer the individual on to other organisations within the area that *were* able to meet that service-user's need:

G4 R: ... *we are mainly supposed to be a very deprived area. So there's an awful lot more resources in Easterhouse. If it is something that the social work phone the* [2nd VO] *group about and they can't cover it,*

Map 6.1 Social Work Districts - Glasgow City

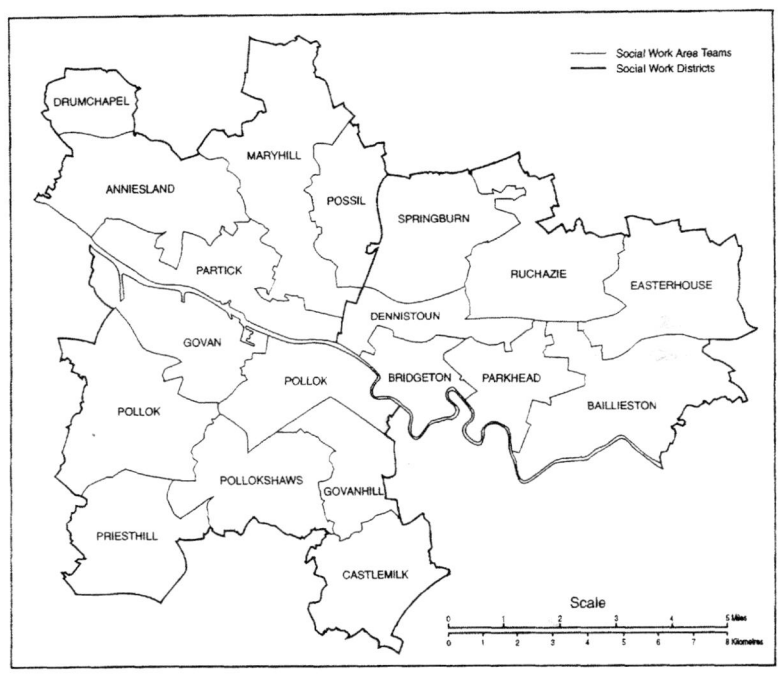

Map 6.2 Social Work Districts – Dumfries and Galloway

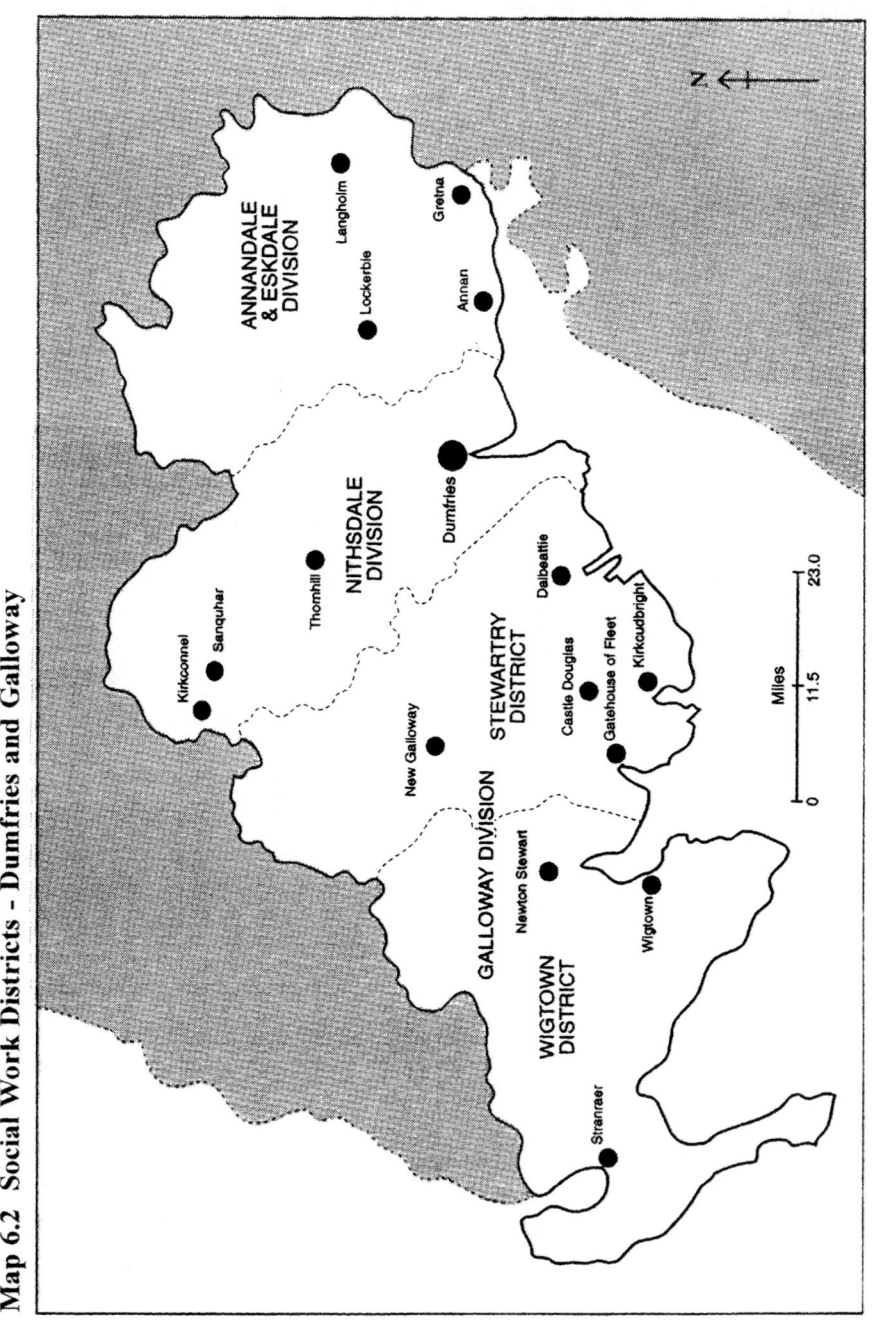

they know they can come to us. If they come to us and we don't have
the space, they will get back to [2nd VO] *to go in and bathe an old*
person, or for them to deliver a bath and our girls will go in and do it.
Its [pause] *I mean its no' just a wee village, Easterhouse is a big, big*
place. But its quite a tight-knit community really, and there's always
other services we can tap in to.

Conversely in Woodside, the sole organisation providing a bathing
service to individuals in the Glasgow North District had experienced a cut
in its mainline funding that threatened the service. If the service is cut,
however, unlike Easterhouse, there are no other provider agencies to
which service-users can be diverted.

A further internal change arising as a consequence of
disaggregation was the restructuring of the internal boundaries of the
social work department districts. In Glasgow City, internal restructuring
changed what had previously been four districts, into three. For some
voluntary organisations this action had no impact. For others, however,
this reorganisation meant that their own geographical boundaries were no
longer coterminous with that of the social services district, while some
further organisations found themselves relocated within a totally new
district. For those organisations experiencing change, this involved the
need to adjust to the different working practices of a new district and the
need to develop new sets of relationships within the statutory sector to
replace those that have often taken years to build up:

G36 R: *Well, the problem that we have just now, is that when the*
Strathclyde Region existed, we worked with South-East District - they
were our Districts in the city at the time, North, East, South and West.
Em, we were responsible to the District management South-East. Now
the Region then ceased to exist, and Glasgow City came up with the
idea of having **three** *districts rather than four, so they amalgamated*
certain areas - they changed the **boundaries**... *so from being in South-*
East, we went to North-East ... So there was **complete** *confusion, and*
years *of working with people, and building up relationships and*
understanding of the way that we worked - earlier I spoke of Finance
[pause] *the only way really, to get round the maze of financial*
difficulties within the region, was to find someone that you could
identify, *and work solely with them. Now we don't* **have** *that. We're*
now in North and East, they've been **dealing** *with people in North and*
East for years - they **know** *people in the North and East, and are*
happy working with them, but they don't **know** *us, so we're just a kind*
of [pause] *actually we're a bit of a 'thorn in their side' just now,*

141

because we keep asking what's going on - but meanwhile, we're just expected to run on fresh air!

In Dumfries and Galloway, where the size and location of the authority has remained the same, local authority restructuring has proven less problematic. However, there is still a need to forge new links with *individuals* within the committee structure (the political arm) of the new local authority, adding to the complexity of the interaction between actors and agencies within the dependency network. This situation is highlighted by what a number of organisations viewed as a lack of awareness by local councillors of the *role* voluntary organisations play within the community, and the difficulties voluntary organisations face in conveying to statutory authorities the varied and complex roles they may undertake. As one organiser commented:

DG11 R: *... the councillors from **** are totally **ignorant** of what the voluntary sector is all about. In my view ... we need to spend some time and effort **educating** councillors as to what the voluntary sector **is.** **Their** [councillors] view is that we go round with meals-on-wheels and that's it!*

In the months prior to the writing of this book, the social services department in Dumfries and Galloway had also undergone internal restructuring. The department has adopted a corporate approach to community-based care, thus care is no longer implemented on the basis of three geographically defined social work districts, but is determined by care group on an authority-wide basis. Due to the very recent implementation of this approach, it is too early to assess what impact this may have on informal sector providers across the region.

External Influences on the Voluntary Sector

A core feature of the voluntary sector, as noted earlier within this chapter, has been its independence. This has enabled organisations to undertake the provision of a service to all individuals falling within the fundamental remit upon which their organisation was founded (which does not necessarily coincide with statutory priorities). Such independence relies on the continued ability of voluntary organisations to take referrals from all sectors of the community (e.g. individuals, friends and relatives; GPs and community nursing; the church). Organisations within this study, however, have commented that increased reliance on local authority funders has transformed their ability to continue open referral. Further, as local authority funders translate policy within a framework of available resources, voluntary sector definitions of need are not only being transformed by the direction of services to individuals falling within social service prioritisations of need, but individuals are increasingly being 'fitted into' available services rather than required need.

Social service departments in both areas now work under a four-tiered priority framework, with levels one and two referring to 'life and limb' situations filtering down to a focus on preventative and social services. Due to funding constraints, however, both authorities now work only within levels one and two. While organisations note that they have fought to preserve their ability to continue open referral, for those with no core funding (e.g. from the Scottish Office) and no significant independent resource base, this ability is declining. In Glasgow for example, at the time of the second round of interviews, organisations commented that they were no longer able to service referrals from individuals, GPs, hospitals and community nursing, unless accompanied by funding through a social services assessment:

G1(2) R: *We used to get referrals from the hospital, and the hospital would refer to us and we would ask social work to contract for that, and* [pause] *we've never been refused before, but now they've started to turn them down.*

Organisations have noted that the need to refer individuals to social services for assessment has impacted on their flexibility. The lack of bureaucratic procedures within the voluntary sector has meant that they have been able to respond quickly to any assessed need, conversely, organisations have drawn attention to the lengthy periods of delay between requests for support and assessment by the statutory sector. While in the first year of interview, for example, delays of up to two to three months were noted, by the second year of interview this had reportedly extended to around six months in some locales:

G37(2) R: *I had a phone call from a woman yesterday, her husband had suffered a stroke. He was transferred from Gartnavel to Drumchapel and they said when he came out, he would get a full package of care ... When her husband came out in May, she was told someone would be out to assess him ... Well she gave them to the end of July, and she phoned them up, and she was told she would get an assessment six months from the 1st August! And she said, 'don't you mean six months from 1st May?' And they said, 'no, 1st August'. One of* *the care attendants put her in touch with me, and you could hear it in her voice - she was at the end of the line in terms of trying to get some help.*

Delays in assessment are as much linked to the lack of financial resources available to social services departments as they are to bureaucratic procedures. Where local authorities lack the resources to meet assessed need, these delays in assessment can be likened to the use of waiting lists as a covert delaying tactic, that has been inherent within a financially straitened NHS. However, given the increased levels of frailty of those individuals towards whom services are increasingly being targeted, it can be argued that these tactics have serious implications for the health and welfare of both carer and cared-for within a community-based system of care:

G1(2) I: *I know that your organisation has gone into people's homes and done assessments in the past, in the knowledge that the social services department will endorse it. Are you still in a position to do that?*

R: *Em, we tend not to approach unless they're looking for carer's support, and I would invite them along to a carers' group - I wouldn't do a full assessment unless I knew the money was there because it raises false expectations, and its a terrible disappointment if someone thinks they're gonna' get help and then it doesn't materialise.*

I: *So what is happening now, are people being re-prioritised or are they just going on a waiting list?*

R: *Yes, uh huh, basically. Well there just isn't **any**!* [care support] ... *The social work have told us that they won't be contracting with us anymore in Glasgow - certainly we see a future where people just won't be picked **up**, I don't know **what** will happen to them!*

While waiting lists for direct service providers were not a key feature of the first round of the interview process, by the second year there had been a noticeable increase in both areas. Some organisations had been able to absorb new demand through 'natural wastage' and a reduction in the level of service (e.g. days of daycare) available to service recipients. Others have sought to lessen the pressures of demand by lowering their profile, through reduced advertising of their services. Such an approach is not uncommon (indeed there was a noticeable lack of any comprehensive statutory source of information regarding resources available to carers and cared-for within the community in both areas). A number of voluntary organisations, however, noted that having reached the limits of their ability to offer direct service provision, they were now only able to offer advice and support to all but existing clients. A number of organisations were now having to turn away requests for services, and had waiting lists in place for daycare, homecare and bathing services - a situation they found hard to equate with the voluntary ethos which underpinned their organisation.

Others providing both direct and indirect provision, noted that if funding constraints reduced their ability to provide advisory and advocacy services, clients may have nowhere else to go. One organisation providing support to carers in Dumfries and Galloway noted that reduced funding had already meant a rationalisation of its services, hence it had opted to retain the service where it had the highest client population base. As a consequence, the service had been cut to those living in more remote rural areas.

Those organisations with some core or independent funding have retained their ability to service some individuals from open referrals, thus contributing to an inconsistency in access to services between places based on the prevailing funding regime within particular locales. Fund-raised resources as noted above, however, are both insufficient and too inconsistent to provide anything other than occasional emergency services. As a consequence, if some element of open referral is to be retained, it is essential that some core funding is made available from sources outwith the local authority resource base.

In reducing the ability of the voluntary sector to take open referrals, the statutory sector is influencing a shift in the internal character of voluntary organisations concerned with service provision. Where organisations are solely reliant on resources mediated by the local authority, the requirement that they conform to social services' interpretations of need, means that local branches of national organisations are increasingly likely to find themselves contravening the basic constitutional by-laws upon which the organisation was founded. One organisation concerned with respite for carers, spoke of being approached by the local authority to take on domestic services to elderly people living alone. They maintained:

DG14(1) R: *This is not our role. People living alone come under a different category of social work, we're there to support the carer - but we're also aware that if we **don't** do it, someone else will, and that might cause problems when we re-negotiate our contract - but its not part of the core philosophy that underpins our organisation.*

The national organisation, however, often provides the information, training and support which allows small locally-based organisations to survive on very limited funding. Placed in the position of trying to serve 'two masters', local branches can find themselves facing a growing dilemma as they seek to reconcile the constraints placed on them by local authorities wielding the purse-strings, and their loyalty to the fundamental ethos upon which their organisation was founded. A number of organisations believed this was creating a "blurring" of their charitable status.

Organisations also voiced concern about the ethical dilemma they faced in undertaking this local authority role in an environment that is increasingly characterised by competition and contracting:

> **G25(1) R:** *Because if you then become a service provider, can you then **comment** on the services? ... em, if you're now being asked to **contract** for services, it changes the relationship quite radically if you think about it.*

One manifestation of this elevation of the voluntary sector within the network of care may thus be a distortion of the meaning of voluntary work (Hedley and Smith 1992). As noted above, a number of voluntary organisations in the Scottish context had already been requested by local authorities to take on the provision of tasks not previously within their remit, and which are at odds with the fundamental premise on which their organisation was founded. 25 percent of organisations within this study, for example, had been asked by local authorities to provide services to groups with greater levels of dependency, to the exclusion of those with less complex needs. Furthermore, as noted above, local branches are increasingly finding themselves being *directed* by social services towards those clients viewed as "in need" of their services, typified by the comment of one co-ordinator of an organisation providing care for the dependent elderly:

> **DG25 R:** *It means they* [social work department] *make a much heavier input into who they perceive as being in need of services - which is sometimes conflicting with our point of view .... they now have a criteria of category one to four, and they only service one and two ... So people that would be within **our** remit - people who are left alone in the morning until night-time, seeing nobody, getting a bit muddled-up as to time and place and what have you, we could, within our aims and objectives, go in to them - but we can't get funding for that, because the*

social work sees that as low priority - they don't matter, they'll have to wait.

This comment highlights the increasing constraints imposed on voluntary organisations by local authority funders. These constraints not only reduce the ability of voluntary organisations to undertake the kind of "open door" approach previously operated, but increasingly imposes on them *statutory* definitions of need. As a consequence, this closes traditional avenues of support for minority groups falling outside such statutory definitions.

The quote further raises the issue of how we view the 'place' of the frail elderly in our society. Implicit in the restructuring of funding and needs criteria to voluntary organisations is that growing numbers of frail elderly will find themselves facing increased social and spatial isolation, reducing their quality of life, and with possible adverse effects to their health. In Dumfries and Galloway, for example, the local authority note that whilst it recognises the preventative value of promoting general social welfare, it nevertheless recommends funding in this area be progressively reduced (Dumfries and Galloway Council Minutes, 1996). Particular mention is made with regard to the funding of social spaces for the elderly, such as daycentres and lunch clubs. Many of these, however, provide far more than simply a space for social interaction. Monitoring non-attendance amongst members (many of whom live alone), visiting the sick, undertaking basic shopping tasks for the unfit, providing low-cost hot meals are just some of the additional functions these services undertake. As illustrated below, such organisations perform a valuable monitoring and preventative function in the care of lone and frail elderly:

DG30(2) R: *.... Arthur ... he's got Senile Dementia, and you know he couldn't play dominoes, he was just playing anything first of all, but with his mind being active, he can play dominoes now and he's winning every dammed thing now! It unbelievable how you see the tremendous difference in people - just that little bit of care and thought! And I have a lady who's blind, if she's got an appointment at the doctor's (we do lots of things we're not supposed to) we'll go up early and take her to the doctor's. And the doctor phones over and says, 'Mary's ready' - because she can't come over on her own - we've got to go and get her. And Amy [a care worker], she'll do bits of shopping for her. I mean we do shopping for loads of people!*

The pressure to focus on the intensive care needs of the very frail, means that services viewed as essentially preventative in nature face the

147

prospect of reduced funding or closure. In 1996, for example, day-centres in Dumfries and Galloway had their local authority grants cut completely. Only in the face of intensive lobbying by the elderly and daycentres themselves, did the local authority rethink the proposed closure. Though funding was re-instated, at the time of the final round of interviews, their future position was still tenuous. Yet, as illustrated above, daycentres provide far more than a space for social interaction for the frail elderly. They also provide a relatively cost-effective method of providing both care and social support to groups of individuals who would otherwise require care supports within the homespace. Where community-based day-centres lack sufficient numbers of trained individuals to undertake such tasks as personal hygiene, the provision of additional care attendants would enable organisations to offset these problems in a manner that would benefit from economies of scale, whilst simultaneously providing respite to the carer. It has, in fact, been suggested by service co-ordinators, that the provision of bathing facilities within these centres could provide an additional advantage to daycare provision.

Faced with increasing demand for their services, voluntary organisations have commented on the lack of understanding displayed by the statutory sector in the face of budgetary cuts. In Dumfries and Galloway, the social work department has sought over the last two years to reduce funding to organisations which, in their view, essentially provide a service for individuals in priority service levels three and four. Following funding cuts in 1996 for example, a daycare organiser commented:

DG12 R: *When I went to a funding meeting not so very long ago ... they* [social work department] *set out what the money was for - organisers salary, all the way down - and one of the chairmen* [of the voluntary management committees] *said, 'I've just been quickly working that out, how much, and we've got £4,000 if we pay what you **say** we should pay! We've got £4,000 left for running the daycentre!' and they said, 'yes, that's right, you should have some sort of **commitment** from your community'. So we said, ' there's **hundreds** of things going on in the community, we're just one of them!' ... So this lady turned round and said, 'you've got to cut your coat according to your cloth'. What do you mean? 'Well if you can't manage on that for five days, you're going to have to cut - you only need to open four hours a day'. We said, 'We can't do that! Care in the community, **we're** here to provide a service!' Do you know what they turned round and said? '**Tough!**' And that was the end of it, **tough!***

Such comments not only indicate a lack of understanding of the role daycare provides within the community but a lack of understanding of the ability and time available to such organisations to fund-raise to the extent that they are able to run a regular service based on these fund-raised resources. Daycare providers, for example, have commented on the increased levels of frailty they are coping with - providing a service to a mix of elderly individuals (with a high proportion in their 80s and 90s) whose health problems range from dementia, to physical and sensory disabilities. Organisations have voiced concern that the emphasis on the need to fund-raise for resources will also reduce the amount of time they have available to spend on the carer/cared for.

In Glasgow, during the second round of interviews, organisations noted a decline in the purchase of contracted services by the local authority due to the increased severity of the local authority's budgetary problems (Sinclair, 1997). Organisations voiced concern regarding the impact of these cuts on service-users as the safety-net is drawn up and preventative services are cut in favour of increasingly complex care needs focused on fewer numbers of people:

G15(2) R: *Em, I think the area of most concern is an indication that perhaps a lot of the preventative work that we do will be pared back - where you're really going in to enhance someone's quality of life rather than, em, intervene in a crisis situation - which we believe in the longer term, even if you were to look at it purely financially, its cost effective, because its preventing, em, people going in to institutional care, or hospital care.*

For organisations providing respite to carers, there is real concern that as funding problems precipitate an increased prioritisation of need, relief to carers will increasingly be seen as a 'luxury'. However, as organisations point out, without these 'luxuries' carers cannot continue the heavy caring role they undertake, with the result that the cared-for will require residential care much more quickly. Others note that while individuals are being assessed by the social work department as in need of a service, the reality is that there is no money to provide the service:

G22(2) R: *Cuts in social work are more severe this year than they were last year, and its more noticeable. And the things that social work **don't** do, and we pick up on, are not there at the moment.*

I: *What kinds of things are you talking about?*

R: *The cuts, em, like occupational therapy departments - we had a lot of people who would have had assessments from the occupational therapy department saying, 'yes, you are entitled, and you should have, and you need' but the answer is there is no money!*

As well as impacting on service users, any reduction in the uptake of spot-contracted services has implications for organisations with no core funding to retain their infrastructure. Further, in the second year of interview, there was a noticeable change in the response of organisations in areas that had previously had substantial provision:

G4(2) I: *One of the things you had mentioned last year, was that it wasn't a problem **finding** services for people within this area.*

R: *There was so much! But they're all closing down now! Eh, to be **honest**, it was a really big shock when **** was closed, because it was a **really** good project. It was **all** elderly care, and there was a day-centre five days a week - and of course these people have **nothing** now. So its whatever we can fit in.*

I: *So there's no day-centre care at all?*

R: *Yea, that's right, that's been done away with.*

As the statutory sector has become increasingly constrained by available funding, voluntary organisations have also expressed concern that the quality of service will lose out to quantity, as statutory purchasers seek out the cheapest option in order to maximise resources as part of a cost-cutting exercise. However, while it is clear that social work departments are themselves faced with increasing demand on a reduced resource base, as yet, there appears little evidence to support these fears. Rather, social work departments appear to be attempting to retain the *quality* of service, but to a reduced number of individuals, through drawing up the safety-net of those qualifying for community-based care. One consequence of this is that as financially straitened social work departments seek to re-prioritise levels of need, funding for social and preventative care services are losing out to the intensive and more complex care needs of increasingly frail members of the community.

Developing Care and the Voluntary Sector

The ability of voluntary sector provisioning to develop over time and space is linked to a number of factors. It was evident in the second round of interviews, for example, that some support groups had folded during the previous year whilst others had opened, which in part reflected changing needs within an area over time. Others under threat of closure had had last minute 'reprieves', with one such organisation now, paradoxically, undergoing a period of expansion. The planned development of others gave way to the increased demand for existing services from statutory purchasers. As a consequence, the development of voluntary services can be as much a response to the priorities of their statutory purchasers as it is a response to user-led needs.

Most organisations participating in the interview process, however, had experienced a decline in income/referrals from their statutory purchasers during the second year of interview. For some, this had stimulated a diversification of services into complementary areas of care in order to supplement demand for their services. Organisations, for example, were looking to develop new ways of utilising their resources and expertise by exploring the concept of a 'one-stop shop'. This focused on offering daycare, residential care and sheltered housing under the same roof as a means of solving the problems and confusion often caused by multiple service providers going into the homespace and creating increased disruption for both carer and cared-for:

> **G14 R:** *We pointed it out to the social work, because you're a **guest** in people's house and people get confused, they don't **like** so many people coming in. Em, there is one girl coming in, we're coming in, somebody else from district nursing is coming in ....*

In one extreme case, an elderly carer in her 80s noted in her diary that a total of twenty three different individuals associated with domiciliary care provision had come into her home over a three month period. The extreme confusion caused, resulted in her allowing a double-glazing saleswoman into her home on the misapprehension that she was yet another care provider!

Pilot schemes

The move toward diversification in the face of reduced funding highlights the innovatory role of the voluntary sector within health and social care. This was evident in the variety of pilot schemes being operated within the study areas. Schemes such as family-based respite (where the dependent is cared for within the home of an approved care-attendant, rather than within the homespace or institutional environment), early-stage schemes (where the focus is on raising awareness of available supports at an early stage of ill-health), ethnic minority outreach programmes, the re-introduction of home-helps (where this is no longer provided by the local authority), domiciliary-based day-classes to the house-bound and occupational therapy schemes, illustrate just some of the innovative programmes that were being piloted across the study areas. The value and success of such schemes is measurable by their expansion and/or eventual absorption by the statutory sector and their implementation at a wider scale (examples, here, being person-centred planning and specialised respite for those with specific health problems). Others, however, whilst successful, have been unable to expand due to a lack of available funding:

G15(2) R: *So its* [family-based respite] *filling a gap, which em, we're certainly **hopeful** will be replicated elsewhere.*

I: *So it just operates in the one area, Maryhill?*

R: *Just in the one area, yep. But certainly I think its proved its worth - albeit on a small scale - its been very successful for the people that have used it. It's certainly filling a gap - and we could do with that option being around in other areas, you know, but so far we haven't managed to do it.*

I: *So that's basically due to funding restraints rather than lack of demand?*

R: *Yes, absolutely ... Its a very normal activity you know, just going to somebody's house for the day, there's no stigma attached to it, there's no big bus coming for you and that kind of thing, you know?*

Though clearly such innovative development plays an important role in service provisioning, organisations note that in the current period of financial stringency within local authorities, available funding is increasingly being directed *away* from development towards crisis management. Where a number of moderate increases in services *have* been achieved by voluntary organisations during the period of study, this has largely been through alternative funding sources such as the lottery, or one-off grants from external philanthropic funding organisations. Time-limited funding opportunities however can be problematic, in that once the funding period has expired, the service can be lost through the lack of alternative sources of funding. While some organisations have sought to recoup some (or all) of the costs, through the introduction of a basic charge, this can have implications for individuals on low incomes. An organisation [G19] piloting the re-introduction of a home-help service in 1997, for example, found lack of demand for its service was linked to two factors:

(i)   the expectation amongst individuals that such a service should be free (based on historical precedence); and
(ii)   the service had been piloted in an area where people could [largely] not afford to pay for the service.

This organisation had, however, noted the higher uptake of its service in a more affluent area located on the geographical periphery of the scheme. As a consequence they were considering whether the scheme should be relocated to a more affluent area, or cut completely. If relocated, this raises questions about future equity in care provision.

The concept of charging for social care provision is problematic. Whilst there is a clear onus on local authorities that no-one should be *denied* access to services on the basis of their inability to pay, to date, there are no clear guidelines with regard to the *level* of charges to be made. Consequently, charges can vary between both individuals and locations, contributing to a growth in geographical inequity in care provision to the service dependent. For voluntary organisations, the whole issue of charging is fraught with problems. While organisations charge the local authority for their services, the issue of charging individuals is more problematic, in that for many organisations it was viewed as undermining the fundamental ethos upon which the organisation was based. Organisations noted, for example, that their voluntary ethos prevented the acceptance of payment for services even if an individual made a specific request to purchase the service (e.g. because they were refused statutory services, or did not want the statutory sector to be involved in their domiciliary care arrangements). While some organisations have sought to overcome these ethical issues through accepting 'donations', they also note that the voluntary nature of this type of giving means that regular services cannot be solely dependent on such income.

Organisations commenting on the decline in monies available for development, felt that any future expansion of services was only likely to occur through attracting specific ring-fenced monies (e.g. lottery awards and independent grants).

Voluntarism - The Social and Spatial Dimensions

As public sector service provision shrinks, any geographically uneven availability of voluntary services implies not only uneven access, but also uneven opportunities to participate. In Los Angeles, for example, Wolch (1990) found the pattern of voluntary services to be one in which middle-to-high income jurisdictions are voluntary service-rich, whilst the lowest income jurisdictions were voluntary service-poor; the 1992 GHS in Britain also appears to reveal a similar volunteer profile (Goddard, 1992). While surveys such as the GHS highlight regional differentials in voluntarism, these are highly *generalised* accounts of participation rates. The GHS, for example, presents Scotland as having a uniform rate of participation which does not reflect its highly differentiated urban and rural geography. Further, in a recent ethnographic study of voluntary work in Teesside, MacDonald (1996) found that contrary to the sort of "middle class" volunteer profile identified by both Wolch and the British GHS, there was evidence of a growing participation of the unemployed and sub-unemployed in voluntary work. He suggests, that in economically depressed localities, unemployed people are increasingly taking up volunteering as they seek to recreate positive working lives for themselves through voluntary work.

Within this study, voluntary organisations were asked to give a volunteer profile by age, employment and gender. As figures 6.1 and 6.2 illustrate, voluntary organisations responding to the questionnaire display a similar pattern in terms of employment category and gender in both areas. Organisational responses appear (in part) to support MacDonald's assertion of the positive role of the unemployed in voluntarism; they also indicate, however, that the volunteer profile of those concerned with health and social care, is one which is dominated *firstly* by retired individuals and *secondly* by the unemployed. Further, when analysed by gender, figure 6.2 reveals this to be (at least in this study) a field of voluntarism that is predominately female - a factor that may in part be linked to traditional gendered perceptions of the caring role (Nissel, 1980).

Further, as figure 6.3 illustrates, while the employment and gender profiles are remarkably similar in both areas, there are some clear differences between the two areas when analysed by age. While the profile in both areas remained similar for the under fifty age groups, there is a clear divergence for those aged fifty and over. Dumfries and Galloway revealed a volunteer profile dominated by 50-70 year olds, while in comparison, the volunteer age profile in Glasgow City, though more evenly spread, was highest in the 35-49 age group. This would seem to reinforce the demographic profile of the areas revealed in chapter three, in which

Dumfries and Galloway was seen to be an area with an ageing population, whilst Glasgow City was dominated by younger adult age groups.

Figure 6.1   Voluntary Organisations Volunteer Profile by Employment Category (%)

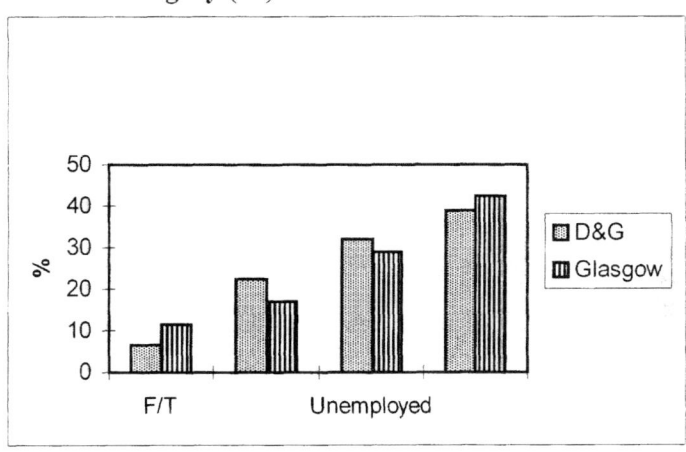

Figure 6.2   Predominance of Volunteers Within Voluntary Organisations by Gender (%)

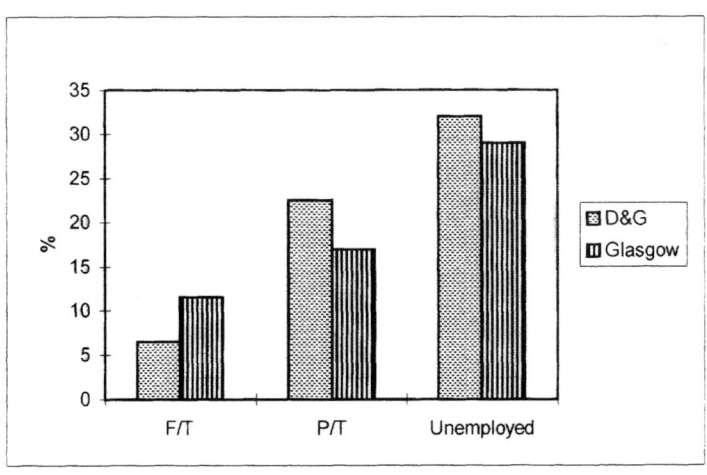

155

Figure 6.3 Voluntary Organisations Volunteer Profile by Age (%)

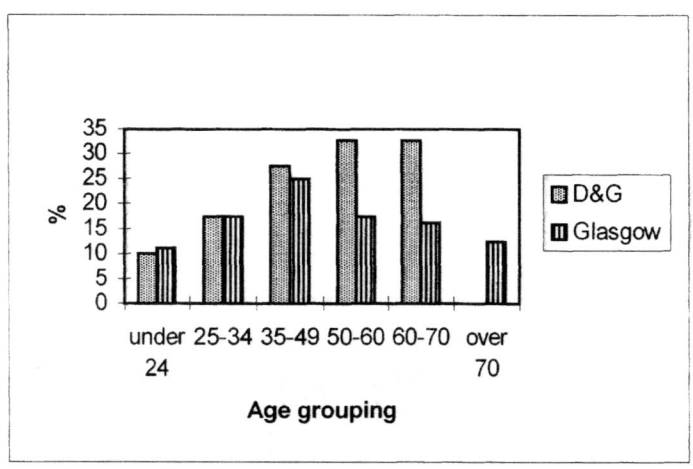

Organisations have noted, however, that the predominance of retired individuals can create problems of seasonality within voluntarism. Elderly volunteers are often involved in the care of grand-children outwith term-time, creating a high seasonal turnover of volunteers which is both costly in terms of training, and problematic for those organisations seeking to offer a regular service. This is clearly an added difficulty for areas such as Dumfries and Galloway whose volunteers have been seen to be drawn predominantly from an older age structure. Further, despite government emphasis on promoting active citizenship through the voluntary sector, organisations noted an increasing difficulty in recruiting new volunteers:

DG2(2) I: *One of the things that struck me last year, was the enormous number of volunteers the* [organisation] *has compared to other organisations. Presumably you have little difficulty recruiting?*

R: *Oh we do, we do. I mean we have a large number,* **but** *its not increasing the way it used to ... We* **do** *have a problem recruiting for meals-on-wheels in a place like Dumfries. In the more rural areas of the region its not so bad, but in Dumfries it* **is** *a problem. And when we were discussing the Good Neighbours Scheme, that's* **one** *hesitation I've got about it, is could we recruit the people? Its quite difficult.*

I: *Is there any particular reason for that?*

R: *There's a general feeling now that people want money for doing things - I think that has a **great** deal to do with it. We tried the job centre, you know, thinking that its something for them to do, and we were prepared to put on their CV that they had worked for the [organisation] - but the first question is, 'how much do I get paid?' ... And I don't think you get that so much in a rural area, because there's no opportunities for part-time work the way there is in a bigger place ... I mean, I've been in the organisation about ten years, and we used to have a list of people we could call on if someone was ill - we don't have that now ... we don't have the number of people we certainly had at one time.*

I: *If you're contracted for a service, does that cause you any problems?*

R: *Well it does, it does. I mean ... well I've said I'll deliver - 72,000 meals I think it was in Dumfries and Galloway last year - well **they're** [social services] hoping obviously that we'll deliver more, but if you've got less and less volunteers, its quite a problem!*

Not all rural areas are receptive to voluntarism, however. Organisations have commented on the difficulties of recruitment in Annan, for example, as compared to Sanquhar or Dalbeattie - both described as having a much stronger community spirit. Voluntary organisations in rural areas have also commented on time/distance difficulties with regard to voluntarism. Service delivery within the domestic sphere, requires more volunteers per head of dependent population who are willing/able to devote more time to delivering a service, than is the case in urban locations - adding considerably to the unit cost of delivery. Additionally, in *very* rural areas *only* those with private transport can realistically participate in any form of voluntarism which requires service delivery within the domestic sphere.

The above interview excerpt also illustrates that [as other organisations also noted] not only is the voluntary sector experiencing a *decline* in volunteers but there are also difficulties inherent in attempting to run contracted services that are dependent on volunteer input. While organisations acknowledge that volunteers can be highly committed individuals, they also note that they are generally unwilling to become involved in the negotiation and administrative processes implicit within contracting. Further, it has been evident that as statutory purchasers draw up the levels of need, services are increasingly being directed towards individuals with higher levels of dependency. This creates difficulties in recruiting volunteer labour, where such volunteers often lack either the training, or will, to cope with increasing levels of dependency and the need to undertake what are often highly personal levels of care:

DG35 R: *...if the numbers had to rise over the hundreds, I don't know if we could cope ... We've got enough volunteers and we've got enough kitchen help, so we cope. But the thing that **does** worry me, is that if our members that are able to come get frailer - because they are, you can see the change every few months - you can see them going down that road, becoming more frail, more dependent.*

I: *So volunteers don't participate in the more personal aspects of hygiene?*

R: *No, because how could you ask them to do that? You've got to make sure that the volunteers don't injure themselves or the person they are taking to the toilet ... and you can't say to volunteers, 'right, can you take' - I mean we've got someone here that's a double amputee, right? So how can you possibly ask a volunteer to do it, you couldna' possibly.*

DG30(2) R: *...volunteers will do **certain** things, but they won't work hard like we work hard! You know, there's a limit to what they'll **do**!*

Such comments indicate that the meaning of voluntary work may be becoming distorted (Hedley and Smith, 1992). While the emphasis on voluntarism has resurfaced, it is as the neo-conservative concept of "active citizenship" with public expenditure increasingly seeking to shift more of the onus of social welfare onto individuals and communities. Yet as the excerpts illustrate, there are limits to the levels of care that volunteer labour is both able, and willing, to undertake - a factor which voluntary organisations argue the statutory sector often fails to acknowledge. As the co-ordinator of one organisation commented:

DG14 R: *Its very **difficult** ... because still nobody takes into account the fact that the voluntary sector is **voluntary**! And if somebody pressurises them too hard, they're going to say, 'I'm going to take my bat and ball home, I'm not going to play anymore!' And they [the statutory sector] **don't** seem to appreciate that, no matter how many times you tell them.*

These factors, combined with the representations of volunteers depicted in figures 6.1, 6.2 and 6.3, reveal a picture of voluntarism within the field of health and social care which may be based more on geography, the local demographic profile and access to female part-time labour, than to neighbourhood status as depicted by Wolch (1990). Implicitly, this points to a need for greater consideration of localised factors affecting the voluntary sector.

Historical Influences on Voluntary Sector Provisioning

While there is a need to explore care outcomes from within the network, as discussed in chapter four, there is also a need for an awareness of the wider temporal and spatial context within which the problem under investigation is located. The remainder of this chapter is thus concerned with the ways in which the spatial expression of voluntary sector provisioning within a locale can, in part, be mediated by temporal influences which arise as a consequence of factors which are both external and internal to the locale.

The spatial patterning of voluntary organisations can be attributed to a number of factors that occur across time e.g. local philanthropic giving, the introduction of different government initiatives, and the personal initiatives of committed individuals. Further, the voluntary sector frequently operates in a climate of uncertainty in relation to the availability of future funding. Opportunism is thus a key element of an organisation's ability to survive. Such opportunism causes organisations to seek out funding wherever new opportunities arise. As new government initiatives have been implemented over time, voluntary organisations have frequently sought to tailor their services in such a way as to harness these new resources for the benefit of the particular client group/s they were set up to serve:

G70(2) R: *See, each area manager is given a community care budget, and approximately 10 percent of that constitutes their flexible budget. Now by law, they cannot use it to employ their own staff on flexi-budgets, they have to involve voluntary organisations or private companies ... we're looking around to broaden our funding base, and as I said, community care is there, that's one way of tapping in to the local authorities, keep some money for ourselves and safeguard our institution for the future - and we could provide a good standard of service ... so I inducted ten people to provide a befriending service ... So this was the service that I'd identified as being the **gap** in the current service provision. So we started to sell that service to Govan social work, and* *then very quickly I started recruiting more and more people and inducting them, and then started to get more calls from Pollock, Gorbals, Pollockshields - so we spread very, very quickly geographically.*

This organisation was set up over ninety years ago, through the philanthropic bequest of a local shipping magnate with a mandate to serve the needs of the local community. Though the organisation has the asset of a large building from which it can derive income, the costs of maintaining such a building also acts as a constraint upon the organisation's resources. To thrive it must constantly seek additional sources of revenue with which to supplement its income. As the above excerpt illustrates, the organisation recognised a potential source of funding within the flexi-budget element of the local authority community care budget, and has sought to harness this by identifying a gap in local services (in this case a befriending scheme) that could be encompassed within its organisational remit. Thus, while the geographical location of an organisation may have arisen as a result of locally-based philanthropy, the geographical boundaries of its services can be as much a factor of its search for alternative sources of funding (in this case community care flexi-budgets).

The historical development of organisations can also derive from external (e.g. government) initiatives. Such initiatives, however, can lead to a voluntary sector development which is often piecemeal and sporadic, owing as much to the availability of resources as it does to any planned action based on identified need. This was particularly well illustrated during an interview with a key figure from within the Glasgow Social Services Department:

*GSWD I: *As well as there being differences between unitary authority areas in the kinds of care that's provided, there's also differences at a more localised level. What do you see as the reason for this?*

R: *Well, I think em.. its probably as much to do with the historical development - the incremental development of services over time - outwith a plan [pause] within the Strathclyde structure. Particularly **Glasgow** division (as it was) **did** fund a substantial level of **mainstream** services using **non-mainstream** budgets [pause] so for example the Urban Programme was much more **heavily** directed to Glasgow than to other parts of Strathclyde. One of the kind of consequences of that, is that a number of services were developed on a sort of Urban Programme project basis in parts of the city, and when the Urban Programme finished they were incorporated into mainstream funding.*

*Now I think if that sort of project based approach becomes a significant feature - as it **was** - then its not surprising that you find there's an inequitable - or unequal at least - distribution of services across the city over time* [pause]. *Em.. there's a sort of unequal range and **spread** of services from area to area.*

* GSWD = Glasgow Social Work District.

Other voluntary organisations have developed within a locale as the result of government initiatives with a completely different focus. Some organisations in both areas, for example, noted that their funding originated in resources made available through the Manpower Services Commission (MSC) during the 1980s - a government initiative whose emphasis focused more on employment initiatives than the needs of service recipients. With the demise of the MSC, the funding for these organisations (as with the Urban Aid example) was either absorbed within mainstream local authority funding, or became transferred to alternative Scottish Office initiatives such as the Urban Programme or (if appropriate) MISG.

As illustrated, organisations have also developed from schemes that were initiated from purely voluntary ventures and which later expanded through attracting statutory sector grants (an explanation given by a number of daycentres), while some arose as the result of the personal initiatives of interested individuals. Others, however, noted that their existence owed less to altruism and more to being in the right place at the right time:

DG35 I: *Why was the decision taken to have a day centre for the elderly in this area? Who made the decision?*

R: *It was a fluke actually! The old councillor happened to be in the right place at the right time when European money was available - and they had so much money left - I think it was about £30,000. This hall was being refurbished at the time, for the community, and there was extra money left, and the councillor said, 'well, can we no' use that money for a day centre?' Right? And it went from there ... And they put £30,000 into this hall, and set up the daycentre. So it was a fluke.*

In identifying newly available sources of funding, organisations have sought to match these funds to identified gaps in service provision within the particular area, or for the particular client group that the organisation was set up to serve. Others have arisen as a consequence of government

161

initiatives set up with an alternative, but complementary agenda, or as a consequence of the active intent of interested individuals. The outcome of such developments over time, however, has meant that to date, voluntary organisations have tended to arise in an *ad hoc* manner which is as much a response to available resources as it is to identified need. While the identification of potential sources of funding is clearly a pragmatic approach to survival, one of the outcomes of such action is that it contributes to a spatially inequitable distribution of voluntary resources over time. If the voluntary sector is to continue to play an elevated role within the provision of community-based health and social care [as current legislation would seem to imply] there is a need for both the statutory and voluntary sectors to recognise the necessity of moving away from such *ad hoc* progression towards a more systematic approach in both the spatial and temporal development of voluntary sector provisioning.

Concluding Comments

This chapter has illustrated how restructuring is playing itself out through *one* of those sets of actors and agencies that form part of the dependency network, and the potential implications for service recipients themselves. The differing funding mechanisms through which voluntary organisations access resources, combined with a geographically uneven distribution of voluntary services and differential opportunities to participate between locales, rather than *increasing* options and client choice can be seen to have contributed to a limitation of services and a growth of geographical inequity in voluntary service provision. This has been exacerbated by the impact that local authority restructuring has had on voluntary organisations. Where contracting is the major funding mechanism, this too can be seen to be contributing to a redefinition of the client-base served by the voluntary sector, with implications for those marginal groups who have traditionally fallen outside statutory definitions of need. Though care reform and the introduction of local authority restructuring have been shown to contribute to the development of geographically uneven provision of voluntary sector supports, this has been exacerbated by:

- the historical legacy of voluntary provision;
- the ad hoc implementation of central government initiatives; and
- differences in the demographic profile between localities.

In terms of the dependency network, the translation of legislation enacted by central government at local government level, can be seen to be

162

impacting differentially not only on voluntary organisations that form part of local dependency networks, but on individuals dependant on community-based care provision. Local authorities have demonstrated different priorities and patterns of spending with regard to the voluntary sector, a situation exacerbated in Glasgow by local authority restructuring, which has contributed to the emergence of a geographically uneven availability of resources. Though this has had less impact in Dumfries and Galloway, participation within rural locales has been problematic. Further, as illustrated, dependency networks are subject to variation, appraisal and reappraisal over both time and space, consequently this chapter has also attempted to illustrate how dependency networks can be differentially embedded within particular places. A more detailed discussion of the implications of these issues for the dependency network will be drawn together in the concluding chapters.

Notes

[1] That is, it excludes such organisations as hospital trusts, museums, universities, which might be charities, but which are not generally thought of as part of the 'true' voluntary sector.

[2] A term used to describe voluntary bodies whose membership consists of other voluntary agencies and whose main role is the provision of advice, information and representation to these agencies.

[3] In 1997, the Scottish Office introduced a moratorium on MISG funding in order to review its continued utility, and at the time of the final interviews, organisations were undergoing re-assessment, contributing to an atmosphere of uncertainty, as organisations expressed fears over the continuation of their funding.

7 Exploring Geographies of Informal Caring

Introduction

The experience of care restructuring arises as a consequence of the inter-relationships between actors operating across multi-levels of the caring process, and the ways in which care outcomes are mediated and translated by actants within the network. As such, the voluntary experience cannot be understood in isolation. While the legislative context acknowledges the role of voluntary service provision, it also notes that 'most care is provided by family, friends and neighbours' (Cm. 849, 1989, para. 2.3). This indicates a need to examine the role of informal carers and how they may serve to influence, and be influenced by, care translations occurring within the network. While the legislative frame identifies the informal carer, this identification is also problematic, in that (as discussed in chapter four) incorporation within the caring process also requires individuals to self-identify as carers. Without an appreciation of this factor, any definition of informal caring is open to challenge. Hence, this chapter considers informal caring in two ways: firstly, it discusses the changing role of informal caring as defined through the wider social and legislative context; secondly, it explores informal caring as defined by informal carers themselves. This highlights the need to examine the *nature* of informal care, its potential and limitations, in order to gain an understanding of such factors as:

- the wider contextual and more localised impacts of social and structural change upon informal caring;
- differences between the social support networks that friends/neighbours are prepared to give, and that which only close kin are prepared to offer;
- variations in access and availability of statutory and voluntary care supports within and between areas; and
- the opportunities available to informal carers to influence other actants located within the dependency network.

Initially, the chapter focuses on the first of these issues by addressing the caring role and the context of informal caring. The remainder of the chapter uses personal geographies of caring to explore the changing role of informal caring, and how this may influence, and be influenced by, the restructuring of health and social care as experienced through the dependency network. In this way, the chapter also aims to provide an insight into the *practice* of the network as experienced by those located at the micro-level.

The Changing Context of Informal Care-giving

Informal caring arrives through, and takes place within, a relationship. A carer can be seen as someone who regularly helps a relative or friend who is disabled or ill, with personal tasks such as dressing, bathing, toiletting, shopping and household tasks, or who offers other sorts of practical or emotional support (Robinson and Yee, 1991). Such individuals may or may not share living accommodation, provide full or part-time care, be employed, or share the caring role with others. While carers can consist of friends or neighbours, the majority are family members - such as a spouse or other relative - and though the causes, histories, needs and illnesses of the cared-for may vary, a thread common to all informal carers is their participation in giving care and support to another person who is unable to live independently within the community. A profile of carers participating in this study is given later in this chapter, in table 7.1.

It is easy to forget that the welfare state rests upon this network of caring. Individuals are more often seen as consumers rather than producers of health and social services. This can lead us to lose sight of the informal help and support provided outwith statutory, voluntary and private services. The extent of this provision, however, has led some commentators to refer to informal carers as "the invisible welfare state" (Finch, 1986). Around 6.8 million people in Britain care for sick, elderly or disabled people, 75 percent of whom care for an elderly person (Tinker et al, 1994, 27). Of these carers, around 1.4 million spend a minimum of twenty hours a week providing care and assistance (OPCS, 1992). In economic terms, it has been estimated that such informal care provision has saved the British taxpayer around £34 billion a year (Brindle, 1998). The contribution of the informal carer to the care and support of the frail elderly can thus be seen as a key element in the successful implementation of any restructured care policy.

Carers can be conceptualised as on the margins of the social care system, that is, they can be seen to form part of the 'taken for granted background to provision' against which other agencies act (Twigg, 1989, 54). Nevertheless, informal carers form a cornerstone of the caring network.

Recent legislation (the 1996 Carers Recognition Act) has formally recognised the rights of carers to be assessed as co-clients in terms of social care needs. The lack of additional resources with which to implement the Act, however, reinforces the fundamental ambiguities regarding their position in a system where services are predominantly structured around the dependent. As a result, variations can occur between different local authorities that arise from the degree of emphasis placed on the subjective well-being of carers as part of the requirement to reduce levels of institutionalisation. There are [at least] three differing frames of reference within which the relationship between statutory, voluntary/private actants, and carers may be identified (Twigg, 1989):

(i) *carers as resources.* Within this frame, social care agencies are seen to operate an essentially residualist role, operating largely in response to deficiencies in the care network. Informal carers are conceptualised as the 'given' against which services are structured, with the central focus of care restructuring placed on the dependent. Carers are viewed as the major form of resource in the support of dependent people, so marginalising carer welfare as a subject of agency concern;

(ii) *carers as co-worker.* Here, carers are seen as co-workers in the care enterprise, intermeshing formal and informal sector provision. The term 'carer' is thus a social construct which semi-professionalises kin and friendship relations, so bringing them within the orbit of the formal system. Within this frame, the aim is to maintain and enable informal care, by recognising that in supporting carers, there is an increased likelihood that [quality] care will continue to be offered. Conflicts of interest are either ignored, on the assumption that carers predominantly *want* to care for their dependent, or are collapsed into individual negotiations at micro-level; and

(iii) *carers as co-clients.* Within this frame, both the carer and dependent are viewed as potential clients for social care services. In general, the focus is on the most heavily stressed individuals with intervention aimed at relieving carer stress. Conflicts of interest between carers and their dependants are fully recognised (as reflected in recent carers' legislation), though even here their status is subsumed to that of their dependent.

These differing perceptions of carers have implications for the inter-relationships between carers and other actants operating within the dependency network, revealing a number of variations that can arise in the translation of policy within and between areas.

The 1989 White Paper stated that "helping carers to maintain their valuable contribution to the spectrum of care *is both a right and sound investment*" (Cmd. 849). Legislative emphasis is thus placed on the 'moral' as a means of accruing the fiscal benefits of tapping into this largely unpaid source of care. Implicitly, community care policy has attempted to invoke a sense of familial responsibility for the dependent, a role many commentators (e.g. Nissel, 1980; Finch, 1987; Glazer, 1990) have maintained falls disproportionately on the female members of the family. Women carers, it has been argued, enable the family to be a provider unit. In this way, the public contribution to community-based care can be limited to discrete tasks with clearly defined boundaries, outwith which care is assumed to be the responsibility of the domestic sphere (Glazer, 1990). Yet despite the fact that many women are increasingly employed outside the home - a factor incompatible with full-time caring - emphasis it is still placed on portraying caring as the natural option, and not undertaking care as unnatural (Brown and Smith, 1993).

Debate over state versus family care has been a major theme running through the history of social policy. However, not only is the notion of 'the family' existing as some form of single institution open to debate (Graham, 1985), but the notion that society should seek to resurrect some pre-existing order of communal and familial responsibility is also argued to be based on evidence that is largely unsubstantiated on two counts. Firstly, it is maintained that the perception that people in the past regularly and unquestioningly cared for ageing relatives misrepresents reality. There is strong evidence to suggest that the frail elderly gained from familial support within the community only where they had sufficient economic resources to offset any burden they may represent to their kin, or where their support was heavily subsidised by charity or poor relief. Where there was no economic support, as noted in chapter three, many of the elderly were placed in Poor Law Institutions. Hence the 'modern' practice of placing elderly populations in institutions is not new. In 1906, for example, 6 percent of those aged 65 and over were living in institutional environs, compared to an overall figure of only 4.4 percent[1] in 1966 (Anderson, 1983, 112). Secondly, the notion that a more stable society existed in the past is also largely mythical. As the 1851 census suggests, well under half the population were living in the place in which they were born. This has lead commentators to argue, that it was only with the development of council housing, rent restrictions, and falling population rates in the 20th century, that Britain began to see the production of communities that were more stable than those existing in previous centuries (Anderson, 1983).

Despite debate over the pre-existence of some communal responsibility that can be resurrected, contemporary political and ideological forces *have* attempted to [re]locate the site of health and social service provision from public space to the homespace. Not only is government policy geared to the assumption that there will continue to be a pool of people prepared to provide unpaid care and support, but it further assumes that the family will willingly take on this increased caring responsibility. It has been argued, however, that such an assumption fails to account for those economic and demographic factors that exert contradictory forces which may undermine such change (e.g. Nissel, 1980; Finch, 1987, Hancock and Jarvis, 1994). More explicitly, it is maintained that this appeal to the ideal of the traditional nuclear family, and an emphasis on the familial roles of women - through social policy - has not been successful for a number of reasons:

(i)   while it is unlikely that *spouse* carers will become less willing or able to care, the ability of other caring groups - in particular married women, or adult children - may well diminish due to changing employment patterns (Hancock and Jarvis, 1994). The increased importance of women's earnings in most households, combined with the growing number of (largely female-headed) lone-parent families receiving inadequate maintenance from the second parent, means that any assumption that such a pool of people will be available to take on this role, may be increasingly out of step with reality;

(ii)   increased mobility has resulted in extended family units becoming increasingly geographically distant from each other, making mutual care arrangements more difficult (Nissel, 1980);

(iii)   the greater tendency to divorce, second families, and single parenthood obscures the pattern of traditional family networks and may reduce the ability/willingness of those relatives who may previously have assumed the caring role (e.g. younger female relatives); and

(iv)   it has been projected that demographic change and declining birth rates will have a large impact on dependency ratios (i.e. those aged over 65 and under fifteen) in future years. By 2030, for example, it has been estimated that for every three people of working age, there will be one elderly person requiring support (Coombes, 1996).

The feminisation of the workforce, increased geographical mobility and changing family structures, illustrate just some of the factors that can mitigate against statutory expectations of an increase in the caring role of women. Nevertheless, it is evident that despite these factors, large numbers of domestic carers are already existent. Thus, while care policy should take account of the wider context of social and cultural change, as other commentators have argued, kinship patterns of obligation, in terms of care-giving and responsibility, are likely to continue (Finch, 1987).

Geographies of Informal Caring

Many carers do not formalise the 'provider' role that they play, rationalising their contribution to community-based care as simply 'looking after mum or dad' or a close relative. As illustrated in figure 4.2, non-recognition of the role they play means that informal carers largely fall within two groups:

(i) the 'invisible carers', i.e. those who do either not recognise the caring role they play, or who do not access care supports outside their own social sphere. Though playing a key role in supporting the frail elderly within the community, the low visibility of this group means that they have no [or limited] contact with other care supports and as such are largely located outside the caring network; and

(ii) 'visible carers', i.e. those who *do* recognise the caring role they play, and as such are linked into other formal and/or informal supports within the dependency network. Their location within the network means they may influence and be influenced by translations occurring within it. It is with this group that this chapter is primarily concerned.

Through focus groups, repeat interviews and carer diaries, the concern, here, has been to uncover some of the ways in which carers cope with the problems of daily life, and how and why they come into contact with formal and informal care services. In doing so, the study has explored those inter-relationships that occur between informal carers and other actants within the network, and examines how carers are affected by, and in turn affect, the process of care restructuring. Carers were prompted to discuss the services they used, issues of accessibility and choice, sources of support, information and advice. While a number of topics for discussion were introduced (hence some degree of structure is inherent to the research process) no direct questions were asked. An indirect approach was seen as the best means of gaining a critical insight of carer's views. This approach was duplicated in the process of gathering data using diary techniques, where different topics for consideration were introduced (as discussed in chapter five) but where carers were free to express themselves on their own terms. The quotes used within this chapter, have been selected on the basis that they best illustrated the key themes emerging from the data.

The analysis focuses on four main themes:

(i)   the relocation of care from public space to the homespace;
(ii)   personal networks of caring;
(iii)   informal caring and external care supports;
(iv)   spatial variations in access and availability of care services.

Table 7.1 reveals the codes used to identify each carer and adds to the carer profile discussed in chapter five. It highlights the relationship between carer and dependent, levels of frailty of the dependent, and illustrates the nature of the formal and informal care supports accessed and available to them, as defined by the carers themselves. In terms of social support networks, the table draws attention to a qualitative difference in support gained from the community that can be grouped into three main categories:

- community supports that comprise regular domiciliary respite including the undertaking of personal hygiene tasks;
- supports that comprise irregular but intensive care supports (e.g. several weeks of respite per year away from the homespace); and
- supplementary care supports that exclude personal care (e.g. shopping, sitting, and transport).

Relocating care from the public space to the homespace

The chapter has drawn attention to the context within which care restructuring is being relocated from public space to the homespace. In-built into the relocation of the site of caring is the assumption that the informal carer will increasingly assume the role previously undertaken by public sector employees. Informal carers often perform tasks formerly undertaken by caring professionals. The experiences of carers within this study, as illustrated in the vignette below, have highlighted, how, in the restructuring of health and social care, there has been a redefinition of an increasing number of formerly medical or nursing tasks as the 'informal responsibility' of carers within the homespace.

DGC1:

> Gillian's mother suffers from Alzheimers and severe epilepsy, and can no longer walk unaided, or communicate verbally. Gillian performs such tasks as lifting, feeding, washing, dressing, toiletting and administering medication to her mother. A bath nurse assists her to shower her mother once a week. Gillian takes her mother to a daycentre five mornings a week Insufficient staffing levels,[2] combined

Table 7.1 Carers' Support Networks

Carer (age)	Name	Dependent condition and age	Social Support Networks	Voluntary Supports	Statutory Supports	Private Supports
DGC1 F 37	Gillian	Mother (70) Advanced Alzheimers and severe epilepsy; poor mobility, no verbal communication	Friends: occasional sitting	Carer support group Daycentre Domiciliary respite	Bathing service Advice & information	Residential respite
DGC2 F early 40s	June	Father (79) & daughter (14 - disabled) Degenerative liver disorder arising from alcoholism and poor mobility	Brother: few weeks respite break per year	Carer's Support Group Advice & information	Advice & Information	None
DGC3 F mid-30s	Jean	Mother (72) & disabled brother (38) early Alzheimers, limited mobility	None	Carers' support group Daycentre Advice & information	Residential respite (infrequent)	None
DGC4 F 70	Jenny	Husband (74) Stroke and severe Alzheimers; very limited mobility and no verbal communication	Daughter: 1.5 days p.wk (including personal care) Son: one evening p.wk Neighbour: daily help with Exercises Friends: occasional visiting	Carer support group Domiciliary respite Advice & information	Community nursing service	Residential respite Physiotherapist
DGC5 F mid-60s	Wilma	Husband (late 60s) Advanced dementia, very limited mobility	Daughter: visiting (no personal care); Son: (occasional personal care)	Advice & information Advocacy	Domiciliary care Advice & information	None
DGC6 M early 70s	Tom	Wife (late 60s) Dementia	Daughter: meals (no personal care)	Carer support group Domiciliary respite Meals-on-Wheels	Hospital daycentre Advice & information	None

Table 7.1 contd.

Carer (age)	Name	Dependent condition and age	Social Support Networks	Voluntary Supports	Statutory Supports	Private Supports
GC1 F early 40s	Susan		Son (lives in): 'sits' one day weekly; (no personal care)	Carer support group Daycentre Advice & information	Bathing service (NHS)	None
GC2 F early 50s	Molly	Mother (93) Advanced Alzheimers; limited mobility	Daughter (lives in) (including personal care) Neighbours - occasional sitting	Daycentre Domiciliary respite Advice & information	None	None
GC3 F 57	Elaine	Mother (88) & aunt (95) mother - severe stroke; no mobility, no verbal communication aunt - blindness and limited mobility	None	Carers' Support Group Advice & information	Bathing service Domiciliary respite Overnight service Advice & information	Domiciliary respite
GC4 F 68	Alex	Husband (70) severe dementia; limited mobility	Daughter & sister: shopping visiting (no (no personal care) Friends: transport and occasional sitting	Carers' support group Daycentre Domiciliary respite Advice & Information	Hospital daycare Bathing service Advice & information	Residential respite
GC5 M 28	William	Grandparents (mid-70s) grandfather - stroke; very limited mobility, no verbal communication grandmother - severe leg impairment, poor mobility	Sister: 2-3 hours daily (no personal care)	Carers' support group Daycentre Advice & information	None	None
GC6 M late 70s	John	Wife (mid-70s) Alzheimers	Daughter: (disabled - lives in)	Daycentre Home-based respite Advice & Information	Bathing service	None

* Dumfries and Galloway carer(DGC) and Glasgow carer (GC); m = male; f = female

> with her mother's high degree of dependency for all personal hygiene and feeding tasks, however, means that she must accompany her mother at the daycentre if she is to continue attending.

The experience of performing tasks formerly undertaken by caring professionals[3] such as lifting, medicating and personal hygiene, was common to most carers within this study. As carers noted, however, while there was an expectation that they would undertake these former professionalised roles, this was largely without the benefit of formal training. Given the intensive levels of care that statutory actants often expect carers to deliver, and despite requests made by a number of participants for some formal training, most carers maintained that they had not been offered even such basic skills such as lifting and handling. That this is being recognised, however, was evident in at least one locality, where opportunities now exist for carers to undertake a coping skills course at a local college. A voluntary organisation provides domiciliary respite [where necessary] to allow the carer to attend. Nevertheless, this is still a highly under-developed area of care support, and one where accessibility is highly uneven. Given the known problems to health arising as a result of poor lifting and handling skills, this is an important issue; a factor recognised by paid nursing and homecare staff who not only receive full training in these skills [4] but are only required to lift an individual if there are two people available to undertake the task.

Carers also noted that while care supports within the home were clearly beneficial, the introduction of formal care to the home environment was creating a change in the relationship normally exhibited within private space. The informal carer no longer felt in control of the homespace. As Wilma commented:

DGC5 R: *I felt they* [statutory services] *were going to send this person in, send that person in - different things, and my home wouldn't have been my own! There would be somebody coming in **all** the time, every other hour of the night and day, and I just couldn't stand that. My home wouldn't have been my own!*

In a restructured landscape of caring, the full weight of the structure of community-based care is borne by clients and carers (Richardson et al, 1989). That is, that though carers may share a socially legitimised perception of services as *caring*, they also feel the loss of independence arising from control from above. Consequently, for carers located within the care network, the introduction of formal care to the home can create a change in the site of caring from private/domestic space, to that of public/domestic space, as the boundaries of what has traditionally been private space and public or 'institutional' space become blurred.

Personal networks of caring

As noted earlier, government policy has sought to 'resurrect' a sense of community and familial responsibility in caring for dependent populations. It was also noted that economic and wider structural change can act to limit this attempt. The in-depth case material and diaries, however, also revealed additional social factors that can contribute to the limiting of the informal support networks available to carer and cared-for. As highlighted in table 7.1, of the twelve in-depth studies undertaken only three carers received regular support from relatives that included help in undertaking the difficult personal tasks often required in caring for frail elderly people. Two carers, had *no* social networks on which they could draw for help and physical support. These individuals maintained that relatives either lived too far distant to provide help, or simply had no interest in undertaking a share in the caring role. In addition to a lack of kinship support, these individuals also lacked community supports - such as friends or neighbours - upon whom they could draw for help. For Elaine, this was the result of a move back into the parental home and the subsequent loss of contact with former friends. The heavy caring role she undertook left her little time to develop new social contacts, and those that she had developed, revolved largely around other carers who were similarly situated. Whilst the remaining six received some degree of support from friends or relatives, this consisted largely of caring tasks such as shopping, brief spells of sitting with the cared-for, or emergency support. As Gillian noted:

DGC1 R: *Em, I have neighbours, like em, they're* **good** *neighbours, but I wouldn't ask them* [for help] *as such. They have helped me out - do you remember the bad snow we had here in February?* **Nobody** *could move, and one of my neighbours came and sat with my mother to let me get out to get the essentials, because we were running out of* **everything** ... *friends have the odd times came and helped me out. Like sometimes if I want to go and get my hair done because I am going out that night, I maybe 'phone up one of my pals and they maybe come and sit with her, just to let me nip up the town. But em, as I say, my brother's not able to, he lives in Perth, and he's got his family. They come and see us obviously, when they can.*

The in-depth studies largely reflected the wider views gained from the focus groups, that while friends and neighbours *did* provide some level of care, this was predominantly in the form of short-term or emergency supports. Examples were given of such supports as: sitting with the cared-for to allow the carer to visit local shops; enabling the carer to make a short social visit; undertaking shopping on the carer's behalf; help with transport; and emergency supports - such as helping the carer to lift their frail elderly relative when they had fallen.

The decline in the physical, and/or mental health amongst many frail elderly is often accompanied by a declining ability to communicate verbally. [5] The difficulties experienced by friends or relatives in adjusting to the changing relationship arising from this decline in health, was noted by a number of carers to have led to declining social contact. The onset of what is often a debilitating illness for the cared-for, also meant that far from gaining support from the community as per statutory expectations, carers had, in fact, experienced a decline in the social networks from which they might have expected to gain support. This was not an uncommon experience, as Alex noted:

GC4 R: *... some people can't **take** it you know, because they knew him the way he **was** before! And oh, he was talking quite a bit you know, he was chatty, and Andy said, 'listen, his face is all twisted', and I said, 'Oh, is it?' - I'd got used to it, you know?*

I: *So do you find that some people don't come to visit quite as often as they used to, because they don't like the idea that your husband is not quite the same person?*

R: *Oh, that's happened from the very **beginning**! Oh yes!*

Tom also remarked:

DGC6 R: *Yes, well some of the more - I think some of them [friends and relatives] felt kind of embarrassed, that she is the way she is, compared to what she used to be. But I mean they understand. They know it's just the illness. But it's [pause] no, no-one's been, but my daughter and myself.*

While the above excerpts have illustrated how social networks can decline as a consequence of the cared-for's reduced ability to communicate, social opportunities were also noted to have declined as a consequence of constraints placed on a carer's own social life due to their caring role. This was raised in an interview with Gillian:

DGC1 I: *So caring's made a big difference to the social side of your life?*

R: *Oh yes. Yes, em very much so. I mean its not as if I can walk out of the door and leave her, or say, "oh bugger this for a carry on, I'm off to the pub". I canny do that. Em everything with me, I've got to arrange everything, it can't be a last minute thing you know? I'm lucky, that all the - I haven't lost any friends through it, you know. But they know if something is coming up, that they have to give me advance warning. They know that they canny phone and say, "Oh, we're doing such-and-such next week." They've got to give me advance warning, so I can get the cover booked so I can go. I've got to have everything done in advance.*

Thus carers described a highly routinised lifestyle that placed both spatial and temporal constraints upon them. Simple tasks were noted to require a high degree of organisation, and without good social networks of support, attending spontaneous events were near impossible. As Elaine noted:

GC3 R: *Sometimes I don't go out, because there's such a lot to catch up on in here* [the home]. *I don't go to the shops or anything. Though I'm really trying to do a bit more. I go to the carers' support group.*

I: *So when you do go out, is it mainly to the carers' support group?*

R: *Yes, I mean your social life is nil!*

For some carers, the telephone became a 'lifeline' - a necessity through which they were able to organise their limited free time, request help and generally communicate with others residing outwith the domestic sphere. Susan, for example, noted that communication by telephone enabled her to sort out problems, arrange meetings, and to keep in contact with friends outside the home. This allowed her to maximise that free time she had to spend away from her caring role, by minimising the 'running around' that she had to do.

It should be noted, however, that not all carers had such abbreviated social networks. Jenny, a carer living in a small community some twenty seven miles from the main urban centre, described a social network that in addition to voluntary and statutory sector supports included neighbours, adult children and friends who continued to visit on a regular basis, despite the fact that her husband was no longer able to communicate verbally. In her view, her ability to draw on a relatively wide social network of support was linked to the size of the community in which she lived. That is, she maintained that smaller communities promoted closer networks of social support, a view also held by other carers living in small communities. This assertion, however, was not borne out by all those living in such communities, a number of whom had no social supports upon whom they could draw. June, for example, had moved to a small village some nineteen miles from the urban core following her husband's change of employment. She had no family living within the area, and though her brother took her frail elderly father into his home for a few weeks each year to give her some respite, she received no care support from neighbours, or the local community. In her view, this was attributable to the fact that she cared for both her father and her disabled daughter, and friends/neighbours felt unable to cope with the degree of care required:

DGC2 I: *What about the notion of community support?*

R: [long laugh]

I: *Do you get **any** help from neighbours and local people?*

R: *No, not at all, no. They've always been sort of wary about* [pause] *I mean even some of my best friends, they are frightened something would go wrong or whatever.*

It has been suggested, that it is the presence of additional family support that encourages neighbours to give care (Ball and Ball, 1982). This is based on the assumption that the presence of familial supports relieves the concerns of friends/neighbours that they may be required to undertake onerous or personal caring tasks. However, whilst it is true that in some of the case studies, those with familial support were also able to draw on additional community supports, these were in the minority, occurring in only three of the twelve case studies. As table 7.1 also illustrates, half of those participating in the in-depth study, despite having some level of familial support, did not in fact benefit from any additional support from friends or neighbours.

The extent of primary familial care was also found to vary. The informal burden of caring is a heavy one, and levels of ability to cope varied. So while a number of carers had undertaken this task for many years (upwards of ten years in several instances), others found their ability to cope declining after relatively short periods of time (typically about a year). This was found to arise largely as a consequence of two factors:

(i)   the health status of the primary carer - a number of elderly spouse carers, for example, also experienced health problems, and several younger carers noted a decline in their own health status as a result of the stress of caring; and

(ii)   variations in the bonds that arise as a result of marriage, parenthood, living together or in close proximity.

While the family may be seen as the bedrock of community care, these bonds cannot be forged (Qureshi and Simons, 1987). Here, for example, whilst some carers devoted many years to caring for a highly dependent spouse or parent (over twenty years in Elaine's case) not all bonds between carers and cared-for were strong enough to survive that level of commitment. Within this study, for example, a number of carers noted that they had put a 'time-limit' on the length of time they were willing to place their own life on the 'back-burner' whilst they undertook the caring role. This is illustrated in an excerpt from Susan's personal geography of caring:

GC1:

Susan noted that she had not initially been very enthusiastic about having Annie coming to live in her home. Annie was Susan's mother-in-law, and even before she had developed dementia, they had never been very close. Susan expressed some resentment at Annie's 'dependency' even during the years when she had been fit and able. Susan, however, saw both herself and her husband as committed Christians, and as such, felt it her duty to care for Annie. She made it clear that she felt this was something she would be unable to sustain long-term. However, after talking the situation over with her husband, she had agreed to place her own life on the 'back-burner' for a period of two years.

Other carers had also noted that prior to the decline in health of the cared-for, relations between themselves and their dependent had been poor. Those who had agreed to undertake the caring role, often did so in response to feelings of guilt and pressure that they felt had been placed upon them by other household members and/or relatives. For others, familial pressure influenced the amount of external support they felt able, or willing, to take. As the co-ordinator of one voluntary organisation noted, families often fail to recognise the primary carer's need for support, making them feel guilty for looking for help:

> **DG19 R:** *I was visiting a lady this morning, and* ***she*** *had a* ***big*** *family. It was her second marriage, so she had children from his family* ***and*** *her family, and they* ***keep*** *saying to her, "do you actually* ***need*** *all this help? My father's not that actually that bad". And that's making her feel quite guilty in looking for help ... she's actually quite torn now, because she does actually feel she* ***needs*** *help, but her children are putting pressure on her not to take it.*

The twin issues of love and guilt play a significant role in the process of informal caring. While a carer's negotiation of space is determined largely by the needs of the cared-for, the social networks available to carers, and the availability of formal and informal support services, a carers' feelings of duty, love and guilt, can also place their *own* restrictions on a carer's movements, preventing them from maximising those supports that *are* available. Carers spoke of a failure to take advantage of residential respite opportunities due to their feelings of guilt at placing their dependent in institutional care:

> **DGC1 R:** *My doctor and the nurse, and even my social workers have tried to get me to have* ***more*** *breaks. Em, and that is just something I just have to work on myself.*
>
> **I:** *Why haven't you taken advantage of that?*
>
> **R:** *At the end of the day it all boils down to money!*
>
> **I:** *Right, and what about if your Mum went into respite for a week, and you just stayed at home?*
>
> **R:** *No, that wouldn't do, no. I couldn't handle that. I can only handle it if I'm away out of the country, or I'm away maybe say to London or Blackpool or Glasgow for the weekend. I just, I just* ***don't*** *feel right* ***being*** *here and she there, to me that's not right!*

Gillian also noted that restrictions on her personal mobility had to some extent arisen as a consequence of her own personal choice. The opportunity did exist for her mother to attend alternative daycare at a day hospital, where Gillian's presence would not be required. Gillian, however, continued to take her mother to daycentre provision, despite the fact that the lack of trained staff meant she must attend to her mother's personal needs. In her view, the change of service would upset and confuse her mother.

Many, however, spend long periods confined within the home with their dependent. When asked how the onset of his wife's frailty had affected his lifestyle, for example, Tom responded:

DGC6 R: *Well, eh, at first I could get out maybe for an hour, or an hour and a half in the morning, and that was it. Then it got that I couldn't get out at all! If I did, I'd to take her with me, and if I was just going down the road for quarter of an hour for groceries, she wanted back home here. She didn't seem secure anywhere, except in the house here.*

I: *Mm hmm.*

R: *It got that I couldn't get out of the house but she was falling, and I couldn't get out, until [VO] came. They came on a Monday and a Thursday, from 10 o' clock to 12, for two hours - which makes all the difference. And then she went to day-care two days a week - roughly from about 10 o' clock to half past three.*

The caring experience highlights the variations that exist between familial/community care. While relatives living outwith the homespace, but within a reasonable travelling distance, were found to offer short, but more regular spells of support, few undertook the intensive and intimate caring tasks required of the 'primary carer'. Only four of the twelve case studies received care support from friends or neighbours. Thus, the social support networks available to primary carers, though important, can be seen to have served largely as a source of complementary care. As a consequence, carers are subject to constraints that can reduce their opportunities to both maintain and develop their social networks and hence the social supports upon which they can draw.

Care *by* the community within this study has, by and large, meant care by one individual. As such, the restructuring of care to community-based environs may be said to strike fundamentally at the notion of care as a shared responsibility (Glazer, 1990). Yet the experience of primary carers, as revealed here and as indicated in table 7.1, suggests that the conditions that best encourage the promotion of community responsibility are those where multiple carers are present and there is a sharing of the caring role.

Informal caring and external care supports

Though the legislative frame highlights the role of informal carers in the caring process, this does not entirely divorce care from other sectors. Further, the limited and [largely] complementary role played by social and familial support networks, as illustrated above, elevated the importance of those supports provided by other actants within the care network (i.e. from voluntary, private or statutory sectors). The role and inter-relationships between these actants and informal carers are considered below.

The notion that caring should increasingly be assumed a collective responsibility incorporates the view that local populations could, and should, take greater responsibility for care delivered within their neighbourhoods through the encouragement of voluntary organisations, the development of self-help groups, neighbourhood care schemes, as well as orchestrating and utilising the support networks of vulnerable individuals. As such, responses to care are concerned with the nature of local geographical communities, or communities of common interest. These factors highlight the utility of the spatial and organisational focus adopted within a networked approach. Such care supports varied between:

- carers' support groups, facilitated by voluntary organisations (and often run by ex-carers);
- domiciliary or home-based respite;
- advice and information;
- campaigning and advocacy; and
- residential respite (in this study, provided only by statutory and private sector providers).

Carers' perceptions regarding each of these forms of support are discussed below.

Carers' Support Groups. Where social support networks were limited, carer support groups were seen to act as the main or sole outlet for the release of tensions amongst individuals who were similarly situated, and who understood the frustrations of caring. Where necessary, voluntary organisations provided domiciliary support to enable carers to attend support groups. As the co-ordinator of one carers' support group noted:

DG20 R: *We act as a safety valve in a lot of ways, where people can come and talk to us if they're feeling really bad, they can vent their wrath on us, and we just take it. ...You know someone working in an office or a shop or somewhere, they don't understand if you say "mum's driving me mad" about someone disabled - its "ooh, that's a terrible thing to say, you should be a loving and caring person" - and so they are, but they're only human. Just because someone's in a wheelchair or* *whatever, doesn't necessarily make them angelic and malleable - and they do have minds of their own!*

Carers' support groups were thus seen to offer an environment within which carers could socialise, listen and share the experiences of others similarly situated. Of the twelve case studies, nine participated in such groups. Of the remaining three who did not use these groups, two (John and Wilma) felt that they would not benefit from group discussion of this kind, whilst the third (Susan) preferred to use any available respite to visit her own friends/family.

As evident from both tables 7.1 and 7.2 (below), support groups were used by carers in a number of ways. Not all those using support groups, for example, cited them as key sites of advice or information. For Gillian, the support group was a site of social contact. The longevity of her caring role (over ten years) outstripped the existence of support groups within her locale. As a consequence, she had developed good links with her GP and community nursing staff, who had become her primary source of advice and information. Tom, though having cared for his wife for a much shorter period, also had a good relationship with his GP whom he viewed as his key source of information. He too saw the carer's group primarily as a source of social support. Consequently, for a number of carers, the loss of social contact arising from the caring role was in part replaced by new friendships gained through voluntary-run carers' support groups. For some, this represented a new social outlet. As Susan noted, while receiving no support from her local community, on becoming a carer, she had discovered a 'new community', one that was not based on notions of a territorially-bounded neighbourhood, but on a commonality of interest and experience, and of whose existence she had not previously been aware. Such communities were viewed as key sites of advice on how to cope with particular caring situations, as well as sources of information on additional resources available in a locale and how to access them. Through other carers, for example, individuals became aware of the resources available in their local community, where to go for help and support, and how to access those supports to which they felt they were entitled but were not receiving.

Carers' support groups also operate at a regional level. Here the aim was not only to establish local carers' groups, but "*to encourage carers' networks - localised forums of carers that bring together a variety of carers' groups, and through that process, to ensure that carers' views and needs are represented by the policy-makers*" (G25). The management committees of voluntary carers' groups consist in large part of past and present informal carers. Both June and Susan, for example, played an active role in the committee structure of carers' organisations within their locale. As both carers and committee members, these actors can be seen to play a role in shaping the internal policy direction of those voluntary organisations with which they were connected. These organisations, in turn, as actants within the dependency network, also seek to influence the translation of care outcomes. Thus, opportunities exist for carers to operate at more than one level of the network, highlighting the complexity of the inter-relationships existing within it.

Table 7.2   Carers' Views of the Main Sources of Information and Advice

Carer	VO	Carers Support Group	GP/ community nurses	Social Services	Other
DGC1	✓	✓	✓ (both)	-	-
DGC2	✓	✓	✓ (GP)	-	-
DGC3	✓	✓	-	-	leaflets in hospital chance discussions
DGC4	✓	✓	-	-	own research (libraries etc.)
DGC5	✓	✓	-	-	-
DGC6	✓	✓	✓ (GP)	✓	-
GC1	✓	✓	-	-	-
GC2	✓	-	-	-	friends
GC3	✓	✓	✓ (nurses)	-	-
GC4	✓	✓	-	✓	-
GC5	-	✓	-	-	-
GC6	-	-	✓ (GP)	-	friends

However, while the voluntary management committees of carers' organisations were largely made up of past and present carers, many of those groups supported through statutory funding also had local authority representation upon their committees. This was seen as a means of informing local authorities of carers' needs, while at the same time ensuring organisations fulfil any obligations attached to their statutory funding. Carers, however, also maintained that this presented a 'double-edged sword' placing constraints on their ability to act in particular ways. One group of carers interviewed noted, that they felt the agenda of their parent organisation had been 'hi-jacked' by social service representatives, to the extent that their own views were being subsumed by a local authority agenda. As a consequence, they had broken away from the organisation to form a new group that was totally independent of any state representation. In this respect, they, like other independently funded organisations, though still affected by the wider caring context, can be seen to have consciously placed themselves outside the network in an attempt to retain their independence.

Thus carers can be seen to experience support groups in different ways:

• as a site of advice and information with regard to their caring role;
• as a community of social contact and support; and
• as a point of access to the policy process.

In this way, some carers become *part* of the voluntary organisation, and in doing so, come to act across multiple levels of the dependency network.

Campaigning and Advocacy. Whilst voluntary support groups play a key role in carer support at the grassroots level, a number of organisations also operate at the wider regional and national scale, participating in campaigning for carers and informing the policy process. Organisations such as Carers National and Alzheimers - Action on Dementia, have played a key role in informing Social Work Committees at national government level, and actively seek to influence policy making at local government levels. Carers National, for example, was seen to play an active role in campaigning for changes to the Invalid Care Allowance in the 1980s [at that time a male only allowance]. More recently, they have played an active role in campaigning for carers' rights, eventually formalised within the Carers Recognition Act (1996), which gave carers the legislative right to have their own needs assessed separately from that of their cared-for. In this way, carers' support groups can be seen to encourage carer networks and to have an impact on the dependency network at the macro-level.

However, though voluntary carers' organisations can play a role in informing the policy process at both the local and national levels, at the local level with which this study is primarily concerned, the degree to which they may be able to transform policy and practice can be limited. As the co-ordinator of one carers' organisation noted:

G25 R: ... *a lot of things go on **centrally** [local government level], for instance previously around the joint community-care plans, we did a lot of representation of carers' views which went to influencing the plans,* *and establishing carers' strategies within the plans. But you know, it wasn't actually done on the ground - you know, providing direct services there, that's a difficulty.*

This is an issue to which the book will return in chapter nine.

Advice and Information. Carers are often isolated or wrapped up in the daily processes of caring; as a consequence, a particular effort is required to get information to them regarding access and the availability of services within their locale. Carers were thus asked to describe not only the services they received, but where they accessed information on services, and to whom they went to for advice on how to obtain services and/or supports. Table 7.2 indicates the main sources of information and advice for those participating in the in-depth study and are largely reflective of the wider study.

As the table indicates, voluntary organisations provided a key site of advice and information for participant carers. What is perhaps more surprising, is the limited level of advice or information that carers were able to glean from the statutory sector - in particular, social services departments. Carers noted, that despite meetings with representatives of social services, they had not been made aware of the care supports to which they were entitled. This role had largely become the domain of informal actants such as voluntary organisations, other carers or friends. Some carers spoke of having to fight for services and the need to repeatedly contact social services to obtain services and their failure to inform carers of available aids:

GC2 R: *If I didn't phone - or **continually** 'phone - I wouldn't get anywhere, I wouldn't even have been told that this is what's available for bath aids. Whether she* [carer's mother] *can walk to the bathroom, or get into the bath by herself - they never even **ask**!*

The process of service delivery was seen to be slow. Delays have been linked to the culture of the service, i.e. the difference between voluntary organisations who aimed to deliver an immediate response, and that of the statutory sector, where response was seen in terms of months (or urgent in terms of weeks) (Wilson, 1993). There was also a difference between agency and user perceptions of services. Agency was seen to be dominated by *process*, whilst clients were seen to be more directly influenced by the services they actually *received.* One carer, with reference to her mother's declining health and her inability to sit upright, spoke of the difficulties she had experienced in obtaining a reclining chair from local authority occupational therapy services:

DGC1 R: *Em, well we had to get a new chair for mother, she started to lean forward, wi' the result that her head was right on top of her knees.*

I: *Did you manage to get that without too much difficulty?*

R: *No. She really **needed** it, but it took a bit of time for things to happen, wi' the result that it went on for a few months, em, and then I just blew my top one day, went ballistic with everybody! And then as I say, I was offered a chair within twenty-four hours!*

In part, this may be linked to the unwillingness of social services to raise carers' awareness to services that they, themselves, have limited funds to deliver. In this respect, failure to inform carers of available supports may be seen to act as a rationing device. One voluntary organisation, for example, noted in the second year of interview, that funding for its advice service to the frail elderly had been withdrawn, with the social services department undertaking to operate this service itself. The co-ordinator pointed out, however, that where they had *proactively* approached service recipients to inquire whether individuals had certain resources, or would like their entitlements checked, statutory actants undertook such checks only in a *reactive* manner. That is, that the onus was seen to fall upon the individual to approach the statutory actant to request that their entitlements be checked. As social services were seen as part of the wider structures of the state, the co-ordinator maintained that carers and cared-for were less willing to come forward for assessment. Elderly people, in particular, associated such checks with the stigmatised 'means testing' of earlier decades. Billis (1993) maintained, that in general, the role of social care services was not seen as one whose aim was to *change* the structure of society, hence, they do not deal with the causes of problems, but are more concerned with outcomes and the distribution of resources. As such, services are seen to be set up more to diffuse discontent than to change existing patterns of resource distribution i.e. they are about containment.

For many carers and cared-for, their initial point of contact with support services was through statutory agents such as GPs, nursing and hospital services. Hospital, nursing services and GP surgeries would thus appear ideal sites for the provision of advice and information to carers and cared for. As table 7.2 indicates, however, the picture was sporadic, with some GPs offering considerable advice and support and others only being visible to the carer in instances of specific medical need.

Medical practitioners, whether hospital or community based, were often seen as lacking in understanding and failing to give advice or information. Carers, for example, spoke of hospital-based medical professionals who raised expectations of services that could not be delivered once the dependent was located in the community. This highlights the need for greater communication between statutory actants operating in institutional environments, and those working in the community:

DGC4 R: *When Bill* [husband] *was in hospital, the doctor said, "Don't worry Jenny, I'll make sure you get* [psychiatric] *respite care", he saw him walking. So the social worker came about a month later and says, "Have you seen about respite yet? I don't think you'll get him in to* [psychiatric hospital] *for respite, Dr - says he's more a nursing than a mental patient". Well, I was at a carers' meeting, so I brought it up, and one of the other carers said, "Oh Jenny, that's what I was told!" So I knew then that the consultant didn't mean it, and I knew Bill wouldn't get back in.*

Of the twelve case studies, half of those respondents from Dumfries and Galloway were offered support and information from their GPs compared to only one in Glasgow. No definitive rationale for this can be offered, although voluntary co-ordinators noted that this may, in part, be linked to the specific medical interests of the GP him/herself, and thus their knowledge of the specific care issues attached to particular client groups.

Domiciliary and home-based respite. Domiciliary and home-based respite was also a key element in sustaining the carer's ability to continue their caring role. As table 7.3 illustrated, however, here provision was seen to comprise a greater mix of voluntary and statutory provision. Only one carer (Elaine) received private domiciliary provision. This carer undertook an extremely heavy caring role, caring for both her mother (aged 88) who could no longer walk or communicate verbally as a result of several strokes, and an aunt (aged 95) whose frailty included both blindness and poor mobility. As a consequence, Elaine chose to buy in *additional* private care provision from her own personal funds, over and above those care supports she received from voluntary and statutory bodies. Of the remaining seven case studies who received some form of domiciliary care, three received a mix of voluntary and statutory provision (in each case, statutory provision comprised community nursing services); two received voluntary care provision only, and of the remaining two, one had opted out of voluntary provision in the belief that it lacked the 'professionalism' of a statutory care service, the other received a bathing service delivered by community nursing services only.

Table 7.3 Sources of Domiciliary Care

Carer	Voluntary Sector	Statutory Sector	Private Sector
DGC1	✓	✓ (nursing)	-
DGC2	-	-	-
DGC3	-	-	-
DGC4	✓	✓ (nursing)	-
DGC5	-	✓ (homecare)	-
DGC6	✓	-	-
GC1	-	✓ (nursing)	-
GC2	✓	-	-
GC3	-	✓ (nursing & homecare)	✓
GC4	✓	✓ (nursing)	-
GC5	-	-	-
GC6	✓	✓ (nursing)	-

Though the statutory sector still provided a considerable proportion of domiciliary care, attempts had been made in Dumfries and Galloway to reduce the levels of in-house homecare provision in favour of contracting out to voluntary and private sector providers. Glasgow, however, with its stronger commitment to public sector provision still claimed to provide the bulk of homecare services (though only two of those carers participating in the in-depth study received their main care supports from the statutory sector). Thus, though over half the case studies received community-nursing services, the voluntary sector was found to provide the majority of non-residential respite. As one carer commented:

DGC1 R: *I don't know what I would **do** without [VO], they are my **lifeline**. They gave me my life back, because without them ..... I mean I've had the odd friend has came and **sat** to let me out. But at least they [VO] em, they put her to bed. Because there is a certain time she **needs** to go to bed, she gets tired. [VO] gave me back my life! I mean, these places have just got to be, because **without** these places, I mean, you'd crack up! It would cost the government **more**.*

Such comments highlight the increasingly important role voluntary activity is coming to play in the provision of support to carer and cared-for. However, as indicated both above and in the previous chapter, the ability of those voluntary organisations located within the network to respond to the needs of carers and cared for appears to be increasingly constrained by their ties to statutory funding and regulatory oversight.

As table 7.1 illustrated, few links exist between informal carers and the private sector within this study. This is due to the fact that, as yet, the role of the private sector in community-based care within the two areas of study is limited largely to residential respite care. While there has been some expansion of private domiciliary care in recent years (as discussed above) only one of the twelve case studies accessed this service. One other carer [Jenny] purchased private physiotherapy for her husband, a service that was not available to her through public or voluntary bodies. The role of the private sector is discussed in more detail in the following chapter.

While health services are often the initial point of contact in regard to care supports, it is the local authorities that are the gatekeepers to community-based care. Social services undertake needs assessments of both cared-for and carer (if requested) and, as indicated in chapter six, increasingly the extent of both public and voluntary care services available to the informal carer and their dependent is determined by social services criteria. Hence, for most informal carers, the social services department of the local authority is the key point of access to care supports. However, as indicated in table 7.1, this is not an indication of statutory support, rather it is indicative of the policy, planning and enabling role played by the social services department (issues discussed in more detail in chapter nine). As the following section highlights, this can vary both between and within local authority areas.

Spatial Variations in Access and Availability of Care Services

It has been argued that the changing level of care to be supplied within the family, and implicit within care reforms, has been deliberately side-stepped by the promise of 'support packages' as a means of avoiding confrontation (Brown and Smith, 1990). The qualifying criteria for receipt of these services, however, is never explicitly identified, nor is there any basic identification of what care packages may be expected to provide. The definition of such criteria is designated as the responsibility of local authorities in collaboration with locally based health professionals, and as such is subject to varying local interpretations and budgetary constraints. Further, though much emphasis is placed on the objective of tailoring services to individual needs, it is with the corollary that decisions regarding care provision "will need to take account of the local availability and pattern of services" (HMSO, 1989, para. 3.3.1). While this implies that location plays a major role in the provision and/or availability of resources, and thus the experience of carers and their dependants over space, as table 7.1 indicates, there appears no obvious spatial pattern to care support. Thus, it is suggested, that spatial variations in caring require a more subtle and detailed analysis. This is not to suggest that differences do not occur across urban and rural areas, or between areas with differing political affiliations, rather it is an issue of scale. So, for example, while a patchwork of different support services over a local authority area may *look* like choice from a planned perspective, it can in fact add up to little choice for the individual carer - there is little comfort in knowing that a carer *could* access a particular service if they lived a few miles away!

While chapter six has highlighted the existence of spatial variations in the availability of voluntary sector supports, carers too noted the existence of variations in care supports that operate at the intra-regional scale. Variations in the availability and accessibility of care supports have implications for the quality of life of both carer and cared-for. Some carers in Dumfries and Galloway, for example, were able to access daycare provision, whilst others, though still resident within the same local authority area, had different experiences of caring. This is illustrated through Jenny's story.

Jenny lives in a former mining village twenty-seven miles from the urban core. She has cared for her husband for fourteen years. Following a stroke, he is unable to walk unaided or communicate verbally. Though she received help from voluntary and nursing services, the informal networks of support available to Jenny were considerably wider than those experienced by other carers interviewed. Family and friends provided substantial support within the homespace despite the fact that her husband can no longer sustain any conversation. Though this carer felt satisfied with the amount of informal and domiciliary-based formal support available, she highlighted a lack of outside services such as daycare or family-based respite. Community care was experienced only within the homespace, no *alternative* sites of caring were available:

DGC4 R: *I mean don't get me wrong, there's nothing - he canny relate to much, I understand - I mean, I know that there's lots of places that have bingo and things, but he's past that now - no' that he ever bothered with they things, but yet when you hear about the change - they've got a lot going for folk in the towns and things.*

I: *Right. So you feel there's less in smaller communities like this?*

R: *Yes, I feel that. But as a whole, we're getting help to work with him. Its pretty good here, I will say that. But I just feel its that when you're no' able to walk - you just feel ....*

Jenny's husband is also incontinent, but cannot use the bathroom, which is up a set of stairs. The living room contains his bed, hoist, commode and wheelchair. This room is now the site in which formal and informal carers attend all his personal hygiene, feeding and medical needs. The merging of domestic space with formal service provision, combined with the lack of alternative sites of caring makes the homespace the sole locus of formal and informal care provision. Jenny's husband, along with others similarly situated within this study (for example, the dependants of Wilma and Elaine) was as much confined within domestic space, as he would have been within institutional space.

The geographical mobility of some carers within this study was also found to be, in part, determined by variable access to services both within and between local authority areas. For many frail elderly, disability is accompanied by poor mobility, requiring the use of a wheelchair or walking aids for any social interaction outside the homespace. For carers with no private transport of their own, the poor provision on public transport, dial-a-bus or similar schemes in their area of residence, meant that any negotiation of space outwith the domestic sphere or its immediate environs, involved the use of taxis. This is a costly option for those reliant on state benefits and other welfare supports and can prove prohibitive.

William cared for his grandparents in the Partick area of Glasgow. His grandmother was unable to walk unaided outwith the home. A lack of adequately adapted public transport or alternative transport schemes for wheelchair users, means that social outings necessarily involve the use of taxis (who charge additional carriage for wheelchairs). A short journey to visit a friend some three miles away, can cost between six to eight pounds for a return journey.[6] William's grandmother was entirely dependent on state benefits, and William himself worked part-time in a hotel kitchen, and as a result had had his carer's 'benefit' reduced. Low income and dependence on state benefits for both carer and cared-for in this instance, made social outings an expensive luxury. Despite the availability of a subsidised taxi-card scheme in the neighbouring district of Govan (part of the same local authority area), no such scheme operated within William's district. This highlights the ways in which differing priorities and patterns of spending between social work districts *within* a local authority area, can contribute to *intra*-authority variations in access to service provision.

Lack of access to private transport cannot be entirely attributed to income status. Carers also illustrated how this was, in part, linked to issues of gender. Whilst a number of female carers within this study had access to private transport for many years, the driving task within their households had been perceived as a male role - the female carer was not able to drive a car. Thus, with the declining health of the male household member, the female carer no longer had access to private transport. Whilst increasing numbers of female drivers mean this is likely to be a declining scenario in future years (Pickup, 1987) it is nevertheless an issue for consideration within contemporary analyses of caring. Further, it was noted that even for those *with* access to private transport, there were practical difficulties in negotiating the dependent in/out of the car without additional aid. Consequently even ready access to private transport can prove prohibitive.

Concluding Comments

By exploring how care supports are experienced at the micro level, this chapter has demonstrated some of the ways in which care restructuring has contributed to more nuanced, site-specific geographies of care. Not only can the experiences of carers and their dependants be affected by the wider context, such as changing patterns of labour and demography, but interpretations of need can differ between locales, as can the availability and ease of accessing particular resources. The picture is further complicated by attempts to redefine the responsibilities of domestic carers - and the inherent contradictions between the needs of carers and their dependants. The chapter has also illustrated, through the case studies, how a sea-change is occurring in the provision of community-based supports, much of which arrives through the voluntary sector.

The issues discussed above have also highlighted how locally-embedded networks of care can arise as consequence of variations in the formal and informal support networks available to carers, which [in part] arise as a consequence of a carer's social and spatial location. For many informal carers, their declining social networks revealed an increased dependence on voluntary and statutory supports. The experience of carers within this chapter suggests, that in terms of the dependency network, the inter-relationship between the voluntary sector and informal carers is a strong one, while that existing between informal carers and the statutory is less so, with only a weak links existing between informal carers and the private sector. The experience of informal caring is thus, to a greater or lesser extent, shaped by the ways in which care policy is translated and transformed by voluntary and statutory actants operating within the dependency network. However, as this chapter has also revealed, this is not a 'one-way street', though the ability to translate care outcomes may be asymmetrical, the inter-linkages between carers and voluntary organisations do offer some opportunities to shape the internal policy and organisational structure of voluntary carers' organisations. The extent to which voluntary organisations are able to influence actants operating at the meso-level of the network has been discussed in chapter six, and is further drawn together in the concluding chapter. Finally, while it has not been the remit of this study to consider the analysis of care restructuring at the macro-level, it is evident that voluntary carers' organisations have played a role in the translation of care at the wider (macro-) scale.

Notes

[1] Broken down, this amounts to a figure of 1.9 percent of the over 65s living in homes for the aged, 1.7 percent located in hospitals, with a further 0.9 percent located in psychiatric institutions.

[2] A factor confirmed by the day-centre manager.

[3] For example, trained nursing and auxiliary staff.

[4] Whilst this was a stated policy of homecare operators, some homecarers interviewed within the course of the study noted that the reality did not always match the policy objective - some had, in fact, received no formal training.

[5] Many of the elderly individuals within this study for example had suffered strokes or were experiencing physical and mental ill-health arising from Alzheimer's Disease or dementias.

[6] At 1997 prices.

8 The Private Sector and a Privatised Geography of Caring

Introduction

The 1989 White Paper noted that community-based care should no longer be seen as the prerogative of the public services, advocating a mixed provision of care including the encouragement of the private sector. In doing so, it noted that government "should make maximum possible use of voluntary and *private providers* and so increase the available range of options and widen consumer choice" (Cmd. 849, para. 1.11, author's emphasis). Thus, in addition to the voluntary sector and informal carers, the private sector is also viewed as a key player within the restructuring of community-based care provision for dependent groups. The private sector is potentially a huge area of study, and one which presents an alternative route through which it is possible to examine how change can be influenced within the dependency network. In considering the private sector as part of the dependency network, emphasis is placed: firstly, on giving a broad outline of the ways in which the private sector may be impacting upon the network in general; and secondly, on how the privatisation of care may be impacting on the voluntary sector in particular.

Insights into the private sector were gained through a detailed questionnaire sent to all nursing homes, domiciliary and homecare providers providing services to the frail elderly within both Glasgow and Dumfries and Galloway. As noted in chapter five, an overall response rate of 63 percent was elicited through these surveys, with a return rate of 78 percent in Dumfries and Galloway and 58 percent in Glasgow City. This gave a 'flavour' of the ways in which the private sector may impact and be impacted upon by health and social care restructuring. It should be noted that this analysis incorporates only those visible private sector providers of social welfare. As also discussed in chapter five, it is important to bear in mind, that there is a substantial level of private domiciliary care provision purchased at the level of the individual that cannot be accessed. The purchase of this care is also dependent on ability to pay, hence such provision is seen to be heavily concentrated in the higher social classes

(Leat, 1993). By focusing only on formal, organised, forms of private care that are participants within the network, these elements are absent.

The Context of Private Sector Care

The private sector has long played a role in the delivery of medical care services, in particular, private hospital and nursing provision. Within community-based health and social care, it has been most prominent in the delivery of private nursing and residential respite care. As noted in chapter three, this has been particularly evident over the last two decades, with changes to the supplementary benefits system in the early 1980s having the impact of enabling poorer frail elderly individuals to claim residential care costs. This change to the benefit system resulted in a 'mushrooming' of private residential places, with a growth of 138 percent in the period between 1981-86 (Parker, 1990 - see chapter three).

While the growth of residential care has continued (albeit at a slower pace) in the 1990s, there has been evidence of an increase in the growth of private sector services aimed at care within the homespace. Within England and Wales, this has been seen as stemming from community care legislation which has required local authorities to spend at least 85 percent of the transfer element of the Special Transitional Grant (STG) on the independent sector (Audit Commission, 1993). Recognition of the poorer development of the independent sector in Scotland meant that while local authorities were counselled to make maximum use of the independent sector wherever possible, unlike England and Wales, there was no legal requirement to allocate specific funds to the purchase of independent care services in Scotland. Within this study, for example, while 77 percent of respondents described their main function as that of residential care, only 21.5 percent were found to be delivering services solely within the homespace. The remaining 1.5 percent delivered daycare services only. However, of the 77 percent who described the delivery of residential respite as their main function, 18 percent were additionally found to be delivering services within the homespace. The majority of this group noted that these services had been initiated over a period of less than three years prior to the completion of the questionnaire. Figures 8.1 and 8.2 reveal the changing balance (as a percentage of the total) of available private care supports in the study areas over time. Both areas reveal a change in the balance of available services over the last ten years. As figure 8.1 reveals, in Dumfries and Galloway there has been a particularly noticeable growth in home-based provision in the last five years. In Glasgow, the picture appears more mixed, figure 8.2 revealing evidence that some private domiciliary care provision has operated within the area for over twenty years, though

Figure 8.1 Growth in Private Care Provision (%): Dumfries and Galloway

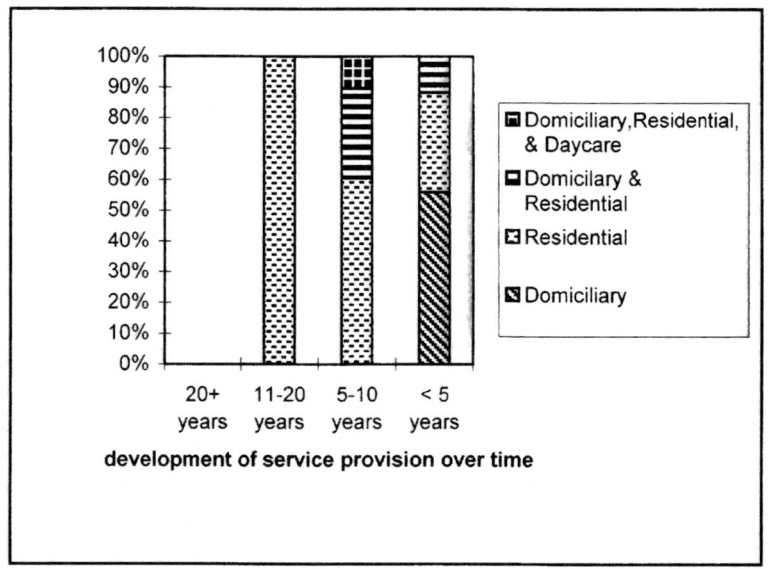

Figure 8.2 Growth in Private Care Provision (%): Glasgow City

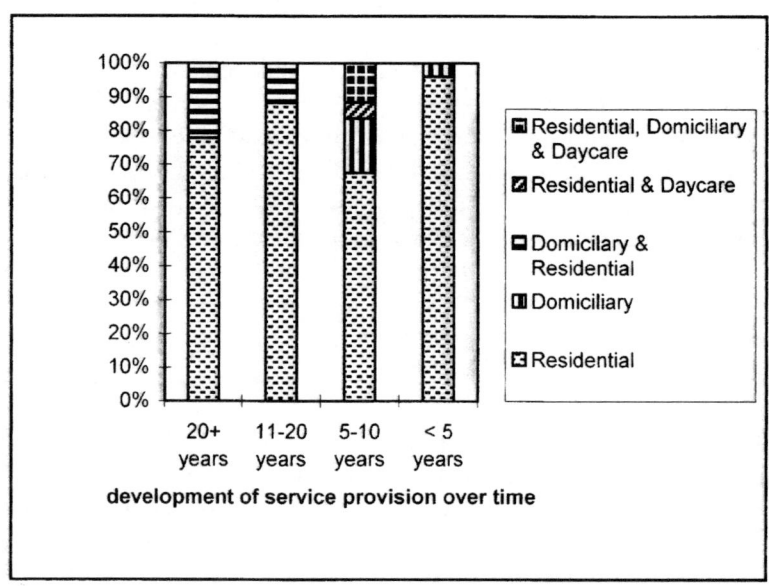

growth over the last two decades has been sporadic. The development of private sector domiciliary and daycare provision appears to be linked to a number of factors. Since 1993, the local authorities have taken over the financial responsibility for new residents of residential and nursing home care from the Department of Social Security (Family Welfare Association, 1995). Given the [re] emphasis on community-based care since 1993, and the lead role allocated to local authorities, this has resulted in a decline in local authority referrals to residential care services. This is to be expected if community-based care is to become a reality and would indicate that people *are* being maintained longer within the homespace. The local authorities, however, have been the main purchasers of private residential bed-spaces, less than 20 percent of respondents cited private clients as their main source of referral. This amounts to a figure of 22 percent in Glasgow City, but only 12.5 percent in Dumfries and Galloway. Hence as local authority referrals decline, the private sector is facing increasing difficulties:

*PG42 Q: *We have experienced difficulties in filling beds which we never had in the past, and due to the financial strictures of the local authority, they have stated funds are not available until April 1997 - a gap of at least five months. This means we are financially reduced, but are still having to maintain all services at a high level to comply with Health Board requirements, which is causing economic difficulty.*

* PG = private sector organisations in Glasgow City; PDG = private sector organisations in Dumfries and Galloway.

Service provision differs from the production of other goods, in that unlike goods, they cannot be readily stockpiled when demand is slack to meet future increased demand, nor can services be shifted with ease from one part of the country to another (Leat, 1993). As a consequence, declining referrals to residential care have meant that a number of private care homes have sought to diversify, and now provide additional services using their existing infrastructure. Private sector providers, for example, were found to be delivering a variety of services such as residential care, residential and domiciliary respite, homecare, homehelp and bathing services, meals-on-wheels, daycare, transport, nursing and telephone care-call services. However, while a large proportion of residential care homes are diversifying into long-term community-based care in Scotland, this is seen largely as a sideline (Filinson, 1998). Further, given that profit is seen as an essential element of private provision (Le Grand and Bartlett, 1993), as evident from the above list of services, those private sector providers who *are* diversifying their services, have sought only to compete in the provision of tangible services. The impact of private provision on the voluntary sector is thus largely restricted to those involved in the delivery of tangible services. Voluntary organisations within this study, for example, also noted an increase in private sector competition for the delivery of care services within the homespace:

> **G7(1) R:** *One of the things that we started off was housework and it went on from there, you know?*
> **I:** *Yes, this is an area that statutory services are increasingly moving out of now.*
> **R:** *Yes, it will be the commercial services that will do it now ... They're taking it over and making it into a bigger thing now there's money to be made in it. The same thing is happening with meals-on-wheels - the commercial services have got one on the go, which is fine. There's a franchise out there just now - people touting round to see if they can get names and addresses to deliver frozen meals and a micro-wave thing. Because there is a market out there for people that can afford it and want a meal delivered.*

The financial constraints currently being experienced by the local authority in Glasgow are also having an impact on the delivery of these additional services. Unlike voluntary care providers, whose immediate response to cuts has been to seek out alternative sources of charitable funding, or to raise additional revenue through fund-raising, this option is not open to private providers. Hence, where no alternative purchaser is available, the private sector response has been to reduce service availability:

> **PG7 R:** *Since December 1996, we have had large problems with funding, particularly with daycare provision. At present, daycare is operating five days a week, and has on average thirty clients. However, at the beginning of the new financial year, we will probably need to reduce this to two days a week. This will result in at least ten clients looking for long-term care. We are unable, due to financial constrictions, to offer home support as an alternative. This in turn will lead to clients being at risk within their own homes.*

As this comment suggests, the reduction in funding for such services as daycare *may* be contributing to a re-institutionalisation of those very individuals whom legislation has sought to maintain within the community. It further raises the question of whether the assumption that a reduction in residential referrals can be equated to a transfer of care resources to *community* environments is a correct one.

Other private sector providers noted that while legislation has aimed to reduce the role of the statutory sector as providers of health and social care in favour of a purchasing and enabling role, the degree to which local authorities have engaged with this can vary. Within Dumfries and Galloway, for example, though the local authority has attempted to withdraw from residential care by selling off its in-house provision, it has met with considerable local opposition (Dumfries Courier, 1997) and to date has been unsuccessful in achieving this goal. Similarly, a further announcement in June 1998, that the local authority proposed to withdraw from homecare provision met with such visible public opposition, that it has withdrawn its proposals (Dumfries and Galloway Standard, June, 1998). In Glasgow City, where local government remains ideologically committed to public care provision, there is no evidence of a statutory sector attempt to withdraw from its provider status. The local authority, here, remains a key provider of residential and homecare services:

PG87 R: *The social work department implies that private care is a negative option to people being assessed. This is not only unfair, but it is untrue, as the vast majority of residential homes provide a superior service at less cost than local authority or domiciliary care. The elderly are being discouraged from going in to private care. Choices, especially with respite care, are being restricted to local authority homes.*

Legislation concerned with community-based care has emphasised the need for joint-working and consultative approaches with both the statutory and informal sectors, as a means of contributing to planned care initiatives based on the knowledge-base of both care purchasers and providers. To this end, statutory authorities have been directed to implement joint planning and consultative mechanisms that involve such statutory agencies as the social work department, the Health Board and housing departments, plus representatives from the informal sector, carers and users (Cmd. 849, 1989). Private sector providers within this study were thus asked a series of questions related to their involvement in joint planning and consultative process.

Private sector input into planning initiatives and processes in both areas was low. Only 35 percent of private sector organisations in Dumfries and Galloway had been consulted in any form by statutory bodies associated with the decision-making process. In Glasgow this figure was even lower, at 31 percent. Further, a number of those who stated that they *had* been consulted, noted that consultation came in the form either of a request to complete and return a questionnaire on some topic determined by local authority researchers, or in the form of an invitation to comment on draft plans. In both cases, opportunities to contribute were limited to a written response to some pre-defined agenda. Input to the decision-making process was limited to late stages of the planning process, so constraining the private sector's ability to influence the important stages of agenda setting.

However, while organisations in Glasgow had a low degree of private sector input into the planning processes, a number of residential care organisations noted the existence of a consultative forum - the Residential Nursing Homes Association (RNHA). This *did* allow some alternative mechanism through which private sector providers could feed into the policy process. Yet despite the rhetoric of community care legislation, there was little evidence that there has been a forging of any stronger links between the private sector and statutory sector funders in Scotland (Filinson, 1998). It has, in fact, been argued, that local authority bias towards *voluntary* care providers has placed constraints on the development of private sector provision in social care (Hardy et. al, 1992). Three main factors have been highlighted:

- voluntary sector providers are seen to engender greater trust, due to their non-profit making status;
- many voluntary organisations have a long track record and a good reputation in the delivery of social care; and
- many voluntary organisations share a similar philosophy and principles to those of local authority funders.

So despite a legislative commitment to public sector withdrawal from service provision, as private sector providers within this study have noted, any encouragement of private provision within both areas has been limited. This indicates variations in the ways that local authorities seek to translate policy within locally embedded networks of care. The local authority in Dumfries and Galloway, for example, have sought to divest themselves (albeit unsuccessfully) of their provider status, whilst in Glasgow there appears a strong commitment to retaining statutory provision. It also illustrates, however, that in Dumfries and Galloway service-users have been able to marshal sufficient resources to transform the ways in which the local authority have sought to translate policy.

In addition, while there was evidence of joint working between voluntary and statutory sectors and inter-sector working within the voluntary sector, there was little evidence of any joint private/voluntary working. Though some voluntary daycare services did take individuals from private residential care without charge, organisations operating within the homespace have expressed concern about joint working arrangements:

G37(2) R: [Private organisation] *for example, they work as an agency, right? So they don't have any insurance, so if anything goes wrong, the burden lies with the carer, or the person carrying out that work. Whereas ourselves, we have insurance, if anything goes wrong, we're covered. And I have had to say to our care attendants, if there is somebody from another agency there, be very aware of what happens if anything did happen. Because there's no way* [VO] *is gonna' pick up the tab for it, you know?*

A Geography of Privatised Care

As noted previously, whilst there is a growth of private domiciliary care, a large proportion of private sector provision within the sphere of health and social care for the frail elderly is focused around residential care. Additionally, as noted, some residential homes are now looking to diversify their services, utilising their existing physical and human resource base. Whilst this is an astute business decision on the part of homeowners, it does raise the issue of access for service users. Few residential homes are purpose built; the majority are located on the basis of suitable properties for conversion. Within this study, 54 percent of respondents in Glasgow and 40 percent in Dumfries and Galloway cited the availability of suitable premises as their primary motivation for service location.

Thus for many private sector respondents within this study, location has been based less on considerations of equitable access, and more on the availability of suitable sites. As Dear and Wolch (1987) have shown, within urban areas, the search for suitable accommodation can lead to an agglomeration of services in the urban core, as the private sector seeks to buy up large, aging properties suitable for conversion made available through the process of suburbanisation. Within more rural areas, however, the search for suitable sites can lead to a reversal of this process and a dispersal of care services as providers seek suitable properties within which to locate their services. As the following comment from a key informant from within the social work department, in Dumfries and Galloway noted:

DGSW R: *We have a number of residential homes you know, they are rather arbitrarily scattered I have to say, I mean the local authority ones are located within the principle rural towns in the Stewartry, you know? That's why they've been so attractive, because they have a visibility, also they're in the local centres of population. Whilst some of the* [private] *ones that struggle, are in the more rural areas. But interestingly, if you talk to some of the more progressive establishments,*

201

the way that they're developing their services is by making them very **relevant** *to people, and I think that there's a clue there, about saying that even though they're disadvantaged in terms of their location, like they're in the middle of nowhere, em [pause] if they make themselves relevant, or offer a service that's* **attractive**, *people will use them.*

Consequently, while such sites may be relatively remote from that core of the population requiring services within the homespace, it may also be the case that in terms of serving more remote rural communities, such a diversification of provision by private residential care providers can, in fact, serve to bring care closer to these local communities.

'Privatising' the Voluntary Sector?

G70 R: *as far as I'm concerned, the local authority have actually* **turned** *voluntary organisations into private organisations.*

This chapter is presented in two parts, the first part has sought to give a flavour of the ways in which private sector organisations within the network are experiencing care restructuring. However, in considering the ways in which actants within the network may be transformed by the influence and actions of others located within the network, it is also necessary to consider not only the role of the private sector within community based health and social care, but also the impact of privatisation on the voluntary sector.

In a climate of increased competition for resources, an organisation's survival may depend on its ability to offer a better/cheaper/more comprehensive service that its competitors. Implicit within the concept of competition, is the notion that there will be winners and losers. However, for voluntary organisations whose ethos is founded on the shared concept of common benefit, competition is an alien concept. One issue for investigation within this study was, therefore, the degree to which the introduction of market principles within the caring network may be impacting upon the ability/willingness of voluntary organisations to work together for the common good.

While organisations in both areas acknowledged that their working environment was becoming increasingly competitive, the emerging picture was mixed. Though a number of organisations were indeed adopting the language and working practices of the marketplace, there was also considerable evidence of continued inter-sector working, and a reluctance to enter the competitive market with other voluntary organisations:

G54(2) R: *You know, where people are fighting for funding, and because there are different pockets of funding that we're looking to, people have said if we work together, we could maximise resources, and try to plan together so that the future is slightly more structured and decisions are clearer. Whereas I think in other situations, what it has done is, its reinforced old barriers, where people are saying, 'well we're protecting our area, you go off and do your thing', you know?*

DG2(2) R: *I think we have to make sure that what we're offering is not already there. [pause] And I think maybe voluntary organisations have to pull together more, and pool their resources - you know, if you're offering something, why should I offer it? We shouldn't really be in competition.*

Evidence from the interview material revealed examples of inter-sector working in areas such as training, shared premises, information and joint events, where voluntary organisations could benefit from economies of scale, and the referral of clients from one organisation to another (where this was viewed as being the most suitable option for the client). A more recent phenomenon was the emergence of voluntary organisations who were sub-contracting with other voluntary organisations for services, for example, the provision of meals to small specialised day-services, or the provision of specialised services as part of a package of care purchased by the local authority. Other examples revealed the mutual dependence of organisations, e.g. those providing transport to day-centres.

The interview material within this study, however, also revealed a growth of voluntary organisations that now viewed each other as competitors and were increasingly reluctant to share information and working practices. Examples of deteriorating working relationships were noted between some local voluntary organisations as the social work department re-directed the purchase of provision away from one organisation toward another:

G70(2) R: *I've been approached by a number of [voluntary] organisations in this part of the city, who have said, 'Oh, you make money from community care, can you tell us how you do it?' And obviously I'm now in the position [pause] in the past, I would happily tell anyone anything, right? Because I feel if you work in the voluntary sector, you're all in it together. But because things have changed, I am more reluctant, right?*

The aim of community care legislation has been to encourage competition for service provision - and thus the above scenario is not unexpected. It does, however, sit poorly alongside a policy whose aim has been to elevate this sector as a means of 'tapping in' to the benefits inherent within philanthropic working practices. Rather than capturing the essence of the voluntary sector (in terms of voluntarism, innovation, flexibility etc.), the translation of policy into competitive practices by local statutory purchasers is transforming the ways in which participating voluntary organisations are mediating care provision, and the internal ethos of some organisations. Indeed, it has been suggested that such change within the voluntary sector could become a stepping stone on the path to true privatisation, and once the private sector has entered the market, the voluntary sector will once again find themselves taking a back seat (Taylor, 1992). It should be noted, however, that whilst voluntary organisations acknowledge the atmosphere of competition, not all feel threatened by this development, some view the uniqueness of their particular organisation, or the specialist sector to whom their service is directed (e.g. expertise in the area of a specific illness), as relative protection from private or other voluntary sector competition.

Concern has also been expressed by voluntary providers that competition for services may inhibit continuity of care, as statutory purchasers seek the cheapest option. The shifting of the purchase of care services incurs costs not only through the loss of purchased hours of care, but also in terms of the costs incurred in the employment and training of individuals on the basis of that care. While this may be a fact of life for those operating in a competitive environment, nevertheless it can be highly detrimental for those organisations working on a non-profit basis:

G37(1) R: *What contracting has done for the various organisations, it* **has** *put us against each other, because we're here for the client, and if the client goes to another organisation - that's so many hours we've lost, and we've maybe **employed** somebody and **trained** them on the basis of having those clients.*

Though organisations have expressed the desire to keep the informal face of the voluntary sector, they have noted increasing difficulty in maintaining this in the face of an increasingly competitive environment.

Voluntary organisations have also expressed concern that in a competitive environment, the needs and wishes of the service recipient may lose out to the desire of cash-strapped statutory providers to find low-cost service alternatives. Such organisations have noted that while they are the main providers of homecare services outside the statutory sector, there is increasing evidence of low-cost private providers entering the market. This has had the impact of forcing some voluntary organisations to cut costs in the face of cheaper bids from the private sector. However, while private sector providers may undertake the basic hours of care, as voluntary organisations have argued, they do not provide the valuable advice, support and informing roles that are also undertaken by voluntary sector providers. The importance of these roles to service recipients was highlighted in the previous chapter. Further, where local authorities are entering into a process of competitive tendering, there is concern that statutory purchasers in their search for low cost options may overlook such factors:

DG11(2) R: *Private companies are out there waiting to grab the homecare, and eh* [pause] *the possibility of the competitive tendering process for homecare is causing great concern, **because** I see some of the private companies tendering is **false**, in that - 'yes, it'll be £2.10 an hour for a basic service, but if you want something else on top of that, it'll be another 90p on top of that, and travel is over and **above** that'. Whereas **** will say, 'Its £6.00 an hour, all-in - you get **everything** for that'. So the councilors sit round the table and say, 'Oh, [organisation] £6.00 an hour. What's this? Private care, £2.10!' But they don't really understand the consequences of the actual cost from the private sector. It's not a level playing field, and that needs to be made absolutely clear.*

In a study by Taylor et al (1995), for example, it was noted that one local authority, on putting homecare out to tender, received bids from a number of industrial cleaning companies. While the bids were rejected, concern was expressed with regard to the long-term prospects for the purchase of domiciliary care services. That is, that as financial constraints continue to bite within the local authorities, there are no guarantees that this attitude will prevail.

As discussed in chapter six, some voluntary organisations noted that competition can encourage an improvement in standards as organisations bid to improve both cost and quality of service provision. Nevertheless, organisations also voiced concern that they may be squeezed from the market by big business concerns. The presence of profit-taking private providers and non-profit voluntary providers creates an imperfect market, in which private providers have the reserves to enable them to undercut the voluntary sector, forcing their exit from the market. However, though organisations reported examples of having been undercut by the private sector in terms of unit cost for services, as yet there is little evidence that they have in fact been squeezed out of the market.

Competition has also encouraged an increased professionalisation amongst the voluntary sector. Though some organisations would claim that they have *always* been professional, others acknowledged that the need to compete has encouraged them to throw off the traditional 'twin-set and pearls' image often associated with the voluntary sector. Organisations have adopted a business-like approach and have increasingly refined their administrative procedures. For some national organisations, this has also included adopting a corporate approach and the rationalisation of branches, as decision-making and administrative roles have moved out of the locale to district or regional level in a bid to increase their competitive edge. In a period when national government is attempting to devolve power closer to the communities they serve (Audit Commission, 1994), this is arguably a precipitous move.

Other voluntary organisations have sought to preserve and increase their presence within the field of health and social care through the formation of associations based on size of turnover, that bear a close resemblance to the formation of cartels:

G25(1) R: *I think that's proving that that's the way that it will go, that it will become like big business, and big organisations will swallow up small organisations - I think those sorts of aspects are there.*

Organisations in Dumfries and Galloway noted that competition for resources has already caused the amalgamation of two complementary service providers. This emphasis on size, and the statutory sector preference for dealing with larger organisations, has also been raised by private sector providers. Those who form part of a wider consortium of private care provision appear to have greater access to provision than do their smaller counterparts:

PG65 Q: [Nursing home] *is part of* [large consortium]. *We are in partnership with the GGHB and all our residents are admitted from* **** *hospital.*

PG59 Q: *Rightly or wrongly, small independent homes have felt under pressure since 'community care' started. The Health Board now states that they wish to encourage such local units, but offer no encouragement or support.*

This was particularly evident in Glasgow City, where 49 percent of all private care providers responding to the questionnaire, were shown to be part of a wider regional, national or international company. This compares to just 25 percent in Dumfries and Galloway, where the size of the potential customer base is more limited. In Dumfries and Galloway, 75 percent of private sector provision was made up of independent locally-based organisations.

Thus there are clearly variations in form, scale, size, distribution and organisation of private providers, that as with the voluntary sector, point to the internal heterogeneity of the private sector (Parker, 1990). Unless steps are taken to counteract the impact of these developments on small organisations, it could [at its most extreme] result in smaller voluntary and private organisations being swallowed up or squeezed out of the market by large private providers, with larger voluntary organisations increasingly taking on the characteristics of the private sector.

As a consequence, it would appear that small private sector care providers can experience similar problems to those experienced by their voluntary sector counterparts. Some smaller organisations have been noted to voice real concerns over caring values with the entry of big corporate firms from other areas of the economy into the market. In particular, there is evidence of an influx of firms whose primary interests lie in such diverse areas as construction, insurance and breweries. Fears have been voiced that these large corporate providers are more likely to be concerned with increased profit margins, than is likely to be the case with small residential homeowners (Taylor et al, 1995).

Concluding Comments

This chapter, has revealed a number of ways in which the private sector may be impacting on, and being transformed by, the dependency network. The growth of private sector provision within the homespace for example, appears to be, in part, mediated by the ways in which local authorities translate policy into practice within locally embedded networks of care. The degree to which local authorities engage with legislation enacted by central government (by seeking to divest themselves of their provider status) combined with the decline in local authority referrals to private residential care, has contributed to a diversification of private providers into domiciliary care. However, it is also evident that the actions of care recipients within the network have also acted to constrain the ability of local authorities to translate policy in a way that would encourage private sector growth. And while private sector diversification has been seen to contribute to increased provision in remote locales, the availability of services has also been seen to be a function of suitable premises rather than considerations of enhanced access for the service user.

With regard to the impact of the private sector on voluntary organisations linked within the network, to date, any growth in private sector provisioning is likely to have a transformative effect only on those voluntary providers concerned with the provision of tangible services. For these organisations, however, increased competition is transforming their voluntary ethos, i.e. through a reduction of their willingness to work together, and through a 'privatisation' of their working practices as they bid to remain competitive. The preference of local authorities to engage with larger, 'professional' organisations, appears to be causing larger voluntary organisations to take on the characteristics of the private sector as they compete for resources and attempt to increase their visibility and power in the decision-making processes. This, however, may well be at the expense of smaller organisations within both private and voluntary sectors.

9 Statutory Influences on the Geography of Caring

Introduction

There are two main aspects to the restructuring of health and social care. The first is concerned with social and spatial change. The preceding chapters of this book, for example, have discussed the move away from institutional care to community-based environs, and the implications of this move for voluntary, private, and informal care-givers. The second aspect of restructuring concerns the redefinition of state responsibilities for the social welfare of the population - effected by public sector retrenchment - and the move toward alternative informal and private sector care provision. The legislative context within which this has occurred has been discussed in chapter three. The concern of this chapter is to examine how the statutory sector can act to translate and transform care and policy outcomes within locally-embedded networks of care, and the impact this may have on the voluntary sector.

The nature of the relationship between the formal and informal sector has been an integral part of this project, in that the study has attempted to illuminate how and why actors and agencies respond in particular ways. As argued in chapter four, to understand the impact of change on any particular agency located within the dependency network it is necessary to negotiate a path *through* it, and investigate the links between actors and agencies located within it. There is also a need to examine power relations, and the ways that these are manifest through such mechanisms as sub-contracting, strategic alliances, and inter-collaborations (Cooke and Morgan, 1993). Within health and social care, this may be particularly evident in the differential ability of agencies to exert influence within the policy, planning, purchasing and implementation processes. As a consequence, this chapter is also concerned to examine the ways in which restructuring has become manifest in shifting power relationships within the statutory sector, relationships between the statutory and informal sectors, and what this may mean for voluntary organisations located within the dependency network.

Revisiting the Network

The dependency network identifies three key statutory agencies as having an integral role to play in the process of health and social care delivery to the community:

- the Social Services;
- the Health Authority; and
- the Housing Department.

While legislation identifies the local authority social services departments as having the lead role, the input of both health and housing are also viewed as essential for the successful delivery of any comprehensive care programme (Cmd. 849). As illustrated in figure 4.1, this has effected a change in the power relationships between local authorities and that of health authorities. Local authorities now have the lead responsibility for defining the care needs of the frail elderly and other community-care groups.

In view of this elevation of the local authority within the caring network, three important issues merit examination:

(i)   the degree of influence social work committees [1] are able to exert on the direction of locally-based care policy;
(ii)   the changing role of the social services (SWDs), the housing departments (H), and that of local health authorities (HAs); and
(iii)   inter- and intra-sectoral relationships.

These issues were examined through the interview responses of key informants from each of the statutory agencies mentioned above, plus social work committees (SWC) in the two study areas. The aim was to examine how statutory agencies operating within localised contexts translate centrally-determined legislation, and the degree to which this is manifest in differentiated policy outcomes, with implications for locally-based care providers.

While the legislative frame has been discussed in chapter three, there are a number of issues that are of key importance to this chapter:

(i) the legislation requires that local authorities should seek to reduce their role as direct providers of health and social care, in favour of an *enabling* role. The emphasis is on increasing the role of the voluntary/non-profit and private sectors (Cmd. 849, para. 10.4). Sub-contracting to locally-based voluntary and private sector care providers is a key mechanism for achieving this objective;

210

(ii) where the distinction between health and social care is blurred, health and local authorities are required to collaborate, and to decide how to share the objectives, responsibilities and funding of different services; and
(iii) there is a need for close co-operation between agencies within both formal and informal sectors for the purposes of joint planning. Local authorities in Scotland are required to prepare clear plans in conjunction with Health Boards, housing authorities, the voluntary and private sectors and informal carers (Scottish Office, 1993).

These issues underscore some of the key linkages and inter-relationships between statutory and non-statutory actants within the dependency network.

Democratising Care and the Local Policy Process

Variations in the implementation of care legislation can impact on other actors and agencies at local level. As a result there can be differences in the interpretation and implementation of care provision, and consequently the emergence of locally-embedded networks of care. In allocating the lead role to local authorities, not only does the legislation redefine care for the frail elderly as a *social* rather than a *medical* provision, but it places local decision-making with regard to care firmly within the democratic process. That is, the interpretation of centrally determined legislation is [at least theoretically] determined by locally elected representatives. One outcome of this is that as the political make-up of the committee structure can differ between local authority areas, so too can the ideological basis upon which local decision-making is taken. This can result in variations in the emphasis placed on particular aspects of health and social welfare.

Within Glasgow, the political make-up of the local government in 1997 was left-of-centre. Members of the Labour party formed the majority of elected representatives within the committee structure. At national government level, political representation for Glasgow was also dominated by the Labour party, presenting unity in the ideological persuasion of elected representatives for Glasgow at both meso- and macro-levels of government. The political make-up of elected representation in the Dumfries and Galloway local government structure differed from that of Glasgow. The largest grouping of elected representatives here, was made up of independent councillors, and - up until the 1997 general election - national representation was firmly right-of-centre Conservative. This last election saw the region split between Labour and Scottish Nationalist representation. Within the time-scale of the study, however, there has been no outwardly visible manifestation of this change in terms of health and social care provision.

One outcome of these differences in democratic representation has been that the local authority in Glasgow has largely retained its commitment to public provision for such services as local authority nursing homes and home-care services. Until recently, these services have been seen as integral to a Labour-based ideology, based on collective provision. Within Dumfries and Galloway, however, there have been attempts to divest the local authority not only of its in-house nursing home provision and (more recently) its home-care services, but also of its commitment to day-centre service for the elderly. Nevertheless, despite a clear willingness of both elected and non-elected bodies within the local authority to divest themselves of these public services, attempts to do so have met with considerable public protest, forcing the local authority to retain its in-house provision (Dumfries and Galloway Standard, 1998). However, [at least] with regard to home-care services, it has been suggested that the social services may be adopting an alternative route to divesting itself of this service. There is evidence, for example, of a gradual reduction of service through natural wastage and its replacement by externally purchased services from both voluntary and private care providers (Dumfries and Galloway Standard, 1998).

Despite local variations in the political make-up of the local committee structure, it was evident that there were limitations to the local authorities' ability to mediate centrally-determined legislation. As a key figure from within the social work committee in Dumfries and Galloway noted, decision-making in regard to community care was largely driven by two factors:

- available resources (indicating decision-making is largely budget-driven); and
- the need to take account of current legislation enacted by central government:

DGSWC I: *How is local policy formulated, is it within the social work* **committee**?

R: *Its formulated within the social work committee. Sadly a lot of it is budget driven. Now, we look at what we have, we've got to take into account, em, legislation that comes to us, like the Children's Bill, which we got this year. We've got to decide as a committee how much we can implement, em ... we've got to decide what we **want** for*

Dumfries and Galloway, and the Director [of social services] *puts it into an acceptable and a legal form.*

This view was reinforced by key figures from within the local authority in Glasgow City. As representatives of the respective local governments have indicated, visibility, and consequent resource targeting, are subject to swings in political favour. It was noted in the final year of interviews, for example, that resource allocation within social services was being driven by the recent implementation of the Children's Act. This required local social services to redirect funding previously allocated to *other* areas, in a bid to put this centrally determined legislation into practice (in essence, 'robbing Peter to pay Paul'). In previous years, the political spotlight on *carers* had had a similar impact on the direction of social services' budgets, inducing the local authority to redirect more resources within the budget to the needs of this particular group. This was seen to have had a variable impact on the ability of voluntary organisations to access resources through local authority actants:

G25 (1) R: *... at the moment with carers, because if you like, carers are 'flavour of the month' ... there is that feeling that, you know, people* [within the local authority] *feel that they've got to be doing something for carers, otherwise how are their services gonna' survive? There's almost a wee 'get out' for us there as an organisation, you know? So we maybe don't have to produce quite the detail and the quantity of evidence to get funding that other areas are doing.*

G25 (2) I: *Last year you commented, that carers organisations were likely to continue being funded because of the high profile that carers had at the time. Has there been any significant change in that, are they still seen as high profile?*

R: *Mmm, no, I think its moving. I think one of the things we've seen - certainly as far as the Children's Act becoming the latest piece of legislation - is all the planning structures and personnel within the local authority and social work, has moved to that sort of area. Em, there seems to be quite a large vacuum - all the work that went on in planning, and getting involved in all of that [for carers' organisations] seems to have disappeared to a large extent. So there's been a move, something else is sort of 'flavour of the month'.*

I: *You seem to be suggesting, that different groups become politically favourable for a while?*

R: *Yeah. I think there was a window for carers, and I think that window disappeared at the same time as reorganisation came about.*

Such responses illustrate, that despite variations in the political make-up of local government, and the [theoretical] devolvement of decision-making responsibilities regarding community-care to the meso-level, political ideology and policy agendas stemming from the national level play an important role in shaping the frame.

Care, Conflict and Co-operation Within the Statutory Sector

Care restructuring and the changing locus of care has effected a move away from the focus on bio-medical models towards social models of care. While legislation requires local authorities to collaborate with health professionals in a joint consultation and planning process, the onus of ensuring the care needs of the elderly are met falls within the remit of local authority departments, and in particular that of the social services. As a consequence, social services departments, rather than health professionals, [2] have the lead role in determining the care needs of the frail elderly residing within their jurisdiction.

At the time that this study was undertaken, funding for the implementation of these services was allocated to local authorities from the Scottish Office on a capitation basis. As key informants from within the local authorities noted, however, this formula took little account of local need, and the differing circumstances experienced by urban and rural authorities. Further, the expectation inherent within the legislative context has been one in which additional funding for the implementation of community-based care initiatives would be made available through Resource Transfer monies (or Decrement) from the Health to the local authority. That is, that as institutional care facilities owned and operated by Health Authorities were gradually run-down in favour of care delivered within the domestic sphere, additional capital would become available from funds released through the phasing out of institutional or hospital care. It was envisaged that such capital would be transferred from Health to local authorities for the implementation of community-based care provision.

While theoretically this appears a rational *modus operandi*, a major drawback has been the lack of clarity regarding the boundary between those services defined as the responsibility of social services and those defined as falling within the remit of community health services (Butcher, 1995; Lewis and Glennester, 1996):

DGHB I: *One of the difficulties in trying to implement community care was argued to arise from the difficulties of determining the boundaries between what was seen to be health and what was social care - and ultimately that came down to a question of who paid for what. Do you find that that has effectively been ironed out now?*

R: *It actually forced a **reinforcement** of the boundaries. People come with very confused labels - you know, they say they're maybe 60 percent health, 40 percent social and vice-versa. I remember one particular service, and **neither** health nor social work wanted to **buy** this service beyond its original pump-priming year, and we said, "why?" - because everybody says this is a good service, and the Health Board said, "Because we don't know what's health, and we don't know want to buy anything else" and Social Work services were saying, "Oh, we don't know what's **social** and we don't want **theirs**!"*

There has, for example, been much debate with regard to such issues as the 'social or nursing bath' and the provision of specialist equipment (Twigg, 1990, 1997). These factors were still much in evidence within both areas in which the study was undertaken. Bathing and tuck-in services, in both Glasgow and Dumfries and Galloway, were still found to be variously undertaken by community nursing and homecare services. Whilst domiciliary bathing services for those suffering frailties and/or ill-health had in the past been the remit of community nursing, following the implementation of the NHS and Community Care Act, this has been increasingly seen as the remit of social services. Though legislation has indicated that agencies involved in community-based care should collaborate where such blurred boundaries occur, the reality has been that in a period of resource shortages this lack of clarity has created tensions. Agencies have sought to achieve cost savings through redirecting responsibilities for such services (and thus the costs incurred) to alternative statutory agencies. Indeed, Twigg (1997, 213) has gone as far as to argue that, "As cost pressures have borne down on the NHS there has been a tendency ... to retreat back to the medical heartlands of acute hospital care ... that represents 'real medicine', the territory whose status is high and unambiguous, as opposed to the grey areas of long-term and community based care whose status is low and whose legitimacy as part of medicine is less certain". This also draws attention to the way in which community-based care has been seen as a less 'professional' aspect of healthcare by the medical community - a factor apparent in the relative lack of training homecarers receive in comparison to nursing and auxiliary nursing staff.

A second issue related to the issue of decrement, is the degree of inertia in the changeover from institutional to community-based service provision. Demand for community-based services has increased, yet some service recipients still remain within hospital care. As a consequence, the freeing-up of resource transfer funds has not been contiguous with the need to implement community-based services. While some bridging finance exists, this has been directed largely at community care groups with learning disabilities and those experiencing mental ill-health - this does not apply to vast numbers of the frail elderly.

As illustrated below, notable tensions have arisen between health and social services, as claims have been made that health authorities have been 'dragging their heels' in releasing available resource transfer monies. In part, this has been linked to increasing unit costs as beds numbers decline but wards remain open. However, it has also been noted that health authorities have been unwilling to divest themselves of capital and infrastructure, and have sought to use released capital to expand their own community nursing services and/or find alternative uses for infrastructure:

DGHA I: *In the past, its been indicated that there are tensions between the social services and health authorities, or that housing in the past hasn't always been seen as integral to community-care - how do you think that is developing within this area?*

R: *Well, the health-social services thing - I think that's a continued area of tension. I think primarily, because so much of the money that's* **needed** *to actually make a reality of community-care policies, is currently tied up in institutional provision in the health service - servicing a very small minority of the overall population in need. And so, wherever you've got a situation where you actually need to effect the* **transfer** *of funding out of one sector into another - and under government policy it actually formally requires Health to* **give up** *resources and pass them on to local authorities, there* **is** *tension, and there will continue to be tension. In Glasgow, that is undoubtedly the case.*

For Glasgow City, tensions between the health and local authorities have been aggravated by the restructuring process. Whilst in Dumfries and Galloway the boundaries between the local and health authorities remain coterminous, for Glasgow City, the local authority now forms one of *six* local authorities whose boundaries overlap with those of the Greater Glasgow Health Board (GGHB). Whilst Glasgow City is the largest of these six authorities, with its boundaries lying entirely within those of the GGHB, the Health Board is, nevertheless, in the position of having to co-ordinate policy with several local authorities.

In contrast to health and social services, housing has tended to take a back-seat in the community-care process:

DGH I: *You touched on your role within strategic planning, how are you **involved** in health and social care policy formulation with regard to your role within the delivery of community based care?*

R: *Not really to any great extent. I mean, I think that's one area that still has to be thrashed out. Em, Social Services and Health, I think, and ourselves in Housing, we agree our own policies, and em, we sort of do our own thing although its run through a sort of corporate core to make sure there's some sort of cohesion to it. But for example, if you had to ask anyone here what Social Services' policy was on x, y, or z - most of them wouldn't have a **clue**! And equally, social services, if you asked them about various things on housing policies - then blank expressions all round from the vast majority! There's still an awful lot of people keen to protect their own turf if you like, whereto it be at management level or at elected member level, or just at that sort of customer level. Customer's of Housing services aren't necessarily perceived as customers of social services - there's still an independent identity, though there are **strands** of policy that are going to overlap.*

Key figures within the Housing departments of the respective local authorities drew attention to the differing attitudes key players within the statutory sector held toward the role of their agency within the process of delivering community-based care. In Dumfries and Galloway, for example, it was evident that community care was viewed as occupying a fairly minor role in the wider housing remit and, as such, the time and human resources that the housing department was willing to devote community care planning was limited:

DGH I: *how important do you think key individuals are in the purchase and delivery of services in the area?*

R: *Absolutely! I mean, I think its one of the important **tricks** in many ways, trying to identify the key players in every organisation. And its*

217

not necessarily the obvious people who can make things happen, or know **how** *the resources work, or have the relevant contacts at the operational level - and make sure they're involved in the appropriate parts of the processes. In some ways, although there's a Joint Strategy Group involving the Director of Social Services, the General Manager of the Health Board and the Director for Housing Services,* **our** *director actually takes the view that she doesn't necessarily want to get involved - she's not the key player - she's involved in a hundred and one things - in many ways, either myself or my op have more* **direct** *contact at an operational level, and we know how things happen.*

A figure within the Housing department in Glasgow also commented on the lack of lack of co-operation they had experienced with other statutory actants, resulting in unsuitable housing options being made available for deinstitutionalised individuals:

GH I: *Do you work together at all [with health and social services] in assessing areas of need and so on?*

R: *We do our assessment and they do theirs! ...er .. its a sore point, because for example, the whole of the Hospital Resettlement Programme -* **nobody** *from Housing has been* **allowed** *in to assess! And I think that's a* **big** *gap, and I think we're suffering the problems as a result. As an anecdote, we'd identified a property for a client coming from the Hospital - the Hospital and Social Work Team had assessed, and told us* **what** *they were looking for. We spent a considerable amount of money taking that property up to standard, the social work department had viewed the property, the care agencies had been to the property - and together we'd done all the work. We took the* **client** *out to view the property, after everything was* **done** *of course - the client doesn't get any say* **really** *in what he's or she's getting. The client arrives - the person had* **lived** *all their life - in* [institutional care] *in a* **flat** *environment, had never* **had** *to walk upstairs, or if they're* **faced** *with stairs, they can't cope with them! And yet medical, social work ....* **nobody** *had picked that up! Now that's just an example of, I believe, where Housing people* **do** *need to be more involved.*

While tension between statutory organisations concerned with community care was still evident in both areas, there was evidence of a growing awareness for the need for co-operation, with attempts being made to overcome intra-sectoral conflict through increased collaboration. At the time of interview, for example, both health and social services in Dumfries and Galloway were in the process of physically integrating their departments within one building. The stated aim of this move was the hope that such close physical proximity would lead to the development of a similarly close working relationship and, to this end, they were in the process of developing a Joint Commissioning Team for community-based services. In Glasgow, Health and Housing authorities had recently developed a joint Housing Procurement Team for the provision of community-based housing for frail elderly, mentally and physically disabled individuals leaving long-term institutional care. Such developments were aimed at overcoming some of the problems identified by key informants above.

Within both areas, however, it was evident that the lack of resources with which to implement community care policies are a key feature. Local authorities - and social services in particular - have been hard hit by budgetary constraints. Contiguous with the legislative requirement that local authorities undertake the lead role in community-based care provision, they have experienced cutbacks in funding from central government and growing demand for services at locality level. The Glasgow City Authority, for example, faced a £3 million deficit in 1997 (Sinclair, 1997). Inevitably such an overall deficit filters through the various local authority departments, percolating down to those voluntary organisations in receipt of local authority funding - either in the form of grants or contracts for purchased services. One voluntary organisation contracting with the social work department in Glasgow, for example, noted a loss of £20,000 of community care funding in 1997. Others had funding cut completely within some social work districts causing some organisations to be unable to continue providing a service in these specific locales.

In part, therefore, it can be seen that the uncertain environment within which the voluntary sector works (as highlighted in chapter six) is a reflection of the uncertainty also faced by local authorities, who are themselves unsure of the funding they are likely to be allocated by central government. Inevitably there is a 'knock on' effect as the local authority passes on these budgetary cuts, through reduced funding to voluntary and other informal service providers. In the process, the local authority is seen to draw up the safety net, as care provision becomes increasingly directed at those most in need. This uncertainty leads to a form of short-term planning, characterised more by reactive, rather than proactive, policies. Such outcomes give rise to a growing mismatch between: a) needs and expectations; and b) the ability to deliver services, given current budgetary constraints.

Thus, as illustrated, while the legislative frame requires co-operation between those statutory actants charged with the planning and delivery of community-based care, a number of factors can also act to shape and constrain these inter-relationships. Three in particular have been highlighted here:

- the lack of clarification of the roles and responsibilities of statutory bodies charged with the implementation of community-based care can create tensions between social services, health and housing;
- constraints on resources available to social services with which to implement community-based alternatives to meet the needs of particular care groups. This can arise from: the changing agendas of national governments; an in-built inertia in the system of decrement; and a tendency to 'turf protection'; and
- variations in the perceived importance of the role particular statutory bodies play in the process of community-based care, can create tensions in the working relationships between actants.

Dependency Networks and Asymmetrical Power

The government wishes to strengthen public accountability for the delivery of community care. Local Authorities will be required to prepare clear plans in conjunction with Health Boards, housing authorities, voluntary agencies including housing associations and the private sector which define objectives and targets and describe procedures for monitoring progress towards the achievement of effective community care (Cmd. 849, para 10.7).

There is an expectation that local authorities will implement joint-planning procedures, involving both statutory and informal agencies concerned with the provision and delivery of community-based care. This indicates that the informal sector is viewed as having more of an elevated role to play in the decision-making process than has been the case in previous care arrangements. To this effect, current statutory sector documentation is littered with references to 'partnership', 'negotiation' and 'empowerment', words that in conjunction with joint-planning, promote the notion that the informal sector has a significant role to play in informing and influencing the planning process. Such references advance the conception that, within the dependency network, symmetry exists in the power relationships between agencies located within the formal and informal sectors. It would therefore be anticipated, that a mutually reflexive influence existed between voluntary and statutory sectors.

Three key factors affect a voluntary agency's ability to influence the planning process:

- the existence of a well-developed joint-planning framework within the local authority area in which they are located;
- the ability of a voluntary agency to *access* that framework - either directly, or through an representative intermediary; and
- the *level* at which the voluntary agency is able to access the planning framework.

The existence of a clearly defined joint-planning framework cannot be taken as a 'given' within local authority structures. Whilst a clear planning framework had existed under the previous Strathclyde regional structure with voluntary sector representation within the higher tiers of the joint-planning framework, following local authority restructuring in 1996, these structures fell into disarray. Though joint-planning still occurred between statutory sector bodies in Glasgow (despite somewhat strained relationships), by the final year of interview, voluntary sector inclusion within any joint-planning mechanism had broken down completely:

G18(2) R: *Last May we went to the social work department and said, 'look, enough is enough, we know that you had a problem last year, we know you had the fallout from local authority reorganisation and we've been very patient, but you really need to get a grip of yourself now in terms of voluntary sector input into community care planning.' ... But despite verbal assurances, still nothing has emerged. Eighteen months after the breakdown of any sort of input from users, carers or voluntary organisations into community care planning - eighteen months after that, we're still waiting for some new structure, which has not yet been implemented, and which we haven't actually seen yet.*

Voluntary organisations also noted that when challenging the statutory sector with regard to their exclusion from the joint-planning process, the response had been that as no framework existed for private sector representation, to include the voluntary sector would be inequitable. Nevertheless, as indicated above, in the final year of interview there *were* indications that the local authority was once again moving toward the development of an integrated joint-planning framework, though this framework still awaited implementation in 1998.

Hence voluntary sector access and influence within the formal policy and planning process in Glasgow since local government reorganisation had been minimal. Access had been reduced to the ability of organisations to exert influence through informal channels, or at grassroots-level, where working relationships may be closer. It was clear, for example, that though variations existed *between* social work districts in Glasgow, within some districts, attempts had been made to implement consultative structures at more localised levels:

> **G54(2) I:** *Last year you mentioned that you had no input into the planning structures and the Joint Planning Forum, has there been any development in that area?*
>
> **R:** *Mhmm! I would say that this year, that just hasn't been a realistic goal, because eh - there's just **not** been a clear process for that kind of Joint Planning. Particularly because in Glasgow, there's been **so** much happening, and social work is about to go though **another** reorganisation! So joint-planning really has been very difficult ... Having said that, we've been involved in decision-making forums in Castlemilk for voluntary organisations involved in community care services. I was involved in that as an advocacy project, and that's been really positive. There's some joint sessions being planned in October, between the forum and the social work teams, so we can exchange information, so that's **beginning** to happen.*
>
> **I:** *Right, so there's little pockets of joint structures developing on a more localised basis?*
>
> **R:** *Yeah, yeah, that's it. As I say, people I think are just trying to make sense where they can of the surrounding chaos basically! And I really don't want to be too hard on the social work, because I think it really has been difficult for people ... I mean I think the voluntary sector certainly has been very **badly** hit, but I think you can see where its hit social work as well, and other agencies.*

Glasgow North West District, prior to reorganisation, had also had a liaison group in place. Voluntary and local project managers were able to put across their views to representatives from the district social services, so offering the informal sector *some* channels through they were able to feed-in to localised decision-making processes. While this form of structure allows for some grassroots participation within the policy process, voluntary sector input at this level was clearly limited and was dependent on the view of one key individual within the statutory sector (in this case the district manager) whether or not these issues would be taken forward to a higher tier of the planning process:

G20 (2) I: *You were saying that you felt that the relationship with the statutory sector could be improved by more collaborative working. I was wondering if you could just clarify what you mean?*

R: *I think that is to do with joint planning and development generally. We're maybe not as involved as we might be. We did have a liaison group that was meeting in the north-west, then it all changed when the personnel changed. But it wasn't really a planning group, it fed **into** the planning system if we had particular concerns about what was going on.*

I: *If that was feeding in to the planning process, was there a representative of the voluntary sector that took that forward?*

R: *No, it was the District Officer - he would present those - we didn't really have a direct link into what happened.*

I: *Right, so to your knowledge, there's no representative from the voluntary sector sitting on the joint planning board?*

R: *None whatever - if they **are**, information certainly isn't being fed back. I don't know WHO they* [social services] *are consulting with on development issues. But if you don't have a voice, then you don't know the best way forward, or you don't understand what all the variables are - and its very difficult to make a difference.*

These interview excerpts illustrate a commitment (at least at the lower levels of the planning and implementation process) to consult with the informal sector. However, as these organisations have noted, the numerous internal changes within the social services, arising, in part, as a consequence of local authority reorganisation in Glasgow City, has meant that ultimately these liaison processes have tended to be sporadic.

Contrary to Glasgow City, Dumfries and Galloway has a clearly defined joint-planning framework. As figure 9.1 illustrates, the framework consist of a two-tier mechanism for planning and policy formulation, the upper tier comprises a Joint Strategy Group (JSG), made up of chief officers (at director/assistant director level) of the Social Work, Housing Department and the Health Board, whose role is to develop strategy based

Figure 9.1 Joint Planning Framework - Dumfries and Galloway

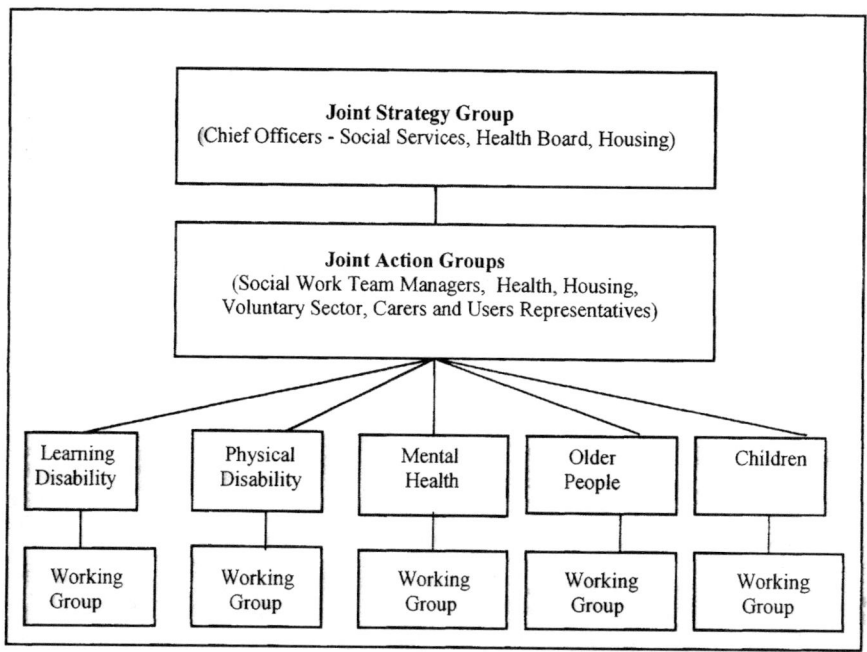

on initiatives spiralling up from the lower tier. The lower tier incorporates a series of fora - five Joint Action Group (JAGs) - one for each of the defined care groups (older people and dementia; mental health; learning disability; physical disability; children and younger people). JAGs are made up of lower-level representatives from each of the statutory agencies (e.g. Team Managers from the social services department) plus representatives from the voluntary sector.

The JAGs are seen as fora through which initiatives formulated at grassroots level can be introduced to the planning process and taken forward - if gaining approval - for consideration and funding approval by the JSG. Statutory officers describe the JAGs as playing a powerful role in the planning and policy process:

> **DGSW R:** *The JAGs are - well they're not called strategic groups, but they are incredibly powerful I think. They don't **think** they are powerful, but I wouldn't dream of commissioning a new service if it hadn't come through a JAG. I feel they are enormously important.*

Examples were given of initiatives passed through the JAGs that included the development of policy for inter-agency guidelines on responses to service-user views, the defining of health and social care, and consideration of issues concerning respite care and day services.

This view of the power of the joint-planning framework, however, is not held universally. Non-statutory bodies have no representation within the upper tier of the planning framework, and as the following response illustrates, contrary to the claim of the statutory sector respondent, voluntary sector respondents view the lower tier as having been constructed more as a consultative body, rather than having an integrated role to play in policy formulation:

DG11(2) I: *Do you see these Joint Action Groups as .... more a consultative body, or do you see them as having a more integrated role in the planning process?*

R: *Mhmm - I think they **should** be more integrated, and more ... authoritative ... but they are essentially consultative roles, where you have a collection - an intellectual collection - of em ... often like-minded people ... its essentially self-selection onto these things, you don't tend to get a ... or rather, you tend to get the kind of people who actually want to **improve** conditions for older people - and there's nothing wrong with **that**, but sometimes you wonder if, if they actually at the end of the day have any **teeth**!*

I: *Yes. What's your **own** opinion of that?*

R: *I don't think they **have** got any teeth.*

The above quote also illustrates the arbitrary selection of voluntary and informal sector agencies onto the JAGs, hence its representativeness is questionable. This issue was further highlighted by a number of smaller voluntary organisations within the study, who were either unaware of the existence of such a body, or lacked any form of representation within it (either in terms of their own organisation, or some intermediary organisation representing their views). Despite the presence of this clearly defined joint-planning framework, as the questionnaires revealed, only 40 percent of respondent voluntary organisations in Dumfries and Galloway had some form of representation within the JAGs. In Glasgow, prior to reorganisation, this figure *had* been higher at 57 percent, though as noted above, restructuring had brought about considerable disruption to the joint-planning process, with the structure collapsing completely by the final year of interview. Thus, with regard to the voluntary sector's ability to *access* the joint planning framework, within this study, (even in the first year of interview) only 51 percent [in total] of voluntary agencies responding to the questionnaire had either participated directly in the joint-planning process or were represented by some intermediary body.

Within Dumfries and Galloway, however, there was evidence of further attempts to consult with voluntary organisations regarding the direction of local policy. Designated Link Officers [3] from within the social services attended the Voluntary Sector Forum to discuss grants, co-operation and voluntary sector policy. Though this forum was only in its second year, it was viewed by the local authority as providing the interface between the voluntary and statutory sector with the aim of generating wider consultation and greater harmonisation between the two bodies. Voluntary sector representatives were viewed as representing *networks* of organisations, thus their role was to feed information out to other organisations, and to collate information from voluntary organisations located within the community, to feed in to the forum itself.

Though such fora are testimony to a nominal commitment to integrated planning and policy approaches, questions are raised here with regard to the *process* by which voluntary organisations gain seats upon these consultative and decision-making bodies. The emphasis within both areas is on *selected* representation; that is, selected by actors from within the statutory sector. However, as the following responses highlight, the ability of the statutory sector to select informal sector representatives has implications for the symmetry of power relationships within the planning process:

G18(1) R: *There is a tendency in Glasgow for statutory organisations to prefer to talk to 'tame' voluntary organisations rather than challenging ones. This is a big problem, especially in relation to the social work department which likes voluntary organisations to be deferential. If you are too articulate or too challenging, they get threatened. There is still a widespread feeling of patronising and controlling attitudes. The word 'empowerment' is widely used but seldom translated into reality.*

G25(1) I: *You were talking about joint planning, how are voluntary sector representatives selected onto the joint planning boards, or do voluntary organisations choose themselves?*

R: *That's a good question! We got onto the Joint planning Forum because we were **asked** on to the Joint Planning Forum! I don't know why they* [social services] *chose us - in some aspects, I suppose* *we're seen as quite a 'clean-cut' organisation. There's a number of bodies who I think **want** to be involved there, in the planning structures, and are **not** represented or whatever. Its a good question, I don't know why, I don't know how.*

The sentiments of this latter comment were reflected in the responses of voluntary sector interviewees in both Glasgow and Dumfries and Galloway.

Though voluntary sector representation is included within the joint-planning structure in Dumfries and Galloway, the level of access is limited to the secondary tier of the planning and policy process. While, as noted, a key informant from within the social services maintained that these are powerful bodies, they are nonetheless largely *consultative* bodies, and as such, their ability to influence the policy process can be limited. Contrary to the statutory view of JAGs [described earlier] voluntary sector actants maintain, these are largely 'rubber stamping' bodies with the real decision-making occurring at the JSG level, within which they have no representation.

As illustrated, the level at which the voluntary sector is included within the joint-planning process is largely at the consultative stage. Consultation refers to the process of seeking information, advice, or the views of actors (in this case the voluntary sector) on issues related to a particular topic under discussion. Implicit in such a process of consultation is the pre-definition of the topics for discussion; that is, that the agenda for planning and policy direction has already been set. Agenda setting is a key stage in any planning process. Further, the power to *exclude* issues from the agenda can be as powerful a tool as the ability to *include* (Lukes, 1974). Opportunities for influencing the policy and planning process within such framework will therefore be confined to the 'fine-tuning' of a pre-determined agenda and, as a consequence, the ability of the voluntary sector to influence strategic decision-making will be reduced. By confining voluntary sector input to a consultative, rather than a formative (or strategic) level, its ability to either include or exclude issues from the joint-planning agenda is constrained. The potential for the voluntary sector to influence strategic policy-making within the policy process is thus also considerably reduced.

DG20(2) I: *When you go into negotiations, do you feel an equal partner?*

R: *Equality, yeah. No, no, I think it is very dangerous to think that way, I mean going back to those who were involved in the joint-implementation process – the community care implementation*

227

*process - they were sitting at the table, but em, they're **not** partners, they're not the ones that draw up the agenda.*

The inability of the voluntary sector to overtly include or exclude issues from the planning agenda, and conversely the statutory sector's *ability* to do so, reveals the existence of a asymmetrical relationship within the dependency network. The local authority can clearly be seen to be exerting what can only be described as an *asymmetrical* level of power within the policy and planning process. And while the actions of some statutory actants appears to be working *towards* some level of symmetry, the empirical evidence presented here points to a much more asymmetrical set of relationships between actants located within the network:

- asymmetry is evident in the existence and absence of joint-planning frameworks and JAGs between areas;
- asymmetry can be seen in the presence and exclusion of some voluntary organisations from the network;
- asymmetry is illustrated in the differing levels of involvement of actants within the network; and
- asymmetry is expressed through the differing levels of influence that actants are able to exert within the network.

Contrary to actor network approaches, therefore, the unequal ability of statutory and informal sector agencies to influence the policy and planning process infers that the power relationships within the dependency network are more closely aligned to the asymmetrical view of power highlighted by Dicken and Thrift (1992) and discussed in chapter four.

Informal Channels of Access

While the above section has highlighted the existence of an asymmetry of power relations within the network, actors within the study also noted their use of informal channels of access. That is, some individuals within the voluntary sector were able to influence key individuals linked to the planning process through informal processes. Key players with energy and enthusiasm for a particular project were thus viewed as having the ability to shape policy outcomes:

DGSW I: *How important do you see the role of key individuals within the purchase and delivery of services?*

228

R: *Yes. I mean there are always key players, it doesn't matter what structure you put in place the key players cut them up! [Laughs]. Individuals with enthusiasm and dedication will always do that - and the structures - however fancy - won't work without their commitment.*

Examples were given of the ways in which ideological and personality clashes between key figures from elected and non-elected bodies concerned with the development of care policy in Dumfries and Galloway had resulted, in the past, in difficult working relationships between statutory agencies concerned with care provision, and a stagnation in the development of policy initiatives.

Conversely, however, the development of services in a particular area can also emerge largely as a consequence of the interests, or enthusiasms, of particular individuals. Service profiles within an area were noted to be (at least in part) linked to the willingness of pressure groups and individuals to lobby for resources for that area. In Dumfries and Galloway, for example, the Stewartry and Annan areas were seen to be well serviced in terms of provision for individuals with learning difficulties; provision for those with physical disabilities, however, was minimal. One informant highlighted the findings of a report which concluded that (in Dumfries and Galloway):

DGSW R: *there was a lot of good work, there was very good links and networks, but they weren't what could be called business-like, they relied **completely** on personal contact, and who knew who, and the work that was really done because somebody wanted to help out.*

Key informants in Glasgow City expressed similar views with regard to the role of individuals. The persistence and initiative of one committed individual within the voluntary sector, for example, had led to the successful development of a liaison group that involved the voluntary organisation, consultant psycho-geriatricians, GPs, social workers and homecarers. This development was unique within Glasgow City, in terms of the organisation's ability to access actors from within both health and social services at various levels. Others had consciously sought out high profile individuals to co-opt onto their committees, in the knowledge that these individuals had good connections with key individuals in positions of influence within the statutory sector:

G70(2): *I identified someone, who I found out was taking early retirement. He was in a very senior position within [organisation] and I approached him, and he's now our Chair of the Board. He's a* *very able guy, and he's got great clout - he's very well connected. This guy has a sort of **galvanising** effect, because where I could say something and they would just go, "Oh right, yes", **he** has the necessary clout, and when he says something, they all **listen**!*

Personalities can thus be crucial in the development of links at locality level. Consequently such links were seen by both formal and informal sectors alike, as key to the development of policy and care provisioning - a process they referred to as 'relationship contracting'.

While the importance of individual links was highlighted by both formal and informal agencies in both study areas, for some agencies located in Glasgow City, restructuring had severely impacted on these informal channels. Organisations spoke of a constant change of individuals in local authority posts, to the extent that some no longer knew who their point of contact was within the social services. Such experiences exert 'transaction costs' (Nicolls, 1997) on voluntary organisations, who are, as a consequence, required to expend both additional time and resources on rebuilding these inter-sectoral relationships. This is a key issue given that individual relationships can often be of more importance to successful outcomes than the contracted terms of any care provision (Hoyes and Means, 1993):

G22(2) R: *Since reorganisation we've dealt with quite a lot of social work staff. We had an area manager who'd been here for a few years, and there was a senior who took care of community care - he dealt with us and the various projects about us. During that time, the **area** manager left, the senior community care worker, he left. Someone came in his place and was here for about five or six weeks, then they'd someone in for three or four **days**! So basically what happened was that the structure we dealt with **collapsed**, there was nothing. There was no senior that we knew, or knew us or the project, there was no **area** manager, there was no supervisory officer. And for the last six months, we've dealt with - we don't **know**!*

Other voluntary organisations noted, that as a result of reorganisation, they now found themselves in different social work areas. This change had impacted on the informal links with individuals within social services in two ways:

(i)   for voluntary organisations who had been affected by the geographical repositioning of social work area boundaries, relationships built-up within their former area no longer existed, or were of limited use. Such organisations were faced with the need to rebuild relationships within a different area; and

(ii) this repositioning placed such organisations at a disadvantage (locally) in comparison to agencies who had experienced no boundary change, and who thus retained networks of inter-personal relationships that had been built-up over time. As indicated above, however, this was clearly dependent on the degree to which officers within social work areas were retained in post.

Informal actants, however, such as voluntary organisations, informal carers and service recipients have the ability to step *outside* the network in order to marshal support for the retention of resources - an option not open to statutory actants. In Dumfries and Galloway, for example, attempts by the local authority to withdraw financial support from day centres for the elderly (leading to closure) met with lobbying and public protest to the extent that councillors were forced to revise their position (Dumfries and Galloway Standard, 1997):

DG30 R: *They were threatening to close **all** the day centres in Dumfries and Galloway - there's actually nine all together. But, however, the pensioners got themselves together and said, "we can't let them **do** this", you know, it was a service that they **valued** and it was under threat and they mobilised. So loads and loads of buses full of pensioners went - any anyway, they decided not to shut them down, and gave them a year's reprieve.*

DGSW R: *Well you see, what happened was, that they* [council] *began to realise that - hang on a minute, there is a **huge** lobbying committee that covers everything - and home carers were out there in force, and the Elderly Forum were out there in force.*

The ability to marshal sufficient human resources to lobby for a particular issue or resource is, however, likely to be dependent on the extent to which it is able to attract public support. Dear and Wolch (1987), for example, pointed to a hierarchy of acceptance in which particular resources (such as daycare for the elderly) are viewed as more acceptable to local communities and thus likely to attract public support, while others (such as drug or AIDS centres) are viewed as noxious, and thus were far less likely to be able to attract local support.

Statutory Responses to the Voluntary Sector: Resources and Control

Despite the expectations raised by the legislative context, as this chapter has illustrated, local authority implementation of the joint-planning mechanism within Dumfries and Galloway has been interpreted largely in terms of a consultative approach to voluntary sector input, rather than through the development of any strategic role within the planning process. Within Glasgow City, the voluntary sector was seen to have no formal input into the joint-planning process. This, as indicated, raises questions about symmetry within the dependency network:

G18 Q: *There is still a widespread feeling of patronising and controlling attitudes. The word empowerment is widely used but seldom translated into a reality.*

G44 Q: *Change of attitudes within councils. They are not necessarily expert in the field but almost assume superior knowledge.*

* Q = qualitative questionnaire response

Voluntary organisations, however, commented that, while locally elected representatives made decisions regarding the allocation of funding to care providers, there was a real lack of awareness of what it *is* that the voluntary sector actually does:

DG1(2) R: *I personally have no faith in councillors - I don't think they are really aware of what the voluntary sector is all about. There's a handful, there's seventy councillors here, and I could count on - maybe ten of them - that are really aware of what the voluntary sector is about. When you here some of them speaking about what the voluntary sector is, they think its meals-on-wheels and nothing else! So there's a huge education problem.*

The issue of resources, and access to resources, also played a key role in determining relative power relationships within the network. The emphasis on symmetry within network approaches to analysis implies that within the dependency network, resources would be expected to flow equally in both directions. Inherent within the concept of a multi-agency approach to the purchase and provision of health and social care is the notion of partnership between the formal and informal sectors. Partnership, in the strictest sense, can be understood as an association of persons for business purposes, the implication being that both parties within the partnership have a relatively equal status within the negotiation and decision-making processes. This would accord with the view that the elevation of the voluntary sector may be leading to the emergence of a 'Shadow State' (Wolch, 1990, xvi), whereby the voluntary sector takes on an increasing share of formerly publicly provided welfare responsibilities, but also develops increasing political and economic resources with which to affect policy.

The concept of partnership implies a process of negotiation in which both partners arrive at a mutually agreeable settlement regarding the issue under discussion. Voluntary organisations are involved in negotiation with the statutory sector largely in relation to the contracting process, and/or the delivery of services. The outcome of negotiation can be seen as the result of the differential ability of agencies to command resources to their best advantage:

G25(1) R: ... *there's a lot of glib use of those type of words, and when it actually comes to it, its not going to happen ... sitting round a table with officials from health services and the social work department, but they* [informal sector representative] *don't have the back-up of all the staff that are there. I mean that person* [statutory sector representative] *isn't sitting at the table alone, they've got the social work - all these people doing their research, providing their stats* [statistics] *and information - and how is that one person supposed to sit there and represent all carers? In a lot of instances, it hasn't been thought through properly ... Empowerment - sure empower organisations and people, yeah, but think through what the actual implications of it are ... Think of yourself sitting there as a professional and all what brings your empowerment to be there, and then put that on to the people that's not there.*

This relationship with the statutory sector was largely characterised as one in which the voluntary sector was very much seen as the supplicant whose voice of dissent was muffled by a statutory agency essentially holding the 'purse strings'. One voluntary organisation, however, commented that under the new arrangements, local authorities were not only smaller (at least in some localities), but that contracting, in its view, had placed the voluntary sector in a more favourable negotiating position:

G4(1) R: *The difference now is that they* **treat** *you as an equal rather than – because they realise you are giving a good* **quality**

service. So now your treated different as well, whereas before, it was 'try her in [VO]*'.*

Nevertheless, this view of a growing equity in the partnership between formal and informal sectors was not universally held. Other organisations highlighted the ways in which contracts were presented to voluntary organisations as a *fait accompli,* offering little opportunity for discussion or negotiation. Organisations also pointed to long delays in the re-negotiation of contracts and constant revisions sent from legal departments within the local authority. Such examples were seen as illustrative of a basic deficiency in understanding of the nature of the voluntary sector. These instances highlight key differences in the internal structure and the material and non-material resources statutory and voluntary sector organisations were able to command:

G70(1) R: *I mean, on the whole I get criticism from individual social workers who seem to think we can compete with the local authority. I don't have a finance department, I don't have a personnel department. Until recently, I've been running all this myself, I've been going out to do assessments, running the training for the employees, matching them up, doing all the co-ordination.*

Voluntary organisations characterised the statutory sector as slow to respond, heavily bureaucratic, but having at its command a considerable range of resources in terms of administration, expertise and the financial backing to utilise these resources. Conversely, the voluntary sector is characteristically viewed as having a high degree of flexibility, minimal bureaucracy - allowing for speedy response to changing situations - but limited access to resources, both human and financial. However, rather than viewing these key differences in organisational structure as beneficial, they were illustrative of a general perception, within the statutory sector, of a 'non-professional' voluntary sector. This view was reflected in the negotiation process, and the preference statutory bodies expressed for dealing with large national voluntary bodies, whose administrative structure were viewed as more closely akin to that of their own:

G70 I: *Do you feel you are an equal partner in the negotiation process?*

R: *No, no. I think its eh,* ***always*** *unequal when you're dealing with the local authority. They've a real arrogance in their attitude - very arrogant. And, eh, well its always, "well we're the local authority,* *its good for you to be involved with **us**", right? The thing with the local authority is, its not just **one** person, its like a whole bureaucracy.*

G36(2) R: *The problem is, that there's no **imagination** within social work. They don't have any flexibility within their own system, so they find it very difficult to recognise the **need** for flexibility, or the **benefits** of flexibility within any other system.*

While, as illustrated in chapter six, voluntary organisations derive their income from a wide variety of sources, for those involved in the provision of care services, much of their income derives from local authority grants/contracts. As a consequence, locally-based voluntary organisations are often constrained by the policy and service preferences of their statutory funders. This has a clear impact on both the services voluntary organisations are able to provide, and the client group that they provide services for. Organisations were being directed to develop services in a particular way, or run the risk of losing funding:

DGSWD R: *Under the new regime, we looked at how much closer we could put a hold on em - with the provision of their [VO] service. What we're saying is, that within our Eligibility and Priority Framework, we're now targeting expenditure towards people within one/two need. So immediately we're saying to [VO] you know, the autonomy you've enjoyed is - we can no longer **allow** you. And so what we've been through, is a process of re-negotiating the relationship we have with [VO], and in terms of the loss of autonomy, it all came under considerable threat from our saying "no, we want to have a greater hold".*

DGSWD I: *One of the traditional roles of the voluntary sector, was the innovation they were able to bring to services - if you are now funding for a specific thing, do you think that may reduce their ability to innovate?*

R: *Well what I would say to them is, "frankly, you can do what you like with your own money" ... but you know, we are looking for **our** money to be directed to the services that we are buying ... we're quite flexible, we're **looking** for new ways to provide care in the community, em, you know? But it has to be directed towards **our** objectives - we're not going to fund somebody to run their pet project. We're not going to fund general or education or community* *development work and we're **not** going to fund **campaigning** organisations.*

As a consequence, this cannot be viewed as a partnership of equals. Organisations have pointed to the clearly uneven playing field upon which they find themselves having to operate, both at the intra- and inter-sectoral level. The rhetoric of partnership is thus seen as a notion that, for most, is far removed from the reality of the statutory/voluntary sector relationship in practice:

G37(2) R: *Yes, there's no doubt about it, its an unbalanced partnership ... They don't start off with a level playing field ... they're a big organisation* [SWD] *they can take the stance that they can spread the work over a number of staff and the work takes a little under a day. Whereas you hand it over to a voluntary organisation with two staff, and its a **massive** task in comparison!*

G54(1) R: *Em, I'd probably say no, we're not in an equal partnership, because although consultation does take place, and its very positive, at the end of the day, em, there's no obligation - and I think you're then dependent on a good working practice from other agencies who will say* [pause] *take on board what you're saying so it will have an impact ... certainly I would like to see the voluntary sector being treated as an equal partner, rather than if you like, the poor relation.*

While the views expressed above are representative of the majority of voluntary organisations participating within this study, not *all* organisations expressed such a negative stance. Two organisations within Glasgow felt that though the position was *initially* unequal, they were beginning to move toward a position in which they envisualised the development of a more equitable partnership with the social work department (though there was little positive movement towards partnership within the health sector). One other organisation indicated, that though there may be little equity in partnership at the decision-making levels, at ground-level the picture could be a very different. When dealing with individual clients, they noted, that in *some* cases, where the voluntary organisation provided the bulk of care to an individual, health and social services professionals may willingly allow the voluntary organisation to take the lead role, given its greater knowledge of the individual case.

Though patronising attitudes toward the voluntary sector from statutory actants were seen to exist, there was increasing acknowledgement of the crucial service that the voluntary sector provide. In addition, some key individuals within the statutory sector recognised the potential benefits the voluntary sector can bring in terms of health and social care provision. They also recognised that the restructuring process was a learning curve for them too, and thus were striving to recognise the difficulties faced by the voluntary sector in the face of restructuring:

DGSWD R: *I think there are real dangers, but we're working through a process where we're learning how to contract with the independent sector in terms of preserving the services they've developed, and their knowledge and expertise. But they are non-profit making, and people working for them are not driving BMWs and so on. So their ethos is very much a public service ethos, and I think there's a real danger we could lose that. So I think we're developing knowledge and expertise and learning how to establish a new type of relationship. We need to have a much more business-like relationship with the voluntary sector, but we shouldn't undo the - em - the service they're providing which is based on a great deal of knowledge, expertise, skill and so on.*

Towards a 'Shadow State'?

Before turning to consider how the issues raised in this, and the preceding chapters, are drawn together, it is worth noting that there are some sharp distinctions between what has been revealed in the this study, and Wolch's (1989, 1990) view of the changing relations between the voluntary sector and the state. Wolch (1989) argued, in relation to welfare restructuring, that the elevation of the voluntary sector and the shift of responsibilities from the public to the voluntary sector has given rise to the emergence of a 'shadow state' apparatus - conceptualised thus:

- the voluntary sector is seen to take on an increasing share of formerly publicly provided welfare responsibilities, whilst simultaneously developing increasing political resources with which to affect policy;
- as a consequence of this increasing role in the provision and planning of welfare services, collective service responsibilities previously undertaken by the public sector are seen to operate outside traditional democratic controls;
- the shadow state is controlled in both formal and informal ways by the State and is strongly affected by State resources and constraints; and

- inherent within the shadow state is the 'statization' of life (increased penetration of state control into matters of everyday life).

If this is correct, this would run counter to the Government's stated objective (as quoted above) of increasing public accountability for the delivery of community based care. Further, in an era of apparent retreat from state intervention, the emergence of the shadow state is seen to imply an extended and increasingly diversified pattern of state intervention via the voluntary sector.

This chapter has illustrated, for example, how the ability of the voluntary sector to influence the policy process within the formal framework at local level has largely been limited to a consultative role. Voluntary organisations were seen to be excluded from important areas of the policy process, such as agenda setting and strategic decision-making. As a consequence, an asymmetry of power exists in which the ability of voluntary organisations to exert influence in these areas has been limited largely to their ability to influence key individuals through informal channels of access, or at grassroots level. Thus, while voluntary organisations have taken on an increased responsibility for the delivery of health and social welfare, evidence pointing to an accompanying increase in political influence as suggested by the concept of the shadow state, appears - at least at the level of the local state - limited.

However, it cannot be said that voluntary organisations are totally devoid of political 'clout'. As illustrated, when issues of service provision are of sufficient community interest, voluntary organisations are able to mobilise support and lobby successfully at local government level. This was highlighted in the case of the threatened closure of day-centres in Dumfries and Galloway. At locality level, however, instances of the ability of voluntary organisations' ability to exert political 'clout' have been limited to those issues that touch the imagination of the general public. As Dear (1992, 292) illustrated, there exists a hierarchy of acceptance within which services to key community-based groups are more likely to gain public support than are those to 'others'. Services for the frail elderly, for example, are viewed as acceptable as opposed to community-based services for the chronic mentally ill. Thus, the ability of voluntary organisations to marshal support for services under threat, is likely to be subject to the vagaries of public perceptions of acceptability.

In addition to these factors, the chapter also illustrates an inequity in the process of negotiation between statutory and voluntary actants. The general lack of recognition of the importance of the role voluntary organisations play in the delivery of health and social care, and the tendency for statutory actors to view and treat their voluntary partners as 'non-professionals' is manifest in a partnership of unequals, with the voluntary sector frequently being viewed as the 'poor relation'. The asymmetry of resources - both financial and human - has reduced the ability of voluntary organisations to exert real influence in the planning and policy process. Voluntary organisations have commented that, as the statutory sector holds the purse strings, this has had the impact of 'muffling' voluntary sector dissent. Negotiation thus becomes reduced to 'fine tuning' pre-defined policy specifications.

Though some larger national organisations *are* able to lobby successfully within the wider political arena - particularly at national and supra-national levels[4] - in general, the experience of voluntary organisations within this study has been one in which local organisations (particularly smaller ones) have been less successful in increasing their political resources.

In tandem with increased political resources within the voluntary sector, Wolch (1990) also viewed the vast economic resources managed by the voluntary sector (in terms of capital and employment) as a signifier of the development of the shadow state. While it seems reasonable to assume that any sector commanding significant resources, and playing a major role as an employer, should have the ability to exert influence in shaping the direction of care policy, in Scotland this does not appear to be the case. A major survey undertaken by the SCVS (1997) noted that despite the fact that the Scottish voluntary sector represents a multi-billion pound industry, its complex and diverse nature means that in reality the political 'clout' it is able to exert is minimal.

In relation to financial resources, this chapter has also illustrated how the ability of voluntary organisations to access financial resources can be subject to changes in emphasis and policy direction emanating from central government, but implemented at local government level. The passing of legislation (e.g. the Children's Act) without accompanying ring-fenced funding for its implementation, was highlighted by both voluntary and local statutory actants as a contributory factor in changing the emphases on care provision and supporting finance.

The evidence highlighted here, thus raises the question of whether the shifting role of the voluntary sector can be characterised as contributing to the emergence of a 'shadow state' - in which the voluntary sector is viewed as gaining increasing political resources with which to affect policy - or whether, in fact, it may be more correctly characterised as becoming a *sub-state* apparatus. At locality level, joint-planning, involving consultation between the statutory, voluntary and private sectors has been promoted by Government as the key mechanism for the production of pro-active community care plans (Cmd. 849, 1989). This is consequently the main

239

forum, at local level, in which voluntary organisations may hope to influence local policy initiatives. However, as noted above, a high proportion of those participating in this study had no representation on these local fora, and had little idea how to go about gaining a voice.

Notes

[1] The 'political arm' of the decision-making structure within the local authority. They comprise representatives of local government responsible for local policy-making within their specific area of jurisdiction. It is to these bodies that the relevant local authority departments (e.g. social work and housing) are deemed accountable.

[2] For example, Health Boards, General Practitioners and specialist consultants (e.g. psycho-geriatricians).

[3] Actors from within the local authority, whose role is to serve as a contact point, linking voluntary sector service providers and the appropriate local authority departments.

[4] Carers National for example highlighted their role in lobbying central government for legislative recognition of the rights of carers, leading to the implementation of the Carers Rights and Recognition Act (1996). However, they also noted that whilst official recognition in legislative terms is a step in the right direction, the lack of any funding attached to the implementation of the Act, meant that in real terms, the Act has had little impact in terms of improved outcomes for carers.

10 A Geography of Care

This book set out with two main aims: firstly, to take a geographical approach to the exploration of change between the formal and informal sectors within the process of care restructuring; and, secondly, to explore change through the conceptual frame of the dependency network. While chapters six to nine have been concerned to examine the experience of care restructuring as viewed by actants located within the network, as noted in chapter four, networked approaches to the analysis of care restructuring maintain that an actant's experience of care reform cannot be understood in isolation. Change, and the manifestation of change, is viewed as arising from the inter-relationships between actants and the ways in which these inter-relationships are played out on the ground. As a consequence, it has not been the role of these chapters to draw out, specifically, how the social and spatial implications of these processes are manifest within the two areas studied. In turning to consider these, there are three sets of issues with which the chapter seeks to engage:

- an examination of the geography of care restructuring at an empirical level and within specific places;
- issues of methodological significance to the analysis of care restructuring; and
- an exploration of care restructuring from within the dependency network.

The chapter concludes with a discussion of the ways in which the networked approach to analysis has contributed to an understanding of the geography of care restructuring.

Care Restructuring - Issues of Space and Place

The claim that there are spatial variations in care provision, and indeed in the restructuring of care provision between areas, is not new. Geographers' interest in welfare reform and the uneven effects of deinstitutionalisation is evident in work that spans over two decades. What *is* of interest regarding the analysis of care restructuring in Dumfries and Galloway and Glasgow City, however, is the way in which the unevenness of care has been seen to have arisen as the outcome of a complex web of differing factors. Thus, while the book set out to examine how care may be differentially experienced in urban and rural settings, it became evident in the course of the research that this was not the only issue of geographical significance. Spatial variations in care were also found to operate *between* local authority areas, incorporating issues of geographical significance that operate regardless of urban/rural difference. In addition, the research revealed variations in the ways in which care is experienced *within* local authority areas, pointing to a more place-based manifestation of care restructuring. These issues of space and place, and the ways in which they are specifically manifest in Dumfries and Galloway and Glasgow City are discussed below.

Urban/rural issues

As noted in chapter three, the impact of policy can manifest itself in very different ways across urban and rural locations. The issue of rurality in this study was of particular note. Statutory and informal actants drew attention to a number of factors that impact on the experience of care restructuring in rural locales. Firstly, the study revealed issues of delivery and access. Actants noted the problems of delivering community-based care to widely dispersed populations where it is difficult to achieve economies of scale in the delivery of services. The provision of daycare, carers' support groups and services such as meals-on wheels, for example, was seen to be problematic where the client-base is highly dispersed. As noted in chapter seven, care support outwith the homespace, in these locales, was found to be limited. Contiguous with the problematic of delivery, is the issue of *access* to services. Some care supports were found to operate *only* in the main centres of population (e.g. daycare), and choice for other services was limited (e.g. locally-based residential respite). Where funding was reduced, as noted in chapter six, some voluntary carer organisations sought to rationalise services, focusing on the most heavily populated areas, exacerbating the problems of access to services in rural areas. Access where services are geographically distant, however, is problematic for those with poor mobility and suitable transport options were found to be limited. This, of course, is not solely a rural issue, but is of heightened significance where distance is a factor.

Both voluntary and statutory actants noted the increased time and higher costs involved in the delivery of services in rural areas given the greater distances involved. Voluntary organisations, in particular, noted that due to time and distance factors, greater numbers of volunteers were required to deliver fewer services than was the case in more urban locales. Further, in *very* rural locales, only those with private transport can realistically participate, further constraining the potential pool of voluntary labour. The above issues point to a limitation in terms of choice in rural locales. Despite covering a geographical area that is significantly larger than Glasgow City (though clearly smaller in terms of population), as revealed by the questionnaires, significantly fewer voluntary and private organisations were found to be operating in Dumfries and Galloway. This infers that where care restructuring seeks to place increased reliance on informal sector provision, it is likely to exacerbate spatial variations in access and choice for service recipients.

Statutory actants also noted that funding to the local authority from the Scottish Office was based on a capitation basis that relies on a combination of population estimates and deprivation. Hence, though urban areas such as Glasgow with their concentrated population can experience high levels of deprivation (Pacione, 1993), the focus on population-based eligibility criteria can result in smaller pockets of deprivation going unchecked, and a failure to account for the higher cost of delivering care in rural locales. This inevitably percolates down in terms of those finances available for the purchase of voluntary care provision. In addition to the problematic arising from such funding allocation mechanisms, the research revealed how voluntary care providers in some urban locales had access to resource opportunities not open to rural-based organisations through the Urban Programme. The greater flexibility of this source of funding (discussed in chapter six) allowed voluntary organisations to retain a greater degree of independence from the local authority. Hence, they have increased opportunities to develop in ways that are independent of local authorities' definitions of care need. However, this has also been something of a double-edged sword in terms of equity of care provision in *urban* locales. As outlined in chapter seven, access to this source of funding has a population-based criteria that has resulted in some larger areas having a significant degree of access and choice in voluntary service provision, whilst smaller pockets of need go [largely] unattended.

A final factor is related to demographic change. As noted in chapter three, Dumfries and Galloway is an area with an aging population, which can, in part, be attributed to its rural status. Changes in both the age structure of the area, combined with the wider social and structural changes discussed in chapter seven, can impact on the available pool of informal care supports. Though there was insufficient evidence from the study to indicate whether there had been a decline in those individuals available to undertake informal caring, voluntary organisations did note increasing difficulties in the recruitment of volunteers. Further, as figure 6.3 revealed, the volunteer profile of Dumfries and Galloway was shown to be an aging one, in comparison to that of the urban area of Glasgow. This, combined with the issues discussed above, points to potential difficulties for rural areas, where care is seen to be increasingly dependent on voluntary participation.

Geographical patterns of difference between areas

As suggested at the beginning of this section, variations both between and within places that did *not* directly arise from the urban/rural dimension were also found to be of significance in shaping the local experience of care. In chapter three, the spatially uneven effects of care were seen to arise [in part] from temporal change in the political and ideological commitment to care provision for the frail elderly at the macro-scale. The move from institutional to community-based care and variations in the extent to which public and voluntary care provision has developed over time and space were seen to arise from changes in the wider political and economic environment, combined with changing societal attitudes to the frail elderly and their care.

A further issue, here, is concerned with the ways in which the uneven experience of care, both within and between local authority areas, has been shaped by variations in the historical development of care and care supports across space and within places. Discussion on the historical geography of care for the frail elderly in chapter three drew attention to the uneven development of care and care policy for the frail elderly over time in response to changing social attitudes and the changing ideological commitment within the wider context of care. The empirical findings of this study have also highlighted more localised issues. Variations in philanthropic giving over time, funding opportunism on the part of voluntary organisations, and the personal initiatives of key individuals within both formal and informal sectors, have all contributed to the development of specific services in specific places at specific times. This, combined with the often *ad hoc* introduction of central government initiatives, whose relevance to particular places has been variable, has also had an impact on the development of care supports across space. Much informal sector care provision within Glasgow, for example, was seen to have arisen as the result of the [often] piecemeal development of voluntary services under the Urban Programme. In Dumfries and Galloway, some voluntary care services were seen to have developed as a consequence of government initiatives that had more to do with *employment* provision than care needs.

The analysis of the empirical data in chapters six to nine further revealed how recent change emanating from central government, combined with a number of other differences between the areas studied, has contributed to a spatially uneven manifestation of care translations at the local level:

244

(a) differences were revealed between the political and ideological orientation of local government in Dumfries and Galloway and Glasgow City, contributing to variations in the ways in which the local authorities have sought to translate care policy. The local authority in Dumfries and Galloway, for example, was seen to have embraced the concept of enablement, and had attempted to divest itself of its in-house provision. As revealed in chapter nine, however, the local authority in Glasgow had remained committed to public provision and resistant to any increase in the purchase of private sector care;

(b) the implementation of structural and [in some instances] geographical change arising from local government restructuring has had a varied impact on local authorities in Scotland. Where significant change *has* occurred, this has been seen to have a considerable impact on the landscape of care. This has been of particular significance in the shaping of differential experiences of care between Dumfries and Galloway and Glasgow City;

(c) the extent of coterminosity was also seen to vary between local authority and health board boundaries in the two areas studied. This variation, combined with the effects of local authority restructuring, had an impact on the ways in which working relationships between these statutory actants had developed;

(d) differences were revealed in the decision-making structures at local level, with voluntary and other informal sector actants within the two areas having differential access to the planning and policy process;

(e) the extent of voluntary and private provision available in Dumfries and Galloway and Glasgow City was seen to vary. Hence, choice and availability of care supports was also seen to vary between the two areas;

(f) funding opportunities available to voluntary actants varied between the two areas. Such differences were seen to have an impact on both the development of voluntary care across space, and the differential ability of voluntary actants to retain a level of independence from their statutory funders. Chapter six also revealed geographical variations in the ability to fund-raise and a territoriality to philanthropic giving. Attention was drawn to the logistical difficulties of fund-raising in widespread areas, and the financial limitations inherent within areas of high unemployment. This points to a scenario in which wealthier, urban-based locales are likely to have greater flexibility in voluntary service provision;

(g) differences were revealed in the demographic profiles of the two areas, that had implications for the expansion of any care provision that places increasing emphasis on voluntary labour.

These factors illuminate a pattern of care provision that can be seen to vary across space. These arise not only as a consequence of the wider social and structural context of care, but also as a result of the ways in which local factors interact with the wider context to produce locally-embedded networks of care.

Geographical patterns of difference within areas

Care policy emphasises the need to tailor services to individual need, with the corollary that needs should take account of local availability and patterns of service. As noted in chapter eight, this implies that location plays a major role in the provision and availability of resources. Some of the factors contributing to locally-embedded experiences of care have been discussed above. However, as the empirical findings of this study have revealed, variations in access to services also operate at the intra-authority scale. In chapter seven, specific reference was made to variations in access to such services as daycare, residential and home-based respite, bathing services, carer support groups and taxi-card schemes. Access to these services was seen to be dependent upon *where* within a local authority area an individual resided. This meant that differential access and availability in services for individuals with the same or similar levels of frailty were found to be operating at a much more localised scale. This was particularly evident in chapter seven, where access for carers was seen to depend on where, within a local authority, an individual resided. This arose from a variety of factors:

- degree of proximity to an area of population density;
- variations in the priorities and patterns of spending within social work districts within a local authority area;
- differences in the funding opportunities available to voluntary organisations across specific locales; and
- the influence and specific interests of key individuals.

The research identified one further change in the relationship between place and care reform that has not so far been referred to in this chapter. This is concerned with the ways in which care restructuring is manifest at a much more place-specific level, and how informal carers and their dependants have experienced care. A key facet of deinstitutionalisation has been the changing locus of care from large institutional environments to community and domiciliary environs. Services are aimed at maintaining the ability of the frail elderly to remain as independent as possible within their own homes. As illustrated within chapter seven, however, this is based on two assumptions: firstly, that informal carers will take on an increasing share of the caring burden; and secondly, on adequate access and availability of services to carers and service recipients.

Within this study, the picture that has emerged is mixed. The uneven availability of social supports and care services between places, combined with the lack of *external* care services for some service recipients, has meant that for these individuals, care support is *only* received within the homespace. No additional sites of caring are available. Further, as also noted in chapter seven, though the local authority in Dumfries and Galloway recognises the preventative value of social welfare to the frail elderly (including daycare, lunch clubs etc.) it is, nevertheless, increasingly withdrawing financial support for these services. This highlights a failure to recognise the valuable monitoring and preventative role such places play in care restructuring, and raises questions about the 'place' of the frail elderly in our society.

Hence, restructuring can been seen to be contributing to the manifestation of new site-specific spaces of care. This has two implications. Firstly, for some individuals, the experience of care restructuring can be more akin to an institutionalisation of their homespace than the deinstitutionalisation of care, raising questions over the reality of *community* care for such individuals and how this might be achieved. Secondly, in relocating the site of caring from public space to private space, there is an increased intrusion of caring professionals within the homespace. Whilst inevitably this is important for the carers' continued ability to maintain their caring role, it is nevertheless creating a changing relationship within the home that adds to debates surrounding the blurring of the boundaries between private and public space (e.g. Tivers, 1987; Bondi, 1998).

A geography of care in Dumfries and Galloway

While the above discussion has drawn together some of the ways in which care restructuring can be unevenly experienced across space and within places, the book set out to examine the experience of care restructuring within the two specific areas of Glasgow City and Dumfries and Galloway. The reasons for this selection were discussed in chapter three. Briefly, however, the concern was to explore: a) how care policy is differentially manifest between urban and rural locales; b) the variable impact of local authority restructuring on care provision in Scotland; and c) how variations in the socio-political and demographic profiles of particular locales can influence the geography of care. Factors contributing to the different ways in which these variations are manifest within the two case study areas are discussed below.

In Dumfries and Galloway, the impact of local authority restructuring has been of limited significance. Geographical boundaries have remained the same. The key difference has been the conflation of two tiers of local government into one authority located in the regional centre of Dumfries. Inter-relationships between the new unitary authority and the Health Board have effectively remained the same. In this area, both local authority and Heath Board boundaries are coterminous, making for easier joint-working practices.

While local authority restructuring was seen to have a limited impact on relationships between actants in Dumfries and Galloway, the political disposition of local authorities themselves can impact on the shape of care outcomes. As noted in chapter three, the democratically elected structures of government within Dumfries and Galloway and Glasgow City were of different political make-up. This has implications in terms of their ideological commitment to change, and the direction of service provision, which may not necessarily be in tune with the desires of central government. In Dumfries and Galloway, the local authority was dominated by independent councilors, whose political disposition was largely in tune with the desires of central government. Thus, while the local authority has been unable [overtly] to implement central policy guidelines to its preferred extent (due to public protest), the trend has nevertheless been toward divesting the local authority of its provider status, in favour of an increased input from private and voluntary providers. Further, in 1998, plans were underway for both health and social service departments to move into shared premises. Though this was seen as a physical rather than an organisational integration, it was significant that a joint-commissioning team for community-based care services was being developed. Such a move is timely given recent government reports on the NHS and Social Services (Cm. 3854, 1998; Select Committee on Health, 1998), which highlight the incumbent government's desire to bridge the divide between health and social care through an increase in joint-working practices.

The analysis of the substantive material also revealed variations in the ways in which actants within places were able to access the policy process, and hence their ability to affect care outcomes. Obstacles to the proliferation of translations were seen to lie in the explicit arrangements that defined the mechanisms for designating the negotiation context, and actants' authorisation to speak on behalf of others located within the network. Inscribed within care restructuring are notions of partnership, negotiation

248

and empowerment, with joint-planning fora forming the key mechanism through which these notions become defined. These fora are the main routes through which voluntary and other informal actants are able to access the planning and policy process.

In Dumfries and Galloway, there is a well-developed joint-planning mechanism that (in theory) provides a forum though which both formal and informal actants can access, and hence influence, the nature of policy and planning outcomes. The views of voluntary and statutory actants with regard to the efficacy of this mechanism as a means of empowering informal actants, however, were seen to vary. Statutory actants maintained that joint-planning provided a significant opportunity for voluntary sector input into the policy process. Hence, the statutory perception of joint-planning was one in which the frame served to empower voluntary and other informal actants, elevating the position of voluntary actants to one of partnership in the policy and planning process. In this way, the statutory actant view of the network was one in which some level of symmetry existed.

The view of voluntary actants, however, was seen to vary significantly from that of the statutory sector. Here, the joint-planning structure was viewed largely as a 'rubber stamping' body. The nature of this linkage was characterised as one that was determined by the statutory sector, with voluntary and informal access confined to consultative levels of the framework only. Hence their access to the strategic levels of planning and agenda setting were limited, pointing to a more asymmetrical relationship between statutory and voluntary actants in Dumfries and Galloway.

Constraints on the ability of some voluntary organisations to influence translations within locally-embedded networks of care were evident within the mechanisms for designating actants' authorisation to speak on behalf of others. Attention here focused on issues of representation. Voluntary and informal representation within the joint-planning process in Dumfries and Galloway was seen to be arbitrary - part determined by statutory actant nomination and part self-selection. Many smaller organisations were seen to lack any form of representation, or were unaware of the existence of a joint-planning frame. While 'umbrella' organisations aimed to represent the views of a wider group of voluntary actants through an 'intermediary' structure, many smaller organisations were not members. Further, some 'umbrella' organisations did not have adequate mechanisms in place for consultation and the disseminating of information. Hence, voluntary sector representation within the joint-planning process can only be said to be partial. Some organisations, for example, noted that rather than being incorporated into the negotiation process, they were being presented with a 'fait accompli', based on discussions between the local authority and intermediary actants. So whilst this kind of framework *can* be a positive mechanism for maximising opportunities to pool resources and strengthen the voice of voluntary actants, the study has revealed how within Dumfries and Galloway, it can also act to isolate smaller voluntary organisations from the decision-making processes.

As discussed above, the research revealed the existence of both *intra*-authority variations in the experience of care, as well as variations that operate at a much more localised, place-based scale. At an intra-authority level, the social services department is a key enabler in community-based care provision. Each department is divided into districts, each with a degree of autonomy, and each with its own budgetary allocation. In Dumfries and Galloway, funding for these districts has been allocated on an historical basis, which is argued by statutory actants to have exacerbated care inequities in its failure to take account of demographic change. The research also revealed that while budgets and general policy emanate from the local authority centre, these can be implemented in differing ways at district level. So, for example, while there was a general commitment by the local authority to contracting as the key mechanism for resource allocation, as voluntary actants revealed, districts can distribute their resources in different ways (e.g. spot or block contracting). As highlighted in chapter four, resource allocation, and the mechanisms through which it is controlled can act to translate how voluntary actants provide care and to whom. This in turn can impact on their internal character, and their ability to retain a level of independence and flexibility.

Statutory actants were also seen to prioritise some services, in some places, over others. In Dumfries and Galloway, variations in access and availability of provision were found to range between such services as daycare, residential respite and taxi-card schemes. These variations illustrate how despite a convergence in thinking between the central and local government with regard to the translation of care in this area, *intra*-authority differences in the interpretation and implementation of care provision can contribute to a highly place-based experiences of care.

A geography of care in Glasgow City

Recent change arising from the implementation of policy emanating from central government was of much greater significance to the manifestation of care restructuring within Glasgow City. Local authority restructuring was seen to have had an impact at both a spatial and an organisational level. The boundaries between the Health Board and the new unitary authority were not coterminous. Further, as a consequence of restructuring, the Health Board has found itself in the position of having to negotiate not only with the new Glasgow authority, but also with five additional local authorities whose boundaries now overlap its borders. While Glasgow is the largest of these authorities, it is having to adapt to being just one of six local authorities now competing for joint-funding and co-operation from the Health Board.

Local authority restructuring in Glasgow has also had a significant impact on the voluntary sector. The physical boundary changes following restructuring meant that some voluntary organisations found their own geographical boundaries straddling two or more different local authorities. Contrary to initial expectations, however, trans-boundary working has proven less problematic than expected. Though peripherally-based organisations have found themselves having to negotiate within a diversity of local authority organisational structures, disaggregation had, in fact, placed them in a (financially) more secure position than those working entirely within the City boundaries.

As revealed in chapter nine, Glasgow City has been particularly hard hit by budgetary cuts. The filtering down of these cuts has meant that a number of those voluntary organisations working entirely within the city boundaries have experienced a significant reduction in income - some to the extent that they were no longer operational. While those located on the periphery of Glasgow City have also been subject to cuts in contracted services, they have, in some instances, been able to 'plug' the gaps by exploring opportunities for expansion into those authorities whose geographical boundaries they now cut across. One impact of this, however, has been the voiced intent of some peripherally-sited voluntary organisations to relocate entirely within the adjoining local authority, in order to focus their attention on building services in an area where funding was more accessible. As non-profit making bodies, voluntary organisations have no financial reserves with which to 'ride out' periods of financial stringency. As a consequence, they face the problem of either having to seek out alternative funding sources, or fold. While this emphasises the essentially pragmatic character of the voluntary sector, it does raise issues of *access* for service recipients, as voluntary organisations become increasingly resource over needs lead. For while the voluntary sector has been shown to have an ethos of community participation, as with the private sector, it has no legislative commitment toward equity in care provision. Any such action by voluntary actants clearly has implications in terms of reduced provision within Glasgow City, and raises questions about the viability of an increased dependence on the voluntary sector as a *replacement* for statutory provisioning where there is no commitment to

251

ensuring equitable access to care. This emphasises the importance of maintaining a spatial awareness in any exploration of care restructuring.

Other voluntary organisations found themselves in a polar situation. Where prior to reorganisation they had served the whole of Strathclyde, disagreggation had placed them in the difficult position of either having to reorganise, themselves, into smaller geographical units, or adjust to the demands and different working practices of twelve different local authorities, justifying expenditure in each area. Disaggregation also placed an increased burden on those organisations that sought to *retain* a regional profile. In these instances, the additional bureaucratic and administrative procedures arising from this spatial and structural reorganisation were noted to be significantly more cumbersome. Each authority [not unreasonably] wanted an accounting of the services provided within their area for the funding allocated. For voluntary actants, this was seen to have the additional effect of constraining their ability to operate in a targeted manner. That is, that where in the past they had been able to channel their resources to specific places in turn, now, they noted, monies from the differing local authorities had, of necessity, to be channelled within the funding authority's area.

The experience of these regionally-based organisations further highlighted the potential for a growth in geographical inequity of care provision between places. Different local authorities within the former Strathclyde region were seen to be placing differing emphases on their priorities and patterns of spending, leading to a shifting pattern of voluntary resources. Voluntary organisations noted gaps in funding from authorities who chose *not* to fund the service either withdrawal of provision from an area that had previously been uniformly served, or the need to search for some alternative sources of funding. As with Dumfries and Galloway, similar variations in access and availability were also found to exist within districts in Glasgow. Access to such basic hygiene supports as bathing services, tuck-in services and taxi-card schemes were found to vary dependent on the social work *district* within which an individual was located.

The discussion on Dumfries and Galloway also revealed how the political disposition of the local authority can act to shape care outcomes. While there is considerable evidence of voluntary and private sector provision in Glasgow City, the local authority's long history of Labour representation has meant that, unlike Dumfries and Galloway, it has made little attempt to divest itself of its in-house provision. In chapter eight, for example, private providers noted the tendency for the statutory sector to prefer in-house or voluntary sector provision over that of the private sector. These factors highlight the importance of the political landscape in the translation of care, and are illustrative of *one* of the ways in which care outcomes become shaped by the local environment within which care policy is translated.

As also noted above, joint-planning provides a key mechanism through which voluntary, private and informal carers become empowered with the means to access and influence policy translations. However, despite legislative direction from central government that such a frame should be developed (Scottish Office, 1993), joint-planning cannot be taken as a given. As this book has revealed, differences exist *between* local authorities. Following local authority restructuring, the joint-planning framework in Glasgow collapsed, and by 1998, there was still no evidence of its reinstatement. Despite evidence of grass-roots consultation between voluntary and statutory actants, there is no formal mechanism, in this locale, through which voluntary organisations can channel their input into the care policy and planning process. Hence the translation of care in Glasgow can be seen to occur within an asymmetrical relationship in which voluntary actants' opportunities to influence care translations within the formal policy process are subject to even greater constraints than that of their counterparts in Dumfries and Galloway. Here, there is little evidence of symmetry in relationships between the statutory and voluntary sectors within the network, and little evidence that, in Glasgow, local authority actants are attempting to work towards a more symmetrical relationship with those informal sectors actants with whom they are inter-linked.

A further consequence of local authority restructuring has been a change in the internal boundaries of the social work districts in Glasgow. The changing geographical boundary of the City authority has resulted a requirement that the social work department reorganise its structure from four to three districts. As a consequence, some voluntary organisations have found themselves located within new districts, so having to develop new working relationships with their statutory funders and adapt to differing working practices. These organisations spoke of being disadvantaged in the bid for funding against organisations that have well developed relationships with their statutory funders, and historical track-record within specific districts.

This further focuses attention on the ways in which the actions of key individuals can impact on the translation of care outcomes between places. Personalities, for example, were seen to be crucial to the development of particular policies and services at the local level, contributing to the emergence of specific patterns of care within places. Similar action was evident in Dumfries and Galloway, where, for example, the origins of a number of daycentres throughout the region were seen to have arisen less in response to a concern for equity in care provision, and more as a consequence of the charitable efforts of local figures.

In 1998, the social work department was in the process of further internal restructuring, which is likely to create additional upheaval for voluntary providers in Glasgow. While internal restructuring has not been as issue in Dumfries and Galloway, it was noted that the social work department *was* planning to undergoing a process of internal restructuring. This, however, was to be an organisational restructuring, which will, in the future mean that the structural organisation of care within the local authority will be based on a division by *care-groups* across the region rather than previously geographically-defined districts.

The uneven effects of care restructuring across space and within places have thus been seen to arise as the result of:

- the influence of the macro-political environment on care translations at the local level;
- variations in the political structure and the implementation of policy *between* local authority jurisdictions;
- variations in the implementation of policy, and hence the ways in which care restructuring is experienced *within* local authority jurisdictions and at the micro-level;
- the differential ability of locales to attract voluntary and private sector resources; and
- variations in the historical legacy of locales.

This draws attention to the ways in which the local experience of care restructuring arises as a consequence of a complex web of factors. These are seen to arise as a consequence of the interrelationships operating between formal and informal actants located within the network, manifest across various spatial scales.

Issues of Research Design

The success of any methodology is dependent on the extent to which it is able to facilitate the aims of the proposed research. Here, the aim has been to take a geographical perspective on the process of change through exploring the inter-relationships and experiences of key actants located within the dependency network. It was not possible within the confines of this book to examine, in depth, the whole of the network, and all those actants located within it, but similarly, the impacts of the inter-relations between actants for the care experience meant that it has not been possible to examine one actant in isolation. Thus, while the voluntary sector has been the lens through which these relationships have been examined, as discussed in chapter five, it was also important to explore the views of other key actants to include informal carers, the private sector (albeit to a more limited extent) and the statutory sector. The order of this investigation was taken with an awareness of the need to devise a method that facilitated the investigation of the notion of symmetry, albeit a tiered symmetry, inherent within a networked approach to analysis.

There is, however, a tension between the separation of sectors and the emphasis on the inter-relations that exist between them. Methodologically, this provided a challenge. The amorphous nature of actants within the network meant that in order to explore these inter-relations, it was not possible to select one key informant from each set of actants. As a consequence, it was necessary to develop different sets of methods and approaches than would have been the case had the book focused only on investigating more formally structured actants, such as the statutory and private sectors. Further, as discussed in chapter four, there is a dynamic to the network that presented a potential difficulty for the interpretation of data. It was thus necessary that the research design should be sufficiently flexible to allow the researcher to investigate possible change within the network during the period of research.

By developing a research design that has incorporated a blend of methods, the book has been able to explore the amorphous sets of relationships that exist both within the network and which operate across various spatial scales. While the main body of information has been gained through in-depth interviewing, the questionnaire data enabled the researcher to access a cohesive set of contextual data that would otherwise have been limited due to the heterogeneous nature of the actants (as with the voluntary sector). Where an understanding of the role an actant plays within the care process (as with informal carers) was not internalised, the repeat interviews and diary techniques provided a mechanism through which these roles could be uncovered. In this way, the research design has allowed not only for an examination of the inter-relationships between actants, but the qualitative methods used also facilitated an exploration of the *nature* of actants, how and why they operate in particular ways. The motivation to locate in a position marginal to the network, or to develop in a particular way, for example, can be the outcome of the internal characteristics of actants and/or the actions of key individuals, rather than the nature of the linkages within the network. A funnelled approach to method is thus viewed as having provided a particularly suitable means of deepening our understanding of how care restructuring is impacting on actants within the dependency network.

What is evident, is that there is a dynamic component to the network. Hence, methodologically, it was desirable that the impact on the voluntary sector should be investigated at several points in time. The aim was to enable an exploration of the effects of change on voluntary actants, the ebb and flow of resources, and the impact on an organisation's ability to provide services. The temporal dimension also allowed the researcher to examine whether the breakdown of inter-relationships (for example, joint-planning processes) would be merely short-lived moments following the confusion of local authority restructuring, or whether they were of longer-term significance.

In Glasgow, the repeat interviews revealed not only how voluntary organisations had experienced a reduction in their ability to undertake open referrals, but how the ability of medical professionals to make referrals had become dependent on a social work assessment. Here, local authority actants were clearly seen to be increasing their influence over health in the translation of care within the network. Nevertheless, the book also revealed how increased delays in undertaking referrals, from 2-3 months in the first year, to around six months in the second year, were linked to growing demand and a reduction of funding allocated from central government. The impact of such change was manifest in the drawing up of the safety net of care provision, and the withdrawal/reduction of funding for some care services (e.g. daycare and bathing services). The study also revealed how the development of new services (the traditional innovatory role of the voluntary sector) was giving way to increased demand for existing services from the local authority. Voluntary sector development was thus seen to be increasingly becoming a response to local authority priorities rather than a response to user-led needs.

In exploring the informal caring experience, the temporal approach revealed less change than had been anticipated. Variations in the need for community care supports over time (raising questions of access and availability) occurred much more slowly than expected, or, in some instances resulted in institutional care for the cared-for. As a consequence, it became evident that by the third set of interviews a point of theoretical saturation had been reached. Carers, however, had been informed at the outset of the time and extent of input they could expect to devote to the research process. This also served the function of facilitating withdrawal where carers came to look on the researcher as a friend or 'confidante'. The decision to continue with the final interviews at this point was thus more an issue of research integrity than the belief that it would further improve the research data.

In sum, the book revealed that whilst there was some evidence of temporal change [within the time-frame of the study] the temporal element was not key to the research process. This is of significance to the research findings in itself. With regard to carers, there are two issues of note. Firstly, the issue of the temporal dimension is intimately linked to the level of frailty of the cared-for. Where extreme levels of frailty were observed, change occurred more quickly than expected. The cared-for either entered institutional care or died (as noted in chapter five). There was no progression of increased community supports as expected. In these cases, it may be that the three-monthly intervals were too long to observe change. However, given the inertia in the care system revealed in the study, it is unlikely that shorter intervals between visits would have revealed much evidence of change in care supports. Secondly, for those experiencing chronic frailty, or whose impairments were less severe, their experience of changes in care supports proved to be much slower to be revealed.

The above issues, however, also indicate that this relative lack of change may be indicative of the complexity identified in the spatial analysis (and revealed in chapters six to nine) and the way in which the network itself operates. That is, while interviews with voluntary and statutory actants suggest a fast moving environment of care restructuring, the mediating roles of actants (such as the voluntary sector) can act to transform care in such a way as to minimise the impact of change on the informal caring experience. Thus, while an exploration of the network can help to reveal the patterns of care restructuring, change occurs more slowly than expected. A three year time-span may thus be insufficient to grasp the dynamics of change in the caring environment. This indicates that the dependency network may be more stable than had been initially presumed.

While this approach revealed change to be of less significance than anticipated, the repeat interviews *did* allow the researcher to explore and develop themes raised in the interview process, and to check for seeming inconsistencies. Further, with regard to carers, the serial interviews served to break down the barriers between researcher and researched, facilitating the uncovering of what often proved to be a highly personalised experience of care.

Each sector explored within the book has given an insight to the whole. The book, however, has not examined all actants in detail. For those reasons discussed in chapter five, there are limitations to the investigation of some actants. The adoption of a questionnaire approach as a means of exploring the private sector experience of care restructuring, for example, has meant that not all aspects of change within this sector have been examined. The themes discussed are derived from the questionnaire itself, hence the analysis presented here claims only to offer a limited understanding of the private sector experience. It is also acknowledged that while the aim of the book has been to investigate the *voluntary* experience of care restructuring, further research in this area could benefit from the incorporation of the experiences of service recipients. While this is clearly an important aspect of care, as with any research, there are limitations to the extent of the study, which it would have been neither practical nor feasible to exceed. Hence, these are seen as issues for further investigation. Further, the emphasis of this book has been on restructuring, hence it does not require a 'view from below' to fulfil its aims.

While it could be argued that the state has been pivotal in the initiation of change, the examination of change through the lens of the voluntary sector, suggests otherwise. Its elevated role through legislation, local state expectations, and the encouragement to conform to state needs via funding, all point to the importance of a detailed understanding of the responses of voluntary organisations to restructuring. As shown in chapter six, the key to the restructuring of care falls largely (but not exclusively) on the ways in which voluntary organisations have responded to the state's call for community-based care. For some organisations, particularly larger or nationally-based organisations, restructuring has provided opportunities for expansion. Such organisations have been seen to take on some of the characteristics of the private sector, adopting competitive, corporate approaches, increasing efficiency in working practices and rationalisation. In the process, such organisations have had to conform to state requirements, losing considerable flexibility and independence, and becoming increasingly dependent on state funding - either through contracts or grants. The state is, thus, in a position to dictate those services it is willing to fund and those it is not. In Dumfries and Galloway, state actants have already noted their intention to withdraw funding from some non-tangible service providers. In essence these organisations have become part of a sub-state apparatus. Chapter eight, however, also revealed how some organisations have moved to form a cartel in a bid to increase both their provider role and their influence in the decision-making processes. Should this move succeed, it may act to counteract increasing state control over such organisations, but in the process, many smaller organisations could find themselves marginalised within the caring process. Others, however, have been seen to have resisted any state encroachment on their independence and voluntary ethos, preferring to relocate outside the network rather than succumb to the dictates of statutory funders.

These issues point to the ways in which it is possible to examine the characteristics of the dependency network, yet still have an initial starting point for analysis.

Care Restructuring: A View from within the Dependency Network

A key feature of this book has been an examination of the extent to which networked approaches are useful in revealing aspects of the geography of change arising from care restructuring. The concept of the 'dependency network' has been employed as a means of interpreting how the voluntary sector is experiencing care restructuring across space and within places. In adopting this approach, however, it has also been necessary to examine not only the voluntary sector itself, but also the roles and distribution of other key actants within the network, the inter-relationships between them, and how their identities and interactions become defined by the translation process. Care restructuring is, thus, seen to arise as a consequence of the interactions between a variety of different associations that occur within the network and that operate across various spatial scales.

The dynamic of the network is highlighted in the changing relationships between actants. Contiguous with the changing role of the voluntary sector, there has been a shift in the power relationships within the statutory sector. Local authorities now take the lead role [over health] in assessing and determining the care needs of the frail elderly. In particular, the research revealed how voluntary actants can no longer accept referrals for services from health professionals unless a care assessment has been undertaken by the social services. This changing balance of power has not gone unchallenged however. Tensions between health and social work actants were evident in both areas, as statutory actants sought to protect their own turf. Working relationships were seen to be strained, though attempts were being made to overcome this. While co-operation and the relationship between housing and social services was also seen to be problematic at times, community care was not viewed as a key housing role by actants within this study, hence it was seen as less of an incursion on housing 'turf'.

The book was also concerned to explore how informal carers within the dependency network experienced care restructuring, and the nature of their inter-relationships with other actants located within the network - in particular the voluntary sector. Further, it sought to explore how carers may act to transform and be transformed by care translations. The study has drawn attention not only to the impact of the wider social and structural change on informal care-giving, but it has also highlighted how the ways in which statutory actants act to translate policy can affect the experience of informal caring. In the attempt to promote the notion of communal responsibility for dependent populations, central government, for example, implemented the Carers Recognition Act. This can be seen to have transformed the relationship between carers and care providers. Hence the

259

character of the linkages has been seen to have changed from one in which carers are conceived of as resources or co-workers, to that of co-client. Within locally-embedded networks of care, however, the character of the inter-relationship between statutory actants operating at the meso-level and informal carers - in both Glasgow and Dumfries and Galloway - was seen to be one in which policy was translated within a frame which viewed carers as co-workers rather than co-clients. In the move to deinstitutionalised care, for example, primary carers in both areas were seen to undertake the bulk of care support to the cared-for, and perform many of the caring roles previously undertaken by caring professionals.

In exploring the ways in which carers experienced care restructuring, the study revealed considerable variation in the social networks available to carers. These variations transformed the character of their linkages with statutory, private and voluntary actants. In particular, the nature of the inter-relationships between carers and the voluntary sector were seen to be considerably more developed, where social networks were seen to be weak. The links between informal carers and the private sector, however, has been demonstrated to be a relatively weak one, largely focused around residential respite, though some individually-purchased care was evident. The characteristics of these relationships, however, are essentially ones that exist at the level of the market. While it is acknowledged that this book does not incorporate all those private sector linkages that can exist at the level of the individual, the nature of this form of support means it is [largely] located outside the network. Hence, its ability to transform the voluntary experience of care restructuring is likely to be minimal.

While the links between carers and statutory actants were stronger, this was largely an asymmetrical relationship. The local authority has the primary responsibility for the assessment of the care needs of the potential care recipient, and hence the external care support likely to be made available to the informal carer. While actants within the local authority take the lead role in the assessment of care needs, the voluntary sector was seen to play a key role in providing the care supports necessary to enable informal carers to continue their caring role. Though these services are, in large part, purchased through local authority funders [who can influence the shape of these services], voluntary actants were nevertheless seen to provide many additional care supports that would not otherwise have been available. Carers' support groups, advice and information on access, and the availability of services were seen to be a key preserve of voluntary actants.

The relationship between statutory actants and informal carers is not an entirely asymmetrical one. Legislatively there is a commitment to notions of empowerment that provides for informal carer representation within the joint-planning frame. Representation is largely through carer voluntary organisations and carer support groups, illustrating the complex nature of the linkages that exist between actants located within the network. The inter-relationship between carers and the voluntary sector is also a reflexive one. Carers' input through the management committee structure of carers' voluntary organisations, for example, as noted in chapter seven, highlights their ability to influence the internal policy direction of such organisations. This inter-relationship opens up opportunities for carers to influence the translation of care outcomes at more than one level of the network. The view that statutory actants had undue influence on the direction one particular organisation, for example, motivated carers to break away to form a new voluntary organisation that was independent of statutory representation. This not only illustrates the complexity of the inter-relationships existing between voluntary and informal carer actants, but it demonstrates the importance of exploring the motivations and intentionality of actants. It further highlights the ability of voluntary and informal actants to step outside the network, should they choose, an option not open to statutory actants.

While voluntary and private sector actants were seen to be located within the same tier of the dependency network, the linkage between them was tenuous. Private sector actants viewed their own location within the network as a weak one, and their relationship with local authorities was limited. Statutory actants (particularly social work purchasers) were viewed as having a preference for developing relationships with voluntary actants, whose philosophy and principles were seen to be closer to those of their statutory purchasers.

The relationship that does exist between voluntary and private sector actants is essentially a competitive one, as the private sector seeks to increase its participation in those areas of care formerly the preserve of public and voluntary sector actants. The presence of the private sector within the network, and the language of privatisation inscribed within the translation of care policy, rather than capturing the essence of the voluntary sector (in terms of its flexibility and innovatory capacity) was seen to be contributing to the growth of competitive practices amongst some voluntary organisations. This was transforming their internal characteristics, and the ways in which they mediate care. Such organisations were seen to be taking on the language and practices of the marketplace, adopting corporate approaches to care provision, sub-contracting and 'adapting' their voluntary ethos to the new contracting climate. Early evidence of a move toward cartelisation by some large voluntary organisations seeking to maximise their influence and provider potential was also evident. If successful, this could effectively marginalise the position of smaller organisations within the network, or result in their exclusion. This was by no means a universal scenario, however, and was found to exist predominantly amongst larger, contracting organisations.

A key issue in exploring the relationship between actants within the network, has been the control of resources, the ability of organisations to access those resources, the mechanisms through which they are deployed, and how this affects translations within the network. The study has illustrated how most voluntary organisations within this study, access their financial resources through central or local government. The predominance of statutory funding has meant that the ways in which statutory actants deploy their resources is likely to impact on the how voluntary organisations are able to mediate care support. In particular, chapter six has revealed how contracting and service agreements have impacted on the ability of contracting organisations to translate care provision. While contracting has been promoted as offering the potential for voluntary organisations to exert influence on the final outcome, the empirical evidence has revealed a mixed picture. Though some organisations have grasped the opportunities and adopted the language and working practices of the marketplace, others have voiced concern about the direction in which this takes the voluntary sector.

As organisations have become increasingly tied to statutory resources, their actions have been increasingly constrained by statutory requirements and definitions of need. This has effected a reduction in their ability to define their own care objectives, and to continue the practice of open referral. Inevitably this has implications for service recipients whose care needs may fall outwith statutory definitions. Contracting has further been shown to be transforming the ability of voluntary organisations to deliver specific services. In particular, statutory funders have been seen to be either reducing or withdrawing their allocation of resources to social and non-tangible supports. This was evident in both areas, though it was more explicit in statutory responses to voluntary organisations in Dumfries and Galloway. The introduction of spot contracting, in particular, while enhancing the flexibility of statutory sector purchasing, has transformed the ability of recipient organisations to act in a proactive manner. Such change has implications for the internal character of contracting organisations. Voluntary organisations noted that the character, remit, and ethos of their organisations were becoming transformed by the requirements of their statutory funders. This points to a scenario in which *these* actants are being subsumed by the statutory sector, effectively becoming part of a sub-state apparatus.

The elevation of the voluntary sector inscribed within care restructuring seeks to harness its characteristic flexibility and innovatory potential. In the move toward service agreements and contracts, however, statutory actants at the meso-level have been seen to exhibit a preference for developing relationships with larger organisations, whose administrative and bureaucratic procedures are more akin to their own. While this does not exclude *all* smaller voluntary organisations, as indicated above, in the search for funding, there are indications that some larger organisations are beginning to form closer inter-relationships *within* the voluntary sector, organising themselves in what is, in effect, a process of cartelisation. This is viewed as a means of enhancing their opportunities to influence the policy process and access funding. Care outcomes were thus seen be shaped not just by agencies operating at different levels of the dependency network, but also by actants operating on the *same* level. These actants actively seek to influence the ways in which resources are mediated, and hence can play an active role in transforming the shape of the network. Individuals within *some* voluntary organisations, also sought to influence care translations through informal channels of access. Chapter six, for example, revealed how such actants have actively sought to increase their opportunities to influence care translations through 'relationship contracting'. Others had sought to enhance their *own* opportunities for interaction within the network though the proactive development of personal relationships with key statutory actants.

The research also revealed how despite constraints on their opportunities to influence the policy process at the meso-level through formal linkages, the voluntary sector *was* able to access the policy process through informal mechanisms. As noted in chapter seven, where issues were of sufficient public interest, local voluntary actants in Dumfries and Galloway have been successful in effecting a reversal of the local authority's decision to withdraw funding to daycentres throughout the region through lobbying and public protest. Collective action was also seen to have been successful in constraining the overt disposal of the local authority's in-house provision.

Not all voluntary organisations are funded through contracting. Where financial resources are accessed through centrally-allocated grants or from a number of diverse sources, the ability of the local authority to influence how voluntary organisations deliver care has been shown to be considerably reduced. These organisations have been able to retain greater flexibility and innovatory potential. In particular, the book revealed how some voluntary organisations, aware of the constraints placed on those dependent on local statutory resources, have actively chosen *not* to become tied-in to such funding in order to retain their capacity for independent action. These organisations are largely reliant on fund-raised resources, and as such, tend to be smaller and more locally-based. This, however, highlights the flexible nature of the dependency network. This action, again, illustrates the importance of examining not just the character of the linkages

263

between actants, but also the characteristics and internal motivations of key actants.

While the control and allocation of resources within the network has been demonstrated to constrain the ways in which voluntary organisations experience care restructuring, it should also be noted that local authorities have *also* been constrained to translate policy within a frame of available resources. The legislative frame has elevated local authorities to the lead agency within care restructuring, while at same time, as illustrated in chapter nine, they have been faced with the dilemma of cutbacks in funding from central government and increased demand for services at the local level. The expectation by central government that community care funding would come in large part from decrement has proven flawed. Continued lack of clarity over the boundaries between health and social care, and 'heel-dragging' by health boards who have sought to retain funds in order to develop their own community-based services has meant the transfer of funds has been slow. Hence, definitions of need are being transformed by the ways in which services to individuals are being channelled by social work priorities, with increasing acknowledgement that individuals are being 'fitted in' to available services, rather than services being developed to fit required needs. Both local authorities within this study, for example, define a priority framework of levels one to four, but resource constraints have meant that the safety-net is being drawn up, with both areas now only servicing levels one and two. Such funding deficits have percolated down to the voluntary sector, causing some to reassess their ability to deliver a service. The uncertain environment within which the voluntary sector operates is thus, in part, a reflection of uncertainty faced by local authorities themselves.

11 Conclusion

The geographical variations in care restructuring that have been explicitly unpacked in the previous chapter illustrate how the experience of care restructuring can vary both *across* space and *within* places. The localities examined in this study have been shown to be implicated in crosscutting sets of relationships that are tied to wider (non-local) processes in a number of differing ways. These linkages reveal a complex set of global-local articulations in which place is seen to be defined, in part, by a set of locally contingent factors that occur within a territorially bounded social world, but also, in Castells's terms as the 'space of flows' (Castells, 1996, 423-428). Hence, the places examined within this thesis can be seen to have been constructed within broader and more complex spaces of integrative networks. As the study has revealed, however, these places can be subject to divergent care outcomes. The differences in provision and the processes through which such provision is translated between Dumfries and Galloway and Glasgow City, for example, has illustrated how local actants are tied into sets of relationships both with other local actants *and* with those located elsewhere. In this way, space can clearly be seen to make a difference to the social processes of care restructuring. What is evident here is that in each place space is significant in a number of ways and at a variety of scales.

The analysis has also focused attention on the notion of local-embeddedess, and the ways in which a networked approach has contributed to the uncovering of place-based difference in the experience and manifestation of care. By focusing on the translation chains, attention has been drawn to the complex inter-relationships between actants concerned with care restructuring and, hence, the importance of examining the spaces *between* actants within the network. The study has unpacked some of the ways in which these spaces act to enable or constrain the proliferation of care. In particular, the empirical evidence has revealed how mechanisms such as joint planning frameworks, contracting and grant aid, act to variously enable and constrain the ability of actants to translate care within the network. Such mechanisms can be equated to Latour's (1988, 299) 'hinges', allowing a selection of what gets in and what gets out, so as to locally increase order or information. As the book has illustrated, such action is seen to be in part determined by the wider context within which

265

action occurs and in part shaped by the local context within the network is embedded.

Given the above, a key issue is the way in which different forms of care provision evolve in different socio-cultural and political contexts. The two case studies have provided empirical examples of the ways in which the local political, socio-cultural and topographic environment have all been seen to contribute to the ways in which care translations are manifest in particular places. The case studies further invite a moral reading of the various aspects of the emerging spatial patterns and relations in these landscapes of care, so adding to current debate surrounding moral perspectives on geography (Smith, 1997).

New forms of care provision require new forms of resources and knowledge. Not only can these be unequally dispersed, but also not all environments are receptive to all innovations. This has been particularly evident in Dumfries and Galloway, where the rural nature of the environment has been seen to inhibit the development of particular forms of care. In Glasgow, the local political environment, combined with change emanating from government operating at the macro-scale, has constrained the ways in which voluntary actants can access the policy process. However, though actants within these locally-embedded networks can be tied to particular places, they can also transcend place, and voluntary actants, in particular, have been seen to extend their networks over ever increasing distances.

Other issues too are of significance in understanding how care restructuring has become locally embedded in particular places. Wider social and structural change, of course, has been instrumental in effecting a changeover from institutional to community-based care. In analysing the impacts of such change, however, an examination of the extent to which places vary in the implementation of care translations, and the availability of human and non-human resources with which to do so is required. Similarly, while the wider political context can have a variable impact on localities, the political landscape of place also plays a significant role in shaping local care outcomes. As noted, local authorities can translate care policy in different ways dependent on their political affiliation and ideological commitment. The restructuring of local authorities has been of particular relevance here, with Dumfries and Galloway and Glasgow City serving to illustrate two very different experiences of the restructuring process.

The role of the political landscape has been compounded by the historical legacy of care within particular locales. Past policies and the geographical outcome of these policies have contributed to variations in the development of care across space, contributing to differential access and availability of care provision for service recipients. The role of place - in

266

particular social and political variations between places - is thus key to understanding the ways in which variations arise in the translation of care restructuring across space.

In moving beyond the specific analysis of care provision in Dumfries and Galloway and Glasgow City, the study has suggested that there is merit in adopting a network analysis approach to this topic. In particular, this approach has enabled the analysis to explore the differing ways in which policy implementation has occurred beyond the particular actor-spaces (Murdoch and Marsden, 1995), or specific situations, in which actants perform their roles. In adopting this approach, it has been possible to highlight and investigate the wide range of associations (or network relationships) which operate in care provision for the frail elderly. These associations occur across a network whose boundaries stretch from the micro-scale of care restructuring within domestic space, to the meso-level of local governance and the wider macro-influences on change. Perhaps crucially, the study has revealed how these associations are tied together in a variety of interrelationships that give rise to various effects and care outcomes. Undoubtedly, this consists of a complex web of relationships, not all of which have been explored fully. Nevertheless, the approach here also reveals how the analysis of care restructuring in different local spheres requires a consideration of the factors that link actors who operate at different scales, and also how these links are constituted. In particular, a network analysis approach has enabled attention to focus on the varying ways and means through which actants formulate care policies in their own settings, and then, through interactions with other parts of the dependency network, implement policies.

In revealing some of the ways in which these associations are made and developed as actants pursue particular goals, and the relative powers of these associations as they come in to conflict, several issues emerge. Actants appear to use whatever resources are available to them to build links and establish their identities. However, outcomes of the engagements in the network seem to depend on which associations are strongest and who dominates as care policy is translated across the network. Equally importantly, where the development of associations conflicts with the internal motivations and characteristics of specific actants, there is a tendency for them to be 'bypassed' as alternative associations - forming differing linkages within the network and with differing sets of outcomes - are created.

In terms of policy, the study has revealed that there are three main sets of issues for consideration:

- there is a need for policy-makers at the macro-scale to place a greater focus on the differing needs of urban and rural dwellers, and the diverse sets of problems faced by urban and rural care providers;
- whilst joint-planning frameworks form an important mechanism through which informal care providers can access the policy process, these frameworks are not accessible to all. If the informal sector is to participate in the provision of social welfare form as more than a 'sub-state' apparatus, local authorities need to realize equitable and democratic systems of access to these frameworks;
- the changing structure through which voluntary organisations access funds has been shown to be having a largely detrimental effect on their organisational ethos, flexibility and innovatory capacity. If these features are to be retained, it is important that some core funding be made available to voluntary care providers.

A combined effect of the above issues is seen to be manifest in diverse translations of need within and between particular places and hence care provision to meet that need.

By undertaking the study in two differing locations, the thesis has revealed that there is nothing inevitable about the way in which care restructuring is manifest across space and within places. Outcomes arise as a consequence of particular sets of circumstances and associations that occur within particular places combined with the impact of wider social and structural change. In assisting the analysis of the particular combinates the dependency network has:

(a) enabled an examination of the spaces of care restructuring by allowing a path to be woven through the various spatial scales within which change occurs; and
(b) focused attention on the ways in which care restructuring becomes locally-embedded.

A network approach, consequently, provides one way of uncovering how the socio-spatial manifestation of care restructuring arises as a consequence of complex web of differing factors. This is a concept that economic geographers have recognised and embraced in their attempt to uncover such issues as inter-organisational networking in regional development, but its potential for exploring other geographical issues remains largely untapped. The book has illustrated one way in which health geographers can usefully adopt a networked approach as an effective tool through which to examine how health and social welfare provision becomes socially constructed and reconstructed across space and place. As Murdoch argues, "network theory never departs from the realm of the spatial and there are no divisions between spatialised interactions and the frameworks which organise their interactions" (Murdoch, 1997, 332). Networks are thus inherently spatial and, as such, offer considerable potential for further geographical enquiry into health related issues.

12 Epilogue

Research into care restructuring is an ongoing process. Care policy and planning are subject to constant revision arising from circumstances that occur at particular points in time. The book gives an account of changes in the landscape of care over a specific three-year period from 1996 to 1998. Since this period, Scotland, and the political environment within which care policy and planning is constructed and implemented has experienced some significant changes.

Following a General Election in May 1997, the British electorate returned a Labour Government committed to holding referenda in Scotland and Wales on the issue of devolved government. Following a Scottish vote in favour of devolution, the new Scottish Parliament was invested in Edinburgh in 1999. National policy-making in relation to health and social care now emanates from this Edinburgh-based Parliament - the Scottish Executive being charged with overseeing its implementation. The Scottish Office has thus been supplanted by a new executive body responsible to the elected members of the Scottish Parliament (MSPs) rather than to Central Government at Westminster. This has a number of implications for future care policy and practice in the Scottish environment. These are briefly addressed below.

Prior to devolution, the newly elected British Labour Government outlined its commitment to tackling poverty and social exclusion through the promotion of active citizenship. To this end, it emphasised the need for closer working relationships between government and the voluntary sector. This commitment was laid out in the 1998 Scottish Compact (Cm. 4083) with similar Compacts introduced for England and Wales. The Compact, as implemented by the Scottish Executive in autumn 1999, makes a commitment to co-operative decision-making in partnership with the voluntary sector and extends voluntary sector opportunities to contribute to the development and implementation of public policy (Cm. 4083, 1998). The Compact thus aims to improve cross-sectoral working and promote effective dialogue between the voluntary sector and the State, so ensuring that the impact of any changes in policy and procedure on the voluntary sector are considered (a process referred to as 'proofing'). Such dialogue will largely be directed through umbrella or intermediary bodies who are seen as the conduits for their members' views. Hearteningly, however, the Scottish Compact does acknowledge the fact that there will be times when these intermediary bodies cannot be assumed to represent the full range of views in their client group area., though it does not make clear how it will seek to redress this gap.

The Scottish Executive has further expressed its commitment to 'joined-up action' which it believes is leading to a considerable growth of collaborative working. Of particular relevance, here, are the new Social Inclusion Partnerships (or SIPs) which have now replaced the Urban Programme and PPAs, with the voluntary sector guaranteed a place on every SIP Board. The eligibility critieria for SIP funding is a mix of those local communities once again defined by geographical boundaries, and theme-based SIPS which may cover a complete local authority area. Interestingly, the community of Milton, in Glasgow, which was seen to have lost its Urban Programme funding due to the population criteria imposed under PPAs, finds itself once again eliglible for funding under the new Social Inclusion Partnerships.

In August 1999, the Scottish Executive announced an additional development that will serve to place the voluntary sector closer to the heart of government by setting up a centrally located Voluntary Issues Unit based in the Executive Secretariat. This is seen to have arisen as a consequence of the increasing profile of voluntary issues both at a UK and Scottish Executive level and recommendations that the Executive seek a more active and strategic relationship with the voluntary sector (Scottish Executive Press Release, 1999).

Though Government has sought to promote the spirit of the Compact at the level of local government, in Glasgow at least, there is little evidence of any change in the relationship between the voluntary sector and the local state. So while there is some evidence of an emerging commitment to meaningful partnership and closer working practices between the voluntary sector and statutory sector at the level of national government, as yet there is no duplication of these developments at the level of the local authority.

Further, it is recognised that not all voluntary organisations will have an interest in seeking partnership with government. Some organisations will prefer to work within their own local spheres of action without reference to the State. For others (such as lobbying and direct action groups) any notion of partnership with the State will represent a direct contradiction of the core mission statement upon which their organisation was founded. As such, these organisations are likely to distance themselves from any attempt to strengthen the inter-relationship between themselves and the State.

The combination of these changes in policy and attitudes toward the voluntary sector within national government is indicative of the emergence of a new political space in which the state and civil society are becoming hybridised (Brown, 1997) so creating a new instrument for implementing policy and delivering care supports. Further, this strengthening of the inter-relationship between the voluntary sector and the state may indeed be indicative of the emergence of a 'shadow state' that is developing increasing political resources with which to affect policy - at least at the level of national government. It is worth remembering, however, that these developments do not represent the changing character of the voluntary sector in its entirety. Significant numbers of smaller organisations are not situated or represented within these new political spaces. It is possible to speculate, that what may emerge from this changing political landscape is a 'shadow state' comprising large and increasingly influential voluntary organisations (the 'third force'), with smaller, more truly philanthropic and lobbying organisations becoming increasingly divorced from the 'shadow state' and increasing their distance from decision-making processes.

What do these changes mean for the Dependency Network? While the overall structure remains the same, new actants in the form of the Scottish Parliament and the Scottish Executive have become enrolled within it and may have a significant role to play in translating care outcomes. Others, such as the Scottish Office, [1] though still located in the network, have come to play a much reduced role. Whilst it is too early to assess the real impact of these changes on other actants within the network - and hence the local-embeddedness of care restructuring - there have been a number of changes that are, perhaps, indicative of how future care policy may be translated within the network. The commitment to closer working relationships through the Scottish Compact and the Voluntary Issues Unit implies a strengthening of the inter-relationships between the voluntary sector and the State at the level of National Government. Though, as yet, it is too early to tell, this may be of some significance in the translation of future care policy within the network. Nevertheless, as indicated within this book, not all voluntary organisations will actively embrace this closer working relationship. Smaller voluntary organisations not affiliated to intermediary organisations may still be excluded from decision-making processes, whilst others will actively seek to exclude themselves.

---

[1] Now renamed the Scotland Office.

Bibliography

Agar, M. (1980) *The Professional Stranger: an informal introduction to ethnography*, Academic Press, New York.

Allen, C. (1997) "The Policy Implementation of the Housing Role in Community Care - a constructionist perspective", *Housing Studies*, 12, 85-111.

Amin, A., Cameron, A. and Hudson R. (1999) Welfare as Work? The Potential of the UK Social Economy, paper presented to the *RGS-IBG Annual Conference*, University of Leicester, Leicester.

Amin, A. and Thrift, N. (1995) "Institutional issues for the European regions: from markets and plans to socio-economics and powers of association", *Economy and Society*, 24, 41-66.

Anderson, M. (1983) "What is new about the modern family: an historical perspective", in *The British Society for Population Studies, The Family*, OPCS, London.

Armstrong, D. (2000) "A survey of community gardens in upstate New York: Implications for health promotion and community development", *Health and Place*, 6:4, 319-328.

Audit Commission (1986) *Making a Reality of Community Care*, HMSO, London.

Audit Commission (1994) *Community Care Bulletin No.2, December*, HMSO, London.

Bachrach, L. L. (1989) "Deinstitutionalisation: A Semantic Analysis", *Journal of Social Issues*, 45, 161-171.

Ball, J. and Ball, M. (1982) *What the neighbours Say: a report on a study of neighbours*, The Volunteer Centre, Berkhamsted.

Barnes, J. A. (1954) "Class and committees in a Norwegian island parish", *Human Relations*, 7, 39-58.

Bell, M. (1996) *Rehabilitating Middle England: the integration of ecology, aesthetics and ethics*, Paper delivered at the VIIth International Symposium in Medical Geography of the Royal Geographical Society with the Institute of British Geographers, Portsmouth.

Berger, P. and Luckmann, T. (1966) *The Social Construction of Reality*, Penguin, Harmondsworth.

Berkowitz, S. (1988) "Afterword: Towards a formal structural sociology", in Wellman, B. and Berkowitz S. (eds.) *Social Structures: a network approach*, Cambridge, Cambridge University Press, 477-497.

Billis, M. (1993) *Sliding into change: the future of the voluntary sector in the mixed organisation of welfare*, CVO, London.

Bondi, L. (1998) "Gender, Class and Urban Space: Public and Private Space in Contemporary Urban Landscapes", *Urban Geography*, 19, 160-185.

Brannen, J. (1992) *Mixing Methods: qualitative and quantitative research*, Avebury, Aldershot.

Brindle, D. (1998) "Carers' plight a 'timebomb'", *Guardian*, London, p.6.

Brown, H. and Smith, H. (1993) "Women Caring for People: the mismatch between rhetoric and women's reality?" *Policy and Politics*, 21, 185-193.

Brown, M. (1997) *RePlacing Citizenship: AIDS Activism and Radical Democracy*, Guilford Press, London.

Burgess, R. G. (1984) "In the Field: an introduction to field research", in Burgess R. G. (ed), *Field Research, A Sourcebook and Field Manual*, Allen and Unwin, London.

Butcher, T. (1995) *Delivering Welfare: The Governance of Social Services in the 1990s*, Open University Press, Buckingham.

Callon, M. (1986) "Some elements of a sociology of translation: domestication of the scallops and the fishermen of St. Brieuc Bay", in Law, J. (ed) *Power, Action and Belief: A New Sociology of Knowledge?* Routledge, London.

Callon, M. (1995) "Four Models for the Dynamics of Science", in Jasanoff, S., Markle, G., Petersen, J., and Pinch, T. (eds) *Handbook of Science and Technology Studies*, Sage, London, 29-63.

Callon, M. and Latour, B. (1981) "Unscrewing the big Leviathan: how actors macro-structure reality and how sociologists help them to do so," in Knorr-Cetina, and Cicourel, A. V. (eds) *Advances in Social Theory and Methodology: Towards and Integration of Micro and Macro Sociologies,* Routledge, London.

Castells, M. (1996) *The rise of the network society*, Blackwell, Oxford.

Checkland, O. (1980) *Philanthropy in Victorian Scotland: social welfare and the voluntary principle*, John Donald, Edinburgh.

Chorley, R. and Haggett, P. (1969) *Network Analysis in Geography*, Edward Arnold, London.

Christaller, W. (1966) *Central Places in southern Germany*, (translated by Baskin, C. W.) Prentice-Hall, Englewood Cliffs, N. J.

Cicourel, A. V. (1981) "Notes on the integration of micro- and macro-levels of analysis", in Knorr-Cetina, and Cicourel, A. V. (eds) *Advances in Social Theory and Methodology: Towards and Integration of Micro and Macro Sociologies,* Routledge, London.

Clapham, D. and Smith, S. J. (1990) "Housing policy and Special Needs", *Policy and Politics* 18, 193-205.

Cliff, A. and Haggett, P. (1988) *Atlas of disease distributions: analytic approaches to epidemiological data*, Blackwell, Oxford.

Cm. 6404 (1942) *The Beveridge Report on Social Insurance and Allied Services*, HMSO, London.

Cm. 3703 (1968) *Seebohm Report of the Committee of Local Authority and Allied Personal Social Services*, HMSO, London.

Cm. 849 (1989) *Caring for People: Community Care in the Next Decade and Beyond,* HMSO, London.

Cm. 4100 (1998) *Compact on Relations between Government and Voluntary Sector in England*, HMSO, London.

Cm. 3854 (1998) *Working Together for a Healthier Scotland*, Scottish Office, Edinburgh.

Collins, H. M. and Yearley, S. (1992) "Epistemological Chicken", in Pickering, A. (ed) *Science as Practice and Culture*, University of Chicago Press, London, 301-326.

Cook, I. and Crang, M. (1995) *Doing Ethnographies, Concepts and Techniques in Modern Geography*, UEA, Norwich.

Cooke, P. and Morgan, K. (1993) "The network paradigm: new departures in corporate and regional development", *Environment and Planning D: Society and Space*, 11, 543-564.

Coombes, Y. (1996) "Demographic Characteristics", in R. B. Shukla, and D. Brooks (eds) *A Guide to Care for the Elderly*, HMSO, London, 11-20.

Cornwell, J. (1982) "Approaches in Medical Sociology to 'Felt Need' for Health Care'", in Cornwell, J., Coupland, V., Eyles, J., Smith, D. and Woods, K. (eds) *Contemporary perspectives on health and health care*, Occasional Paper No. 20, Queen Mary College, University of London.

Cornwell, J. (1984) *Hard earned lives: accounts of health and illness from East London*, Tavistock, London.

Crang, M. A, Hudson, A. C., Reimer, S. M. and Hinchcliffe, S. J. (1997) "Software for qualitative research: 1. Prospectus and overview", *Environment and Planning A*, 29, 771-787.

Curtis, C. and Taket, A. (1996) *Health and Societies: changing perspectives*, Arnold, London.

Curtis, S. (1989) *The Geography of Public Welfare Provision*, Routledge, London.

Curtis, S., Petukhova, N. and Taket, A. (1995) "Healthcare reforms in Russia: the example of St. Petersburg", *Social Science and Medicine*, 40, 755-765.

Daly, M. and Lewis, J. (2000) "The concept of social care and the analysis of contemporary welfare states", *British Journal of Sociology*, 51:2, 281-298.

Dear, M. (1992) "The NIMBY Syndrome", *Journal of the American Planning Association*, Summer, 289-299.

Dear, M. and Taylor, S. (1982) *Not on Our Street: community attitudes to mental health care*, Pion, London.

Dear, M. and Wolch, J. (1987) *Landscapes of Despair - From Deinstitutionalization to Homelessness,* Polity Press, Cambridge.

Dearlove, J. and Saunders, P. (1984) *Introduction to British Politics,* Polity Press, London.

Department of Health and Social Security (1977) *The Way Forward: priorities in Health and Social Services,* HMSO, London.

Department of Health and Social Security (1978) *A Happier Old Age*, HMSO, London.

Dicken, P. and Thrift, N. (1992) "The organization of production and the production of organization: why business enterprises matter in the study of geographical industrialization", *Transactions of the Institute of British Geographers*, NS 17, 279-291.

Dorling, D. (1995) *A New Social Atlas of Britain*, Wiley, Chichester.

Dorling, D. (1996) *Explanations for the Polarization of Life Chances in Britain,* paper presented to the VIIth International Symposium in Medical Geography, Portsmouth, UK.

Dumfries and Galloway Council (1996) *Report to Social Services Committee*, 3, 28 May 1996.

Dumfries and Galloway Standard (1997) *"Carers Reprieve"*, SUN Newspapers, 14th February, 1.

Dumfries and Galloway Standard (1998) *"Angry Protesters Picket Social Services Meeting"*, SUN Newspapers, 12th June, 1 and 3.

Dumfries Courier (1998) *"Care Cuts Fury"*, May 15th, 9-10.

Duster, T. (1981) "Intermediate steps between macro and micro integration: the case study of screening for inherited disorders", in Knorr-Cetina K. and Cicourel, A. V. (eds) *Advances in Social Theory and Methodology: Towards and Integration of Micro and Macro Sociologies,* Routledge, London, 109-135.

Dyck, I. and Kearns, R. (1995) "Transforming the relations of research: towards culturally safe geographies of health and healing", *Health and Place*, 1, 137-147.

Ecob, R. and Macintyre, S. (2000) "Small area variations in health related behaviours; do these depend on behaviour itself, its measurement, or on personal characteristics?" *Health and Place*, 6:4, 261-274.

Eyles, J. (1987) *The geography of the national health,* Croon Helm, London.

Eyles, J. and Donovan, J. (1986) "Making sense of sickness and care", *Transactions of the Institute of British Geographers*, 11, 415-27.

Eyles, J. and Smith, D. M. (1988) *Qualitative Methods in Human Geography*, Polity Press, London.

Eyles, J. and Wood, K. (1983) *The Social Geography of Medicine and Health*, Croon Helm, London.

Family Welfare Association (1995) *Guide to Social Services*, 83rd Edition, Family Welfare Association Publications, London.

Filinson, R. (1998) "The Impact of the Community Care Act : views from the independent sector", *Health and Social Care in the Community*, 6, 241-250.

Finch, J. (1986) *Research and Policy: The Users of Qualitative Methods in Social and Educational Methods*, Falmer Press, London.

Finch, J. (1987) "Whose responsibility? Women and the future of family care." in Allen I, Wicks, M., Finch, J. and Leat, D. (eds), *Informal Care Tomorrow*, Policy Studies Institute, London.

Foucault, M. (1979) *Discipline and punish: the birth of the prison*, translated by Alan Sheridan, Penguin, Harmondsworth.

Fountain, J. (1993) "Dealing With Data", in Hobbs, D. and May, T. (eds) *Interpreting the Field: accounts of ethnography*, Clarendon Press, Oxford, 145-173.

Frazier, L. J. and Scarpaci, J. (1998) "Landscapes of State Violence and the Struggle to Reclaim Community", in Kearns, R.A. and Gesler, W. (eds) *Putting Health into Place: Landscape, Identity and Well-Being*, Syracuse University Press, New York.

276

Gardener, M. J., Winter, P. D. and Barker, D. J. P. (1983) *Atlas of Cancer Mortality in England and Wales, 1968-1978*, Wiley, Chichester.

Geertz, C. (1973) *The Interpretation of Cultures: selected essays*, Basic Books, New York.

General Records Office (Scotland) (1994) *1992 based GAD population projections, Scotland,* GRO, Edinburgh.

Gesler, W. (1991) *The Cultural Geography of Healthcare*, University of Pittsburgh Press, Pittsburgh.

Gesler, W. (1992) "Therapeutic landscapes, medical issues in the light of the new cultural geography", *Social Science and Medicine*, 34, 735-746.

Gesler, W. (1993) "Therapeutic landscapes: theory and case study of Epidaurus, Greece" *Environment and Planning D, Society and Space,* 11, 171-189.

Gesler, W. (1996) *Lourdes, Healing in a Place of Pilgrimage*, Paper delivered at the VIIth International Symposium in Medical Geography of the Royal Geographical Society with the Institute of British Geographers, Portsmouth.

Giddens, A. (1981) *A Contemporary Critique of Historical Materialism*, Macmillan, London.

Giddens, A. (1984) *The Constitution of Society*, Polity Press, Cambridge

Giddens, A. (1993) *New Rules of Sociological Method: A Positive Critique of Interpretative Sociologies*, Polity Press, Cambridge.

Giggs, J. (1973) "The distribution of schizophrenics in Nottingham", *Transactions of the Institute of British Geographers*, 59, 55-76.

Gilligan, C. (1982) *In a Different Voice*, Harvard University Press, Cambridge MA.

Girt, J. L. (1972) "Simple chronic bronchitis and urban ecological structure", in McGlashan, N. (ed), *Medical Geography*, Methuen, London.

Glasgow City Council (1997) *The Council and the Voluntary Sector: Working Together for the Good of the City*, Glasgow City Council Publications, Glasgow.

Glasgow Unitary Authority (1996) *New Councils in Strathclyde: 1996 Guide,* Strathclyde Regional Council Publications, Glasgow.

Glazer, N. (1990) "The home as workshop: women as amateur nurses and medical care providers", *Gender and Society*, 4, 479-500.

Goddard, E. (1992) "Voluntary Work", *General Household Survey No.23*, Supplement A., HMSO, London.

Goddard, E. and Savage, D. (1991) "People aged 65 and over", *OPCS General Household Survey No.22 Supplement A,* HMSO, London.

Gough, I. (1979) *The Political Economy of the Welfare State*, Macmillan, London.

Government Statistical Office (1995) *Regional Trends 30 (1995 edition)*, HMSO, London.

Graham, H. (1985) *Health and Welfare*, Macmillan Education Ltd., London.

Griffiths, R. (1988) *Community Care: Agenda for Action*, report to the Secretary of State for Social Services, HMSO, London.

Grigg, D. (1967) "Regions, Models and Classes", in Chorley, R. and Haggett, P. (eds) *Models in Geography,* Methuen, London, 461-509.

Guillebaud Report (1956) *Report of the Committee of enquiry into the cost of the national Health Service*, Cmd. 9663, HMSO, London.

277

Hägerstrand, T. (1968) *Innovation Diffusion as a Spatial Process* (translated by Pred, A.), University of Chicago Press, Chicago.

Haastrup, K. (1992) "Writing Ethnography: State of the Art" in Okely, J. and Calloway H. (eds) *Anthropology and Autobiography,* Routledge, London, 116-133.

Haggett, P. (1967) "Network Models in Geography", in Chorley, R. and Haggett, P. (eds) *Models in Geography,* Methuen, London, 609-664.

Haggett, P. (1972) "Contagious Processes in a Planar Graph: An Epidemiological Application", in McGlashan, N. (ed), *Medical Geography: Techniques and Field Studies,* Methuen and Co. Ltd, London, 307-324.

Ham, C. and Hill, M. (1984) *The Policy Process in the Modern Capitalist State: First Edition,* Harvester Wheatsheaf, Hertfordshire.

Hancock, R. and Jarvis, C. (1994) *The Long Term Effects of Being a Carer,* Age Concern Institute of Gerontology, HMSO, London.

Harding, T. (1992) *Great Expectations - and Spending of Social Services,* National Institution for Social Work, London.

Hardy, B., Wistow, G. and Rhodes, R. (1990) "Policy Networks and the Implementation of Community Care Policy for People with Mental Handicaps", *Journal of Social Policy,* 19, 141-168.

Harris, A. (1961) *Meals on Wheels for Old People,* National Corporation for the Care of Old People, London.

Harris, A. (1968) *Social Welfare for the Elderly: a study of thirteen local authority areas in England, Wales and Scotland,* HMSO, London.

Haynes, R. (1987) *The Geography of Health Services in Britain,* Croon Helm, London.

Haynes, R. and Bentham, C. (1979a) *Community hospitals and rural accessibility,* Saxon House, Farnborough.

Haynes, R. and Bentham, C. G. (1979b) "Accessibility and the Use of Hospitals in Rural Areas", *Area,* 11, 186-191.

Haynes, R. and Gale, S. (2000) "Deprivation and poor health in rural areas: inequalities hidden by averages" *Health and Place,* 6:4, 275-286.

Hedley, R. and Smith, J. D. (1992) *Volunteering and Society: Principles and Practice,* Bedford Square Press, London.

Henwood, M. (1990) *Community Care and Elderly People,* Family Policy Studies Centre, London.

Hinchcliffe, S. J., Crang, M. A., Reimer, S. M. and Hudson, A. C. (1997) "Software for qualitative research: 2. Some thoughts on 'aiding' analysis", *Environment and Planning A,* 29, 1109-1124.

Hogwood, B. and Gunn, L. (1984) *Policy Analysis For The Real World,* University Press, Oxford.

Howe, G. M. (1963) *A National Atlas of Disease Mortality in Britain,* Nelson, London.

Howe, G. M. (1976) *Man, Environment and Disease in Britain: a medical geography through the Ages,* Harmondsworth, London.

Hoyes, L. and Means, R. (1993) "Quasi-markets and the reform of community care", in Le Grand, J. and Bartlett, W. (eds) *Quasi-markets and Social Policy*, Macmillan, London, 93-124.

Huberman, A.M. and Miles, M. B. (1994) "Data management and Analysis Methods", in Denzin, N. K. and Lincoln, Y. S. (eds) *Handbook of Qualitative Research*, Sage Pubs., London, 428-443.

John, P. and Cole, A. (1995) "Models of Local Decision-making Networks in Britain and France", *Policy and Politics*, 23, 303-312.

Johnston, R., Gregory, D. and Smith, D. (1994) *The Dictionary of Human Geography*, 3rd Edition, Blackwell, Oxford.

Jones, K. and Duncan, C. (1995) "Individuals and their ecologies: analysing the geography of chronic illness within a multilevel modelling framework", *Health and Place*, 1, 27-40.

Jones, K. and Moon, G. (1987) *Health, Disease and Society: an introduction to medical geography*, Routledge and Kegan Paul, London.

Jones, K. and Moon, G. (1993) "Medical Geography - Taking Space Seriously", *Progress in Human Geography*, 17, 515-524.

Joseph, A. and Phillips, D. (1984) *Accessibility and utilization: geographical perspectives on health care delivery*, Harper and Row, New York.

Joseph Rowntree Foundation (1991) *National Survey of Volunteering*, Social Policy Research Findings, No. 22, December, JRF, York.

Kazanjian, A. and Pagliccia, N. (1996) "Key factors in physicians' choice of practice location: findings from a survey of practitioners and their spouses", *Health and Place*, 2, 27-34.

Kearns, R. (1993) "Place and Health: towards a reformed medical geography", *The Professional Geographer*, 45, 139-147.

Kearns, R. (1998) "Contracting Opportunities: Interpreting Post Asylum Geographies of Mental Health Care in Auckland, New Zealand", *paper presented to the VIIIth International Symposium in Medical Geography*, Johns Hopkins University, Baltimore.

Kearns, R. and Barnett, J. (1997) 'Consumerist ideology and the symbolic landscapes of private medicine', *Health and Place*, 3, 171-180.

Kearns, R. and Smith, C. (1994) ' Housing, Homelessness, and Mental Health: Mapping an Agenda for Geographical Inquiry,' *Professional Geographer*, 46, 418-424.

Kramer, R. (1986) "The future of voluntary organizations in social welfare," in Independent Sector Inc. & United Way Institute (ed), *Philanthropy, voluntary action, and the public good*, Independent Inc., Washington DC.

Kramer, R. and Grossman, S. (1987) "Contracting for Social Services - Process Management and Resource Dependencies", *Social Services Review*, 61, 32-55.

Laing and Buisson (1992) *Laing's Review of Private Healthcare, 1992*, Laing and Buisson, London.

Latour, B. (1986) 'The Powers of Association', in Law, J. (ed) *Power, Action and Belief: A New Sociology of Knowledge?*, Routledge, London.

Latour, B. (1987) *Science in Action*, Open University Press, Milton Keynes.

Latour, B. (1988) "Mixing Humans and Nonhumans Together: The Sociology of a Door-Closer", *Social Problems*, 35, 298-310.

Latour, B. (1991) "Technology is society made durable", in Law, J. (ed), *A sociology of monsters: essays on power, technology and domination*, Routledge, London, 103-130.

Latour, B. (1994) "On technical mediation - philosophy, sociology, genealogy", *Common Knowledge*, 4, 29-64.

Law, J. (1986) "On power and its tactics: a view from the sociology of science", *Sociological Review*, 35, 404-425.

Law, J. (1999) "After ANT: complexity, naming and topology" in Law, J. and Hassard, J. (1999) *Actor Network Theory and After*, Blackwell, Oxford, 1-14.

Law, J. and Hassard, J. (1999) *Actor Network Theory and After*, Blackwell, Oxford.

Leat, D. (1993) *The Development of Community care by the Independent Sector*, PSI, London.

LeGrand J. And Bartlett, W. (1993) *Quasi-markets and Social Policy*, Macmillan, Basingstoke, 93-124.

Lewis, J. (1993) "Developing the mixed economy of care: Emerging issues for voluntary organisations," *Journal of Social Policy* 22, 173-192.

Lewis, J. (1994) "Voluntary Organisations in 'New Partnership' with Local Authorities: The Anatomy of a Contract", *Social Policy and Administration*, 28, 206-220.

Lewis, J. and Glennester, H. (1996) *Implementing the New Community Care*, Open University Press, Buckingham.

Ley, D. (1983) *A Social Geography of the City*, Harper Row, New York.

Lipskey, M. (1980) *Street Level Bureaucracy*, Russell Sage, New York.

Litva, A. and Eyles, J. (1995) "Coming Out: exposing social theory in medical geography", *Health and Place*, 1, 5-14.

Litva, A. and Eyles, J. (1996) *The good, the bad and the self-righteous*, paper given to the V11th International Symposium in Medical Geography, Portsmouth.

Lösch, A. (1954) *The economics of location*, Oxford University Press, Oxford.

Lukes, S. (1974) *Power a Radical View*, MacMillan Education Ltd., Basingstoke.

Macdonald, R. (1996) "Labours of Love: Voluntary working in a depressed local economy," *Journal of Social Policy*, 25, 19-38.

MacIntyre, S. (1994) "Understanding the social patterning of health: the role of the social sciences", *Journal of Public Health Medicine*, 16, 53-59.

MacIntyre, S. , MacIver, S. and Sooman, A. (1993) "Area, class and health: should we be focusing on places or people?", *Journal of Social Policy*, 22, 213-234.

McCracken, G. (1988) *The Long Interview: Qualitative research Series, 13*, Sage, London.

McDowell, L. (1992) "Social Divisions, Income Inequality and Gender Relations in the 1980s", in Cloke, P. (ed), *Policy and Change in Thatcher's Britain*, Pergamon Press, Oxford.

Madge, C. (1998) "Therapeutic landscapes of the Jola, the Gambia, West Africa", *Health and Place*, 4, 293-312.

Marsh, D., and Rhodes, R. (1992) "Policy Communities and Issue Networks: beyond typology", in Marsh, D., and Rhodes, R. (eds) *Policy Networks in British Government*, Clarendon Press, Oxford, 249-268.

Marshall, C. and Rossman, G. (1989) *Designing Qualitative Research*, Sage, London.

May, J. (1952) *International Geographical Union XVII International Geographical Congress: First Report of the Commission of Medical Geography (Ecology of health and Disease)*, UNESCO, Washington.

Mayer, P. (1966) *Socialization, the approach from social anthropology*, Tavistock, London.

Mead, G. (1927) "Class lectures in social psychology", in Miller, D. (ed) (1982) *The Individual and the Social Self. Unpublished Work of George Herbert Mead*, University of Chicago Press, Chicago and London, 106-175.

Means, R. (1991) "Community Care, Housing and Older People: continuity or change?", *Housing Studies*, 6, 273-284.

Means, R. and Smith, R. (1985) *The Development of Welfare Services for Elderly People*, Croon Helm, London.

Means, R. and Smith, R. (1994) *Community Care: Policy and Practice*, Macmillan, Basingstoke.

Miles, M. and Crush, J. (1993) "Personal narratives as interactive texts - collecting and interpreting migrant life-histories", *Professional Geographer*, 45, 84-129.

Milligan, C. (1996) "Service Dependent Ghetto formation - a transferable concept?", *Health and Place*, 2, 199-211.

Mitchell, J. C. (1969) "The Concept and use of Social Networks" in Mitchell, J. C. , *Social Networks in Urban Situations*, Manchester University Press, Manchester.

Mohan, J. (1995a) *A National Health Service? The restructuring of health care in Britain since 1979*, St. Martin's Press, New York.

Mohan, J. (1995b) "Post-Fordism and Welfare: an analysis of change in the British health sector", *Environment and Planning A*, 27, 1555-1576.

Mol, A. (1999) "Ontological politics. A word and some question" in Law, J. and Hassard, J. *Actor Network Theory and After*, Blackwell, Oxford, 74-89.

Moon, G. (1990) "Conceptions of space and community in British health policy", *Social Science and Medicine*, 30, 165-171.

Moyser, G. (1988) "Non-Standardized Interviewing in Elite Research," in Burgess, R. G. (ed) *Studies in Qualitative Methodology: Conducting Qualitative Research - Vol. 1*, Jai Press, London, 109-136.

Murdoch, J. (1994) "Actor-networks and the evolution of economic forms: combining description and explanation in theories of regulation, flexible specialization, and networks," *Environment and Planning A*, 23, 731-757.

Murdoch, J. (1997a) "Inhuman/nonhuman/human: actor-network theory and the prospects for a non-dualistic and symmetrical perspective on nature and society," *Environment and Planning D: Society and Space*, 15, 731-756.

Murdoch, J. (1997b) "Towards a geography of heterogeneous associations", *Progress in Human Geography*, 21, 321-337.

Murdoch, J. and Marsden, T. (1995) "The spatialisation of politics: local and national actor-spaces in environmental conflict" *Transactions of the Institute of British Geographers*, NS 20, 368-380.

Murphy, J. (1992) *British Social Services: the Scottish Dimension,* Scottish Academic Press, Edinburgh.

Nissel, M. (1980) "A greater place for family responsibility?" in *The Welfare State - Diversity and Decentralisation*, Policy Studies Institute - Discussion Paper 2, London.

NISW (1990) *The Kaleidoscope of Care,* HMSO, London.

Nyland, J. (1995) "Issue Networks and Non-profit Organisations", *Policy Studies Review*, 14, 195-205.

OECD (1994) *Caring For Frail Elderly People: new directions in care,* Social Policies Study No. 14, OECD, Paris.

Olssen, G. (1980) *Birds in eggs/eggs in bird,* Pion, London.

OPCS (1992) *OPCS Social Survey Division,* HMSO, London.

Pacione, M. (1993) "The Geography of the Urban Crisis: some evidence from Glasgow," *Scottish Geographical Magazine,* 109, 87-95.

Parker, R. (1990) "Elderly people and Community Care: the Policy Background" in Sinclair I, Parker R, Leat D, and Williams J (eds) *The Kaleidoscope of Care: A review of Research on Welfare Provision for Elderly People*, HMSO, London, 5-22.

Parr, H. (1996) *Mental Health and Places of Therapy within the City: Questions of Individual and Collective Definitions*, paper presented to the VIIth International Symposium in Medical Geography, Portsmouth, UK.

Parr, H. (1997) "Mental Health, Public Space and the City: Questions of Individual and Collective Access", *Environment and Planning D: Society and Space*, 15, 435-454.

Parr, H. (1998) "Mental health, ethnography and the body" *Area*, 30, 28-37.

Pearson, G. (1993) "Talking a Good Fight: Authenticity and Distance in the Ethnographic Craft", in Hobbs, D. and May, T. (eds) *Interpreting the Field: accounts of ethnography*, Clarendon Press, Oxford, vii-xx.

Phillips, D. (1981) *Contemporary Issues in the Geography of Healthcare*, Geo Books, Norwich.

Phillips, D. (1990) *Health and healthcare in the third world,* Longman, Harlow.

Philo, C. (1987) "'Fit localities for an asylum': the historical geography of the 'mad business' in England, as viewed through the pages of the Asylum Journal", *Journal of Historical Geography*, 13, 398-415.

Philo, C. (1989) "'Enough to drive one mad': the organization of space in 19th-century lunatic asylums", in Wolch, J. and Dear, M. (eds*), The Power of Geography: How territory Shapes Social Life*, Unwin Hyman, London, 258-289.

Philo, C. (1996) "Staying In? Invited comments on 'Coming out: exposing social theory in medical geography", *Health and Place,* 2, 35-40.

Pickering, A. (1992) *Science as Practice and Culture*, University of Chicago Press, Chicago.

Pickup, L. (1987) "Hard to Get Around: a study of women's travel mobility", in Little, J. , Peake, L. and Richardson, P. (Eds) *Women in Cities: gender and the urban environment*, Macmillan, London, 98-116.

Pinch, S. (1997) *Worlds of Welfare: understanding the changing geographies of social welfare provision*, Routledge, London.

Pinfold, V. (1996) Community connections in the Cityscape: a methodology for analysing observed rehabilitation geographies among people with complex and long-term mental health problems in Nottingham, *Proceedings of the VIIth International Symposium in Medical Geography*, Portsmouth University, Portsmouth.

Prior, L. (1993) *The Social Organization of Mental Illness*, Sage Publications, London.

Pyle, G. (1973) "Measles as an Urban Health Problem", *Economic Geography*, 49, 344-356.

Pyle, G. (1974) "The Geography of Healthcare", in Hunter, J. (Ed), *The Geography of Health and Disease*, Studies in Geography No. 6, University of North Carolina, North Carolina, 154-184.

Pyle, G. and Lauer, B. (1974) *Comparing Spatial Configurations: Hospital Service Areas and Disease Rates*, paper prepared for the Association of American Geographers, Seattle, Washington.

Pyle, G. and Rees, P. (1971) "Modelling patterns of death and disease in Chicago", *Economic Geography*, 47, 475-88.

Qureshi, P. and Simons, R. (1987) "Resources within families: caring for elderly people", in Brannen, J. and Wilson, G. (eds) *Give and Take in Families: studies in resource distribution*, Allen and Unwin, London.

Rhodes, R. (1981) *Control and Power in Central-Local Government Relations*, Gower, Farnborough.

Rhodes, R. (1986) *The National World of Local Government*, Allen and Unwin, London.

Rhodes, R. (1988) *Beyond Westminster and Whitehall: the Sub-Central Governments of Britain*, Allen and Unwin, London.

Rhodes, R. and Marsh, D. (1992) "Policy Networks in British Politics: a critique of existing approaches", in Marsh, D. and Rhodes, R. (eds) *Policy Networks in British Government*, Clarendon Press, Oxford, 1-26.

Richardson, A., Unell, J. and Aston, B. (1989) *A New Deal for Carers*, King's Fund Centre, London.

Rist, R. C. (1994) "Influencing the Policy Process with Qualitative Research", in Denzin, N. K. and Lincoln, Y. S., *Handbook of Qualitative Research*, Sage Publications, London.

Robb, B. (1967) *Sans Everything: A Case to Answer*, Nelson, London.

Robinson, J., and Yee, L. (1991) *Focus on Carers*, Kings Fund Centre, London.

Rosenberg, M. (1988) "Linking the Geographical, the Medical and the Political in Analysing Health Care Delivery Systems", *Social Science and Medicine*, 26, 179-186.

Rowles, G. (1978) *Prisoners of Space: Exploring the Geographical Experience of Older People*, Westview Press, CO.

283

Rowles, G. (1986) "The geography of ageing and the aged: toward an integrated perspective", *Progress in Human Geography*, 10, 511-539.

Rowntree, J. (1901) *The Temperance Problem and Social Reform*, Hodder and Stoughton, London.

Sabatier, P. and Mazmanian, D. (1981) *Effective Policy Implementation*, Lexington, Massachusetts.

Scarpaci, J. (1996) *Healing Landscapes: Revolution and Health Care in Post-Socialist Havana*, paper presented to the VIIth International Symposium in Medical Geography, Portsmouth, UK.

Schoenberger, E. (1991) "The Corporate Interview as a research Method in Economic Geography", *Professional Geographer*, 43, 180-189.

Scottish Office (1991) *The Structure of local Government in Scotland - A Consultation Document*, HMSO, Edinburgh.

Scottish Office (1993) *Community Care in Scotland - Community Care Plans: directions on consultation*, Amends Circular: SW1\91 (SHHD\DGM (1991)1), Scottish Office, Edinburgh.

SCVS (1997) *Head and Heart: report of the commission on the future of the voluntary sector in Scotland*, SCVS, Edinburgh.

Seamon, D. (1979) *A Geography of the Lifeworld: Movement, Rest and Encounter*, St. Martin's Press, New York.

Select Committee on Health (1998) *Minutes of Evidence: Relationship Between Health and Social Services HSS 32*, 18:05:05, 21st May.

Shanon, G. and Dever, G. (1974) *Health Care Delivery: Spatial Perspectives*, McGraw-Hill, New York.

Shukla, R., and Brooks, D. (1996) *A Guide to Care of the Elderly*, HMSO, London.

Sibeon, R. (1991) *Towards a New Sociology of Social Work*, Avebury, Aldershot.

Silverman, D. (1993) *Interpreting Qualitative Data: Methods for Analysing Talk, text and Interaction*, Sage Publications, London.

Sinclair, K (1997) "Police Cordon Ensures City Council Sits Undisturbed by Protest Against Cuts", *Herald*, 4th May, Glasgow.

Smith, C. J. and Giggs, J. A. (1988) *Location and Stigma*, Unwin-Hyman, London.

Smith, D. M. (1977) *Human geography: a welfare approach*, Edward Arnold, London.

Smith, D. M. (1997) "Geography and ethics: a moral turn?" *Progress in Human Geography*, 21:4, 583-590.

Smith, S. (1988) "Constructing Local Knowledge: the analysis of self in everyday life", in Eyles, J. and Smith, D. M. (eds), *Qualitative Methods in Human Geography*, Polity Press, London, 17-38.

Smith, S. (1989) Housing and Health. A review and research agenda, *Discussion Paper 27*, Centre for Housing Research, Glasgow University, Glasgow.

Smith, S., Alexander, A. and Easterlow, D. (1997) "Rehousing as a health intervention: miracle or mirage?" *Health and Place*, 3, 203-216.

Snow, J. (1855) *On the mode of communication of cholera*, Harvard University Press, Cambridge, MA.

Social Services Committee (1985) *Second report: Community Care, House of Commons Paper 13-1, Session 1984-5*, HMSO, London.

Stamp, D. (1964) *The Geography of Life and Death*, Fontana, London.

Strauss, A. (1987) *Qualitative Analysis for Social Scientists*, Cambridge University Press, Cambridge.

Takahashi, L. (1997) "Stigmatization, HIV/AIDS, and communities of color: exploring response to human service facilities," *Health and Place*, 3, 187-199.

Taylor, M. (1992) "The Changing Role of the Nonprofit Sector in Britain: Moving Toward the Market", in Gidron B *et al.* (eds) *Government and Third Sector*, Jossey-Bass Publications, San Fransisco, 147-175.

Taylor, T. and Cameron, D. (1987) *Analysing Conversation: Rules and Units in the Structure of Talk*, Pergamon, Oxford.

Thornton, P. R., Williams, A. M. and Shaw G. (1997) "Revisiting time-space diaries: an exploratory case study of tourist behaviour in Cornwall, England", *Environment and Planning A*, 29, 1847-1867.

Thrift, N. (1983) "On the Determination of Social Action in Time and Space", *Environment and Planning D: Society and Space*, 1, 23-57.

Tinker, A., McCreadie, C., Wright, F., and Savage, A. V. (1994) *The Care of Frail Elderly People in the United Kingdom*, HMSO, London.

Tivers, J. (1987) 'Women with young children: constraints on activities in the urban environment', in Little J, Peake L and Richardson P (eds) Women in Cities: gender and the urban environment, Macmillan, London, 84 - 97.

Townsend, P. (1962) *The Last Refuge: A Survey of Residential Institutions and Homes for the Aged in England and Wales*, Routledge and Kegan Paul, London.

Townsend, P. and Wedderburn, D. (1965) *The Aged in the Welfare State: the interim report of a survey of persons aged 65 and over in Britain, 1962 and 1963*, Occasional Papers on Social Administration, No. 14, London.

Tronto, J. C. (1993) Moral Boundaries. *A Political Argument for and Ethic of Care*, Routledge, London.

Twigg, J. (1989) "Models of Carers: How do social care agencies conceptualise their relationship with informal carers?", *Journal of Social Policy*, 18, 53-66.

Twigg, J. (1990) "The interface between the NHS and the SSD", in Davies, B. et. al. *Resources, Needs and Outcomes in Community Based Care*, Avebury, Aldershot.

Twigg, J. (1997) "Deconstructing the 'Social Bath': Help with Bathing at Home for Older and Disabled People", *Journal of Social Policy*, 26, 211-232.

Vidich, A. J. and Lyman, S. M. (1994) "Qualitative Methods", in Denzin, N. K. and Lincoln, Y. S. (eds) *Handbook of Qualitative Research*, Sage, London, 23-35.

Waxler, N. (1981) "Learning to be a leper: a case study in the social construction of illness", in Mishler, E., AmaraSingham, L, Hauser, S., Liem, R., Osherson, S. and Waxler, N. (eds) *Social Contexts of Health, Illness, and Patient Care*, Cambridge, Cambridge University Press, 169-194.

Williams, A. (1998) "Therapeutic landscapes in Holistic Medicine", *Social Science and Medicine*, 46, 1193-1203.

Wilson, G. (1993) "Users and Providers: different perspectives on community care services", *Journal of Social Policy*, 22, 507-526.

Wistow, G., Knapp, M., Hardy, B. and Allen, C. (1992) "From providing to enabling: Local Authorities and the mixed economy of social care," *Public Administration*, 70, 25-46.

Wolch, J. R. (1989) "The Shadow State: transformations in the voluntary sector", in Wolch, J. R. and Dear, M. (eds) *The Power of Geography: how territory shapes social life*, Unwin Hyman, Boston, Ch.9.

Wolch, J. R. (1990) *The Shadow State: Government and Voluntary Sector in Transition*, The Foundation Centre, New York.

Wolch, J. and Geiger, R. (1983) "The Distribution of Urban Voluntary Resources: an exploratory analysis", *Environment and Planning A*, 15, 1067-1082.

Wolch, J. and Geiger, R. (1986) "Urban Restructuring and the Not-for-Profit Sector", *Economic Geography*, 62, 3-18.

Wolcott, H. F. (1995) *The Art of Fieldwork*, Altimira Press, London.

Wolfenden Committee (1978) *The Future of Voluntary Organisations: a report of the Wolfenden Committee,* Croon Helm, London.

Wolpert, J. (1977) "Social Income and the Voluntary Sector", *Papers of the Regional Science Association*, 39, 217-229.

Wolpert, J. and Reiner, T. (1981) "The Non-Profit Sector in the Metropolitan Economy", *Economic Geography*, 57, 23-33.

Wolpert, J. and Wolpert, E. (1976) "The relocation of released mental hospital patients into residential communities," *Policy Sciences,* 7, 31-51.

Index